Pony Express &
Overland Stage

Pony Express & Overland Stage
Two Accounts of the Opening of the American Western Frontier

ILLUSTRATED

Seventy Years on the Frontier
Alexander Majors

A Thrilling and Truthful History of the Pony Express
William Lightfoot Visscher

Pony Express & Overland Stage
Two Accounts of the Opening of the American Western Frontier
Seventy Years on the Frontier
by Alexander Majors
A Thrilling and Truthful History of the Pony Express
by William Lightfoot Visscher

ILLUSTRATED

FIRST EDITION

First published under the titles
Seventy Years on the Frontier
and
A Thrilling and Truthful History of the Pony Express or Blazing the Westward Way

Leonaur is an imprint of Oakpast Ltd

Copyright in this form © 2017 Oakpast Ltd

ISBN: 978-1-78282-690-3 (hardcover)
ISBN: 978-1-78282-691-0 (softcover)

http://www.leonaur.com

Publisher's Notes
The views expressed in this book are not necessarily those of the publisher.

Contents

Seventy Years on the Frontier   7

The Thrilling and Truthful History of the Pony Express   205

Seventy Years on the Frontier

Contents

Preface	13
Reminiscences of Youth	17
Missouri in Its Wild and Uncultivated State	25
A Silver Expedition	31
The Mormons	39
The Mormons' Mecca	55
My First Venture	61
Faithful Friends	68
Our War with Mexico	75
Doniphan's Expedition	79
The Pioneer of Frontier Telegraphy	86
An Overland Outfit	89
Kit Carson	93
An Adventure with Indians	104
Crossing the Plains	112
"The Jayhawkers of 1849"	122
Mirages	129
The First Stage into Denver	134

The Gold Fever	137
The Overland Mail	141
The Pony Express and Its Brave Riders	149
The Battle of the Buffaloes	158
The Black Bear	164
A Boy's Trip Overland	169
The Denver of Early Days	176
Buffalo Bill from Boyhood to Fame	180
The Graves of Pioneers	184
Silver Mining	191
The Surgeon Scout	195
Conclusion	198

DEDICATION.
AS A TRIBUTE OF
MY SINCERE REGARD FOR
W. F. CODY
AS BOY AND MAN,
MY FRIEND FOR TWO SCORE YEARS,
I DEDICATE TO HIM
THIS BOOK OF BORDER LIFE.
ALEXANDER MAJORS.

Preface

As there is no man living who is more thoroughly competent to write a book of the Wild West than my life-long friend and benefactor in my boyhood, Alexander Majors, there is no one to whose truthful words I would rather accept the honour of writing a preface.

An introduction to a book of Mountain and Plain by Mr. Majors certainly need hardly be written, unless it be to refer to the author in a way that his extreme modesty will not permit him to speak of himself, for he is not given to sounding his own praise, being a man of action rather than words, and yet whose life has its recollections of seventy years upon the frontier, dating to a period that tried men's souls to the fullest extent, and when daring deeds and thrilling adventures were of every-day occurrence. Remembrance of seventy years of life in the Far West and amid the Rocky Mountains!

What a world of thought this gives rise to, when we recall that a quarter of a century ago there was not a railroad west of the Missouri River, and every pound of freight, every emigrant, every letter, and every message had to be carried by wagon or on horseback, and at the risk of life and hardships untold.

The man who could in the face of all dangers and obstacles originate and carry to success a line of freighter wagons, a mail route from the Atlantic to the Pacific, and a Pony Express, flying at the utmost speed of a hare through the land, was no ordinary individual, as can be well understood. And such a man Alexander Majors was. He won success; and today, on the verge of four score years, lives over again in his book the thrilling scenes in his own life and in the lives of others.

Family reverses after the killing of my father in the Kansas War, caused me to start out, though a mere boy, in 1855 to seek to aid in the support of my mother and sisters, and it was to Mr. Alexander

Majors that I applied for a situation. He looked me over carefully in his kindly way, and after questioning me closely gave me the place of messenger boy, that was, one to ride with dispatches between the overland freighters—wagon trains going westward into the almost unknown wild dump of prairie and mountain.

That was my first meeting with Alexander Majors, and up to the present time our friendship has never had a break in it, and, I may add, never will through act of mine.

Having thus shown my claim to a thorough knowledge of my distinguished old friend, let me now state that his firm was known the country over as Majors, Russell & Woddell, but it was to Mr. Majors particularly that the heaviest duties of organising and management fell, and he never shirked a duty or a danger, as I well remember.

Severe in discipline, he was yet never profane or harsh, and a Christian and temperance man through all; he governed his men kindly, and was wont to say that he would have no one under his control who would not promptly obey an order without it was emphasized with an oath. In fact, he had a contract with his men in which they pledged themselves not to use profanity, get drunk, gamble, or be cruel to animals under pain of dismissal, while good behaviour was rewarded. Every man, from wagon-boss and teamster down to rustler and messenger-boy, seemed anxious to gain the good will of Alexander Majors and to hold it, and today he has fewer foes than anyone I know, in spite of his position as chief of what were certainly a wild and desperate lot of men, where the revolver settled all difficulties.

It was Mr. Majors' firm that originated and put in the Pony Express across the plains and made it the grand success it proved to be.

It was his firm that so long and successfully carried on the business of overland freighting in the face of every obstacle, and also the Overland Stage Drive between the Missouri River and Pacific Ocean, and in his long life on the border he has become known to all classes and conditions of men, so that in writing now his memoirs, no man knows better whereof he speaks than he does.

In each instance where he has written to his old-time comrades for data, he has taken only that which he knew could be verified, and has thrown out material sufficient to double his book in size, where he felt the slightest doubt that it could not be relied upon to the fullest extent.

His work, therefore, is a history of the Wild West, its pages authentic, and though many of its scenes are romantic and thrilling, it is what has hitherto been an unwritten story of facts, figures, and reality; and now, that in his old age he finds his occupation gone, I feel and hope that his memoirs will find a ready sale.

W. F. Cody,
"Buffalo Bill."

CHAPTER 1

Reminiscences of Youth

My father, Benjamin Majors, was a farmer, born in the State of North Carolina in 1794, and brought when a boy by my grandfather, Alexander Majors, after whom I am named, to Kentucky about the year 1800. My grandfather was also a farmer, and one might say a manufacturer, for in those days nearly all the farmers in America were manufacturers, producing almost everything within 'their homes or with their own hands, tanning their own leather, making the shoes they wore, as well as clothing of all kinds.

My mother's maiden name was Laurania Kelly; her father, Beil Kelly, was a soldier in the Revolutionary War, and was wounded at the battle of Brandywine.

I was born in 1814, on the 4th day of October, near Franklin, Simpson County, Kentucky, being the eldest of the family, consisting of two boys and a girl. When I was about five years of age my father moved to Missouri, when that State was yet a Territory. I remember well many of the occurrences of the trip; one was that the horses ran away with the wagon in which my father, myself, and younger brothers were riding. My father threw us children out and jumped out himself, though crippled in one foot at the time. One wheel of the wagon was broken to pieces, which caused us a delay of two days.

After crossing the Ohio River, in going through the then Territory of Illinois, the settlements were from ten to twenty miles apart, the squatters living in log cabins, and along one stretch of the road the log cabin settlements were forty miles apart. When we arrived at the Okaw River, in the Territory of Illinois, we found a squatter in his little log cabin whose occupation was ferrying passengers across the river in a small flatboat which was propelled by a cable or large rope tied to a tree on each side of the river, it being a narrow but deep stream. The only thing attracting my special attention, as a boy, at that point was a pet bear chained to a stake just in front of the cabin where the family lived. He was constantly jumping over his chain, as is the habit of pet bears, especially when young.

From this place to St. Louis, a distance of about thirty-five miles, there was not a single settlement of any kind. When we arrived on the east bank of the Mississippi River, opposite the now city of St. Louis, we saw a little French village on the other side. The only means of crossing the river was a small flatboat, manned by three Frenchmen, one on each side about midway of the craft, each with an oar with which to propel the boat. The third one stood in the end with a steering oar, for the purpose of giving it the proper direction when the others propelled it. This ferry would carry four horses or a four-horse wagon with its load at one trip. These men were not engaged half their time in ferrying across the river all the emigrants, with their horses, cattle, sheep, and hogs, who were moving from the East to the West and crossing at St. Louis.

Of course, the current would carry the boat a considerable distance down the river in spite of the efforts of the boatmen to the contrary. However, when they reached the opposite bank the two who worked the side oars would lay down their oars, go to her bow, where a long rope was attached, take it up, put it over their shoulders, and let it uncoil until it gave them several rods in front of the boat. Then they would start off in a little footpath made at the water's edge and pull the boat to the place prepared for taking on or unloading, as the case might be. There they loaded what they wanted to ferry to the other side, and the same process would be gone through with as before. Reaching the west bank of the river we found the village of St. Louis, with 4,000 inhabitants, a large portion of whom were French, whose business it was to trade with the numerous tribes of Indians and the few white people who then inhabited that region of country, for furs of various kinds, buffalo robes and tongues, as this was the only traffic out of which money could be made at that time.

The furs bought of the Indians were carried from St. Louis to New Orleans in pirogues or flatboats, which were carried along solely by the current, for at that time steam power had never been applied to the waters of the Mississippi River. Sixty-seven years later, in 1886, I visited St. Louis and went down to the wharf or steamboat landing, and looking across to East St. Louis, which in 1818 was nothing but a wilderness, beheld the river spanned by one of the finest bridges in the world, over which from 100 to 150 locomotives with trains attached were daily passing. Three big steam ferryboats above and three below the bridge were constantly employed in transferring freight of one kind or another. What a change had taken place within the memory of one man! While looking in amazement at the great and mighty change, a nicely dressed and intelligent man passed by; I said to him:

"Sir, I stood on the other bank of this river when a little boy, in the month of October, 1818, when there was no improvement whatever over there" (pointing to the east shore), I also stated to him that a little flatboat, manned by three Frenchmen, was the only means for crossing the river at that time.

The gentleman took his pencil and a piece of paper and figured for a few moments, and then turning to me said: "Do you know, sir, those three Frenchmen, with their boat, who did all the work of ferrying, and were not employed half the time, could not, with the facilities you speak of, in 100 years do what is now being done in one day with our present means of transportation."

Since that time, which was six years ago, another bridge has been built to meet the necessities of the increasing business of that city, which shows that progress and increase of wealth and development are still on the rapid march.

The next thing of note, after passing St. Louis, occurred one evening after we camped. My mother stepped on the wagon-tongue to get the cooking utensils, when her foot slipped and she fell, striking her side and receiving injuries which resulted in her death eighteen months later.

On that journey my father travelled westward, crossing the Missouri River at St. Charles, Mo., following up the river from that point to where Glasgow is now situated, and there crossed the river to the south side, and wintered in the big bottoms. In the spring of 1819 he moved to what afterward became La Fayette County, and took up a location near the Big Snye Bear River.

In February, the winter following, my dear mother died from the injuries she received from the accident previously alluded to. The Rev. Simon Cockrell, a Baptist preacher, who at that time was. over eighty years of age, preached her funeral sermon. He was the first preacher I had ever seen stand up before a congregation with a book in his hand.

Although my mother died when I was little more than six years of age, my memory of her is apparently as fresh and endearing as though her death had occurred but a few days ago. Many acts I saw her do, and things I heard her say, impressed me with her courage and goodness, and their memory has been a help to me throughout the whole career of my long life. No mother ever gave birth to a son who loved her more, or whose tender recollections have been more endearing or lasting than mine.

I have never encountered any difficulty so great, no matter how threatening, that I have not been able to overcome fearlessly when the recollection of my dear mother and the spirit by which she was animated came to me. Even to this day, and I am an old man in my eightieth year, I cannot dwell long in conversation about her without tears coming to my eyes. There are no words in the English language to express my estimate and appreciation of the dear mother who gave me birth and nourishment. I would that all men loved and held the memories of their mothers more sacred than I think many of them do. One of the greatest safeguards to man throughout the meanderings of his life is the love of a father, mother, brother and sister, children and friends; it is a great solace and anchor to right-thinking men when they may be hundreds and thousands of miles away. Love of family begets true patriotism in his bosom, for, in my opinion, there is no such thing as true patriotism without love of family.

Returning to the events of 1821, we had in the neighbourhood of the Snye Bear River a great Indian scare. This happened in the month of August, when I was in my seventh year, after my father had built a log cabin for himself in that part of the country which afterward became Lafayette County, Mo My mother had died the winter before, leaving myself, the eldest, a brother next, and a sister little more than two years old.

Mrs. Ferrins, a settler who lived on the outskirts of the little settlement of pioneers, was alone, except for a baby a year old. She left the child and went to the spring for water. When she had filled her bucket, and rose to the top of the bank, she imagined she saw Indians. She dropped her bucket, ran to the cabin, took the child in her arms, and fled with all her might to Thomas Hopper's, the nearest neighbour. As soon as she came near enough to be heard, she shouted "Indians" at the top of her voice. Polly Hopper, a young girl of seventeen, hearing Mrs. Ferrin shouting "Indians," seized a bridle and ran to a herd of horses that were nearby in the shade of some trees, caught a flea-bitten grey bell mare, the leader of the herd, she being gentle and easier to catch than the others, mounted the animal without saddle, riding after the fashion of men, and started to alarm the settlement.

My father was lying in bed taking a sweat to abate a bilious fever. A family living nearby were caring for us children, and nursing my father in his sickness. My brother and I were playing a little distance from the cabin when we heard the screams of the woman, shouting "Indians" with every jump the horse made, her hair streaming out behind like a banner in the wind. We were on the very outside boundary of the settlement, and some signs of Indians had been discovered a few days previous by some neighbours who were out hunting for deer. This fact had been made known to the little settlement, and the day this scare took place had been selected for the men to meet at Henry Rennick's to discuss ways and means for building a stockade for the protection of their families in case the Indians should make an attempt of a hostile nature.

So, the first thoughts of the families at home were to start for Rennick's, where the men were. This accounts for the young woman going by our house, as she had to pass our cabin to reach that place. My father, sick as he was, jumped out of bed when she passed giving the alarm, took a heavy gun from the rack, hung his shot pouch over his shoulder, took my little sister in his arms, and, like the rest, started for Rennick's, my little brother and I toddling along behind him.

A family living nearby, consisting of the mother, Mrs. Turner, two daughters, a son, and a little grandson, also started for Rennick's. They would run for a short distance, and then stop and hide in the high weeds until they could get their breath. The old lady had a small dog she called Ging. He was on hand, of course, and just as much excited as all the rest of the dogs in the neighbourhood, and the people themselves. The screams of the girl Polly Hopper, and the ringing of the bell on the animal she was riding, aroused the dogs to the highest pitch of excitement. In those days dogs were a necessity to the frontiersman for his protection, and as much of a necessity on that account as any other animal he possessed, and consequently every settler owned from three to five dogs, and some more. They were the watch-guards against Indians and prowling beasts, both by night and day, and could not have been dispensed with in the settling of the frontier.

To return to our trip to Rennick's: When the old lady and her flock would run into the weeds to hide and regain their breath, this little dog Ging could not be controlled, for bark he would. The old lady when angry would use "cuss words," and she used them on this dog, and would jump out of her hiding-place and start on the trail again. Of course, when the dog barked he exposed her hiding-place. They would run a little farther, and when their breath would fail, they would make another hiding in the weeds, but would scarcely get settled when the dog would begin his barking again. The old lady, with another string of "cuss words," would jump out of the weeds and try the trail again a short distance. This was repeated until they reached Rennick's almost prostrate, as the distance was considerably over a mile, and the day an exceedingly hot one about noon.

My father, though sick, was more fortunate with his little group of children. When he felt about to faint, he would turn with us into the high weeds and sit there quietly, and, not having any dog with us to report our whereabouts, we were completely hidden by the high weeds, and had a hundred Indians passed they would not have discovered our hiding-place.

In due time we arrived safe at Rennick's, and strange to say, my father was a well man, and did not go to bed again on account of the fever.

When Polly Hopper reached Rennick's and ran into the crowd, she was in a fainting condition. The men took her off the horse, laid her on the ground, and administered cold water and other restoratives. She soon regained consciousness and strength, and of course was regarded as a heroine in the neighbourhood after that memorable day. One can well imagine the excitement among the men whose families were at home and exposed, as they thought, to the mercies of the savages. They scattered immediately toward their homes as rapidly as their horses would carry them, fearing they might find their families murdered. For hours after we reached Rennick's there continued to be arrivals of women and children, many times in a fainting condition, and all exhausted from the fright, the heat, and the speed at which they had run.

Mr. Rennick, who was one of the first pioneers, soon had more visitors than he knew what to do with, and more than his log cabin could shelter. These people remained in and around the cabin for two days, and until the men rode the country over and found the alarm had been a false one and there were no Indians in the neighbourhood.

One of the first occurrences of note in the early settlement of the West was the visitation of grasshoppers, in September, 1820, an occurrence which had never been known by the oldest inhabitants of the Mississippi Valley. They came in such numbers as to appear when in the heavens as thin clouds of vapor, casting a faint shadow upon the earth. In twenty-four hours after their appearance every green thing, in the nature of farm product, that they could eat or devour was destroyed. It so happened, however, that they came so late in the season that the early corn had ripened, so they could not damage that, otherwise a famine would have resulted. The next appearance of these pests was over forty years later, in Western Missouri, Nebraska, and Kansas, which all well remember, as there were two or three seasons in close proximity to each other in the sixties when Western farmers suffered to a great extent from their ravages.

For five years, from 1821 to 1826, nothing worthy of note occurred, but everything moved along as calmly as a sunny day.

In the month of April, 1826, a terrible cyclone passed through that section of the country, leaving nothing standing in its track. Fortunately, the country was but sparsely settled, and no lives were lost. It passed from a south-westerly direction to the northeast, tearing to pieces a belt of timber about half-a-mile wide, in that part of the country which became Jackson County, and near where Independence was afterward located, passing a little to the west of that point.

The next cyclone that visited that country was in 1847; this also passed from the southwest to the northeast, passing across the outskirts of Westport, which is now a suburb of Kansas City. The third and last cyclone that visited that section of the country, about eight years ago, blew down several houses in Kansas City, and killed a number of children who were attending the High School, the building being demolished by the storm.

POLLY'S WARNING

Chapter 2

Missouri in Its Wild and Uncultivated State

There was about one-fourth of the entire territory of Missouri that was covered with timber, and three-fourths in prairie land, with an annual growth of sage-grass, as it was called, about one and one-half feet high, and as thick as it could well grow; in fact the prairie lands in the commencement of its settlement were one vast meadow, where the farmer could cut good hay suitable for the wintering of his stock almost without regard to the selection of the spot; in other words, it was meadow everywhere outside of the timber lands. This condition of things would apply also to the States of Illinois, Iowa, and some of the other Western States, with the exception of Missouri, which had a greater proportion of timber than either of the others mentioned. The timber in all these States grew in belts along the rivers and their tributaries, the prairie covering the high rolling lands between the streams that made up the water channels of those States.

Many of the streams in the first settling of these States were bold, clear running water, and many of them in Missouri were sufficiently strong almost the year round to afford good water power for running machinery, and it was the prediction in the commencement of the settlement of these States by the best-informed people, that the water would increase, for the reason that the swampy portions in the bottom lands, and where there were small lakes, would, by the settlement of the country, become diverted, its force to run directly into and strengthen the larger, streams for all time to come. And to show how practical results overthrow theories, the fact proved to be exactly the reverse of their predictions. There has been a continuous slow decline in the natural flow of water-supply from the first settlement of the country.

Many places that I can now remember that were ponds or small lakes, or in other words little reservoirs, which held the water for months while it would be slowly passing out and feeding the streams, have now become fields and ploughed ground. Roads and ditches have been made that let the water off at once after a rainfall. The result has been that streams that used to turn machinery have become not much more than outlets for the heavy rainfalls that occur in the rainy season, and if twenty of those streams, each one of which had water enough to run machinery seventy years ago, were all put together now into one stream, there would not be sufficient power to run a good plant of machinery. The numerous springs that could be found on every forty or eighty acres of land in the beginning, have very many of them entirely failed.

The wells of twenty or thirty feet in depth that used to afford any quantity of water for family uses, many of them in order to get water supplies have to be sunk to a much greater depth. Little streams that used to afford any quantity of water for the stock have dried up, giving no water supply only in times of abundance of rain. All the first settlers in the State located along the timber belts, without an exception, and cultivated the timber lands to produce their grain and vegetables. It was many years after the forest lands were settled before prairie lands were cultivated to any extent, and it was found later that the prairie lands were more fertile than they gave them credit for being before real tests in the way of farming were made with them. The sage grass had the tenacity to stand a great deal of grazing and tramping over, and still grow to considerable perfection.

It required years of grazing upon the prairie before the wild grass, which was universal in the beginning, gave way, but in the timber portions the vegetation that was found in the first settling of the land gave way almost at once. In two years from the time a farmer moved upon a new spot and turned his stock loose upon it, the original wild herbs that were found there disappeared and other vegetation took its place. The land being exceedingly fertile, never failed to produce a crop of vegetation, and when one variety did appear and cover the entire surface as thick as it could grow for a few years, it seemed to exhaust the quality of the soil that produced that kind, and that variety would give way and something new come up.

The older the country has become, as a rule, the more obnoxious has been the vegetation that the soil has produced of its own accord. But there has been in my recollection, which goes back more than seventy years, a great many changes in the crops of vegetation on those lands, showing to my satisfaction that there is an inherent potency in nature, in rich soil that will cover itself every year with a growth of some kind. If it is not cultivated and made to produce fruit, vegetables, and cereals, it will nevertheless produce a crop of some kind.

The first settlers in the Mississippi Valley were as a rule poor people, who were industrious, economizing, and self-sustaining. From ninety-five to ninety-seven per cent of the entire population manufactured at home almost everything necessary for good living. A great many of them when they were crossing the Ohio and Mississippi to their new homes would barely have money enough to pay their ferriage across the rivers, and one of the points in selling out whatever they had to spare when they made up their minds to emigrate was to be sure to have cash enough with them to pay their ferriage. They generally carried with them a pair of chickens, ducks, geese, and if possible a pair of pigs, their cattle and horses.

The wife took her spinning wheel, a bunch of cotton or flax, and was ready to go to spinning as soon as she landed on the premises, often having her cards and wheel at work before her husband could build a log cabin. Going into a land, as it was then, that flowed with milk and honey they were enabled by the use of their own hands and brains to make an independent and good living. There was any quantity of game, bear, elk, deer, wild turkeys, and wild honey to be found in the woods, so that no man with a family, who had pluck and energy enough about him to stir around, ever need to be without a supply of food. At that time nature afforded the finest of pasture, both summer and winter, for his stock.

While the people as a rule were not educated, many of them very illiterate as far as education was concerned, they were thoroughly self-sustaining when it came to the knowledge required to do things that brought about a plentiful supply of the necessities of life. In those times all were on an equality, for each man and his family had to produce what was required to live upon, and when one man was a little better dressed than another there could be no complaint from his neighbour, for each one had the same means in his hands to bring about like results, and he could not say his neighbour was better dressed than he was because he had cheated some other neighbour out of something, and bought the dress; for at that time the goods all had to come to them in the same way—by their own industry. There was but little stealing or cheating among them. There was no money to steal, and if a man stole a piece of jeans or cloth of any kind he would be apprehended at once.

Society at that time was homogeneous and simple, and opportunities for vice were very rare. There were very few old bachelors and old maids, for about the only thing a young man could do when he became twenty-one, and his mother quit making his clothes and doing his washing, was to marry one of his neighbour's daughters. The two would then work together, as was the universal custom, and soon produce with their own hands abundance of supplies to live upon.

The country was new, and when a young man got married his father and brothers, and his wife's father and brothers, often would turn out and help him put up a log cabin, which work required only a few days, and he and his spouse would move into it at once. They would go to work in the same way as their fathers had done, and in a few years, would be just as independent as the old people. The young ladies most invariably spun and wove, and made their bridal dresses. At that time there were millions of acres of land that a man could go and squat on, build his cabin, and sometimes live for years upon it before the land would come into market, and with the prosperity attending such undertakings, as a general thing would manage in some way, when the land did come into market, to pay $1.25 per acre for as much as he required for the maintenance of his family.

Men in those days who came to Missouri and looked at the land often declined to select a home in the State on account of their having no market for their products, as above stated, everybody producing all that was needed for home consumption and often a surplus, but were so far away from any of the large cities of the country, without transportation of either steamboats or railroads, for it was before the time of steamboats, much less railroads—for neither of them in my early recollections were in existence—to make them channels of business and trade. Men in the early settlement often wondered if the rich land of the State would ever be worth $5 per acre.

Missouri at that time was considered the western confines of civilization, and it was believed then that there never would be in the future any white settlements of civilized people existing between the western borders of Missouri and the Pacific Coast, unless it might be the strip between the Sierra Nevada Mountains and the Pacific Ocean, which the people at that time knew but little or nothing about.

In 1820 and 1830 there were a great many peaceable tribes of Indians, located by the government all along the western boundary of Missouri, in what was then called the Indian Territory, and has since then become the States of Kansas, Nebraska, and Oklahoma Territory. I remember the names of many of the tribes who were our nearest neighbours across the line, and among them were the Shawnees, Delawares, Wyandottes, Kickapoos, Miamis, Sacs, Foxes, Osages, Peorias, and Iowas, all of whom were perfectly friendly and docile, and lived for a great many years in close proximity to the white settlers, even coming among them to trade without any outbreaks or trespassing upon the rights of the white people in any way or manner worth mentioning.

There was a long period existing from 1825 to 1860 of perfect harmony between these tribes and the white people, and in fact even to this day there is no disturbance between these tribes and their neighbours, the whites. The Indian troubles have been among the Sioux, Arapahoes, Cheyennes, Apaches, Utes, and some other minor tribes, all of which, at the present time, seem to have submitted to their fate in whatever direction it may lie. There is one remark that I will venture here, and it is this, that while the white people were in the power of the Indians and understood it, we got along with the Indian a great deal better than when the change to the white people took place.

In the early days white men respected the Indian's rights thoroughly, and would not be the aggressors, and often they were at the mercy of the Indians, but as soon as they began to feel that they could do as they pleased, became more aggressive and had less regard for what the Indian considered his rights. Then in the early days Indians were paid their annuities in an honest way, and there was no feeling among them that they were mistreated by the agent whose duty it was to pay them this annuity.

I was acquainted with one Indian agent by the name of Major Cummings, who for a long time was a citizen of Jackson County, and for a great many years, agent for a number of the tribes living along the borders of Missouri. There never was a complaint or even a suspicion, to the best of my knowledge, that he or his clerks ever took one cent of the annuities that belonged to the Indians. The money was paid to them in silver, either in whole or half dollars, and the head of every family received every cent of his quota. Therefore, we had a long period of quiet and peace with our red brethren. It is only since the late war that there has been so much complaint from the Indians with reference to the scanty allowances and poor food and blankets.

CHAPTER 3

A Silver Expedition

In the summer of 1827 my father, Benjamin Majors, with twenty-four other men, formed a party to go to the Rocky Mountains in search of a silver mine that had been discovered by James Cockrell, (an uncle of Senator Cockrell of Missouri), while on a beaver-trapping expedition some four years previous.

At that time, men attempting to cross the plains had no means of carrying food supplies to last more than a week, or ten days at the outside. When their scanty supply of provisions was exhausted, they depended solely upon the game they might chance to kill, invariably eating this without salt. These twenty-five men elected James Cockrell their captain, as he was the only man of the party who had crossed the plains. Being the discoverer of what he claimed was a rich silver mine, they relied solely upon him to pilot them to the spot. The only facilities for transportation were one horse each. Their scant amount of bedding, with the rider, was all the horse could carry.

Each man had to be armed with a good gun, and powder and ball enough to last him during the entire trip, for the territory through which they had to pass was inhabited by hostile Indians. No cooking vessels were taken with them, as they depended entirely upon roasting or broiling their meat upon the fire. When they could not find deer, antelope, elk, or buffalo they had to do without food, unless they were driven to kill and eat a wolf they might chance to. get. When they reached the buffalo belt, however, 200 miles farther west, there was no scarcity of meat. The country where they roamed was 400 miles across, reaching to the base of the Rocky Mountains, and extending from Texas more than 3,000 miles, very far north of the Canadian line.

The buffalo were numbered by the millions. It often occurred in traveling through this district that there would be days together when one would never be out of sight of great herds of these animals. They stayed in the most open portion of the plains they could find, for the country was one vast plain, or level prairie. The grass called buffalo grass did not grow more than one and one-half to two inches high, but grew almost as thick in many places as the hair on a dog's back. Other grasses that were found in this locality grew much taller, but one would invariably find the buffalo grazing upon the short kind, especially so in the winter, as the high winds blew the snow away from where this grass grew.

There were millions of acres of this grass. The buffalo's teeth and under jaw were so arranged by nature that he could bite this short grass to the earth; in fact, no small animal, such as a sheep, goat, or antelope, could cut the grass more closely than the largest buffalo. Strange to say this short grass of the prairie is rapidly disappearing, as the buffaloes have done. In crossing the plains with our oxen in later years we found it impossible for them to get a living by grazing on the portions of the plains where this grass grew.

The party in question soon reached the Raton Mountains not far from Trinidad, now on the Atchison, Topeka & Santa Fé Railroad. It is proper to state that after leaving their homes in Jackson and Lafayette counties, Mo., they traveled across the prairie, bearing a little south of west, until they reached the Big Bend, or Great Bend, as it is lately called, of the Arkansas River. At this point they found innumerable herds of buffalo, and no trouble in finding grass and water in plenty, as well as meat. They followed the margin of the river until they reached the foothills of the Rocky Mountains; then their captain told them he was in the region where he had discovered the mine.

He found some difficulty in locating the spot, and after many days spent in searching, some of the party grew restless and distrustful, doubting as to whether he ever discovered silver ore, or if so, if he was willing to show them the location, and became very threatening in their attitude toward him. He finally found what he and they had supposed was silver ore. This fact pacified the party and perhaps saved his life, as it was a long way for men to travel through peril and hardships only to be disappointed, or, as they expressed it, "to be fooled." They were disappointed, however, when they found nothing but dirty-looking rock, with now and then a bright speck of metal in it. Not one of them had ever seen silver ore, nor did they know anything about manipulating the rock in order to get the silver out of it.

Many of them expected to find the silver in metallic form, and thought they could cut it out with their tomahawks and pack home a good portion of wealth upon their horses. They thought they could walk and lead their horses if they could get a load of precious metal to carry, as their captain had done a few years before, when he sold his beaver skins in St. Louis, took his pay in silver dollars, put them in a sack, bought a horse to carry it, and led him 300 miles to his home.

It must be remembered that this was the first prospecting party to look for silver that ever left the western borders of Missouri for the Rocky Mountains. After finding what they supposed was a silver mine, each one selected some of the best specimens and left for their homes. Everything moved along well with them until they arrived at about the point on the Arkansas River where Dodge City now stands. They camped one evening at the close of a day's travel, ate a hearty supper of buffalo meat, put their guard around their horses, and went to bed. Two men at a time guarded the horses, making a change every three hours during the night. This precaution was necessary to keep the Indians, who were in great numbers and hostile, from running off their horses.

But on that fatal night the Indians succeeded in crawling on their bellies where the grass was tall enough to conceal them from the guard. It was only along the river bottoms and water courses that the grass grew tall. When they got between the guard and the horses, they suddenly rose, firing their guns, shaking buffalo robes, and with war-whoops and yells succeeded in frightening the horses to an intense degree. Then the Indians who were in reserve, mounted on ponies, ran the horses off where their owners never heard of or saw them afterward. Part of the Indians, at the same time, turned their guns upon the men that were lying upon the bank of the river. They jumped out of their beds, over the bank and into the water knee-deep. The men, by stooping under the bank, which was four feet perpendicular, were protected from the arrows and bullets of the enemy. There they stood for the remainder of that cold October night.

One of the party, a man named Mark Foster, when they jumped over the bank, did not stop, but ran as fast as he could go for the other side. The water was shallow, not being more than knee-deep anywhere, and in some places not half that depth. The bottom was sandy, and at that place the river was some 400 yards wide. In running in the dark of the night, with the uneven bottom of the river, Mr. Foster fell several times. Each time it drew a yell from the Indians, who thought they had killed him, for they were shooting at him as he ran. After being three times ducked, he reached the other side and dry land. His clothes were thoroughly drenched, and his gun, which was a flint-lock and muzzle-loader, entirely useless.

Just think of a man in that condition—his gun disabled, apparently a thousand wolves howling around him in all directions, the darkness of the night, the yelling of the Indians on the other side, and 400 miles from home; the only living white man, unless some of his comrades happened not to be killed. He remained there shivering with the cold the rest of the night. When daylight appeared, he started to cross the river to the camp to find out whether his comrades were dead or alive. He reached the middle of the river and halted, his object being to see, if possible, whether it was the Indians or his party that he could see through the slight fog that was rising and slowly moving westward and up the river.

His comrades, who fortunately were alive, could hear, in the still of the morning, every step he made in the water. After standing a short time, he decided that the men he saw moving about were Indians, and he was confirmed in the belief that all his party were killed, so he ran back to where he had spent such a doleful part of the night and there remained until the fog entirely cleared away. He then could see that the men at the camp from where he fled were his comrades. He returned within about sixty yards from where they were, stopped and called to my father, who answered him, after some persuasion from the rest of the party, for they all felt ugly toward him, thinking he had acted the coward in doing as he did.

When my father answered his call, he asked if they would allow him to join them. After holding a consultation, it was agreed that he might come. He walked firmly up to them and remarked:

> I have something to say to you, gentlemen. It is this: I know you think I have acted the d———d coward, and I do not blame you under the circumstances. When you all jumped over the bank I thought you were going to run to the other side, and I did not know any better until I had got so far out I was in greater danger to return than to go ahead. For, as you know, the Indians were sending volleys of bullets and arrows after me, and really thought they had killed me every time I fell. Now, to end

this question, there is one of two things you must do. The first is that you take your guns and kill me now, or if you do not comply with this, that every one of you agree upon your sacred honour that you will never allude, in any way, or throw up to me the unfortunate occurrences of last night. Now, gentlemen, mark what I say. If you do not kill me, but allow me to travel with you to our homes, should one of you ever be so thoughtless or forgetful of the promise you must now make as to throw it up to me, I pledge myself before you all that I will take the life of the man who does it. Now, I have presented the situation fairly, and you must accept one or the other before you leave this spot.

The party with one accord, after hearing his story, agreed never to allude to it in any way in his presence, and gave him a cordial welcome to their midst. They treated him as one of them from that time on, for he was a brave man after all. Think of the awful experience the poor fellow had during the night, and in the morning, to reach an amicable understanding with his party. One can readily see that he was a man of very great courage and physical endurance, or he could not have survived the pressure upon him. It was a sad time for those twenty-five brave men for more reasons than one. Knowing that they were 400 miles from home, late in the fall, without a road or path to follow, no stopping place of any kind between them and their homes on the borders of the Missouri, which was as far as civilization had reached westward.

The thought that impressed them most deeply was in reference to one of their comrades by the name of Clark Davis, whom they all loved and honoured. He was a man weighing 300 pounds, but not of large frame, his weight consisting more of fat than bone. It was the universal verdict of the party that it would be impossible for him to walk home and carry his gun and ammunition as they all had to do. They would go aside in little groups, so he would not hear them, and deplore the situation. They thought they would have to leave him sitting in the prairie for the wolves to devour, or hazard the lives of all the rest of the party.

Some actually wept over the thought of the loss of such a dear comrade and noble-hearted man. Should they chance to reach their own homes, for they were all men with families, the idea of telling his family that they were obliged to leave him was more than they felt their nerves could endure. In my opinion there never was a more brave and heroic group of men thrown together than were those twenty-five frontiersmen. All were fine specimens of manhood, physically speaking, between thirty and forty years of age, and with perfect health and daring to do whatever their convictions dictated.

They went to work and burned their saddles, bridles, blankets, in fact everything they had in camp that they could not carry with them on their backs. This they did to prevent the Indians from getting any more "booty." After all their arrangements were made for leaving their unfortunate camping-place, they started once more for their homes. They traveled at the rate of twenty to twenty-five miles per day. They could have gone farther, but for the fact that they had no trail to walk in. The grass in some places, and the drifting sand in others, made it exceedingly irksome for footmen.

My father was frequently asked after his return:

"Was there no road you could follow?"

He would answer:

"No, from the fact that the drifting sand soon filled every track of a passing caravan and no trace was left of a trail a few hours afterward."

A few years later on this shifting of sand discontinued, and grass and small shrubbery soon began to grow and cover many places that were then perfectly bare. One-half of the distance they had to walk was covered with herds of buffalo, the other half was through desolate prairie country, where game of any kind was seldom seen. It was on this part of their journey that they came near starvation. It only took them a few days after leaving the buffalo belt to consume what meat they had carried on their backs, as men become very hungry and consume a great deal of meat when they have long and tiresome walks to make.

In the first week of their march their convictions in regard to Clark Davis were confirmed, as they thought, for his feet blistered in a terrible manner, his fat limbs became exceedingly raw and sore, so he of necessity would lag. Then they would detail of a morning when they started, a guard of five or six men to remain with him for protection from the Indians. The rest of the party would walk on to some point they would designate for camping the next night, and he with his little guard would arrive some three or four hours later. This went on for seven or eight days in succession, each day they expecting the news from the guard that he had given up the hope of going any farther.

But in time his feet began to improve, in fact his condition every way, and he would reach camp sooner each day after the arrival of the party. After they had passed the buffalo belt, where meat was abundant, and struck the starvation belt in their travels, Mr. Davis' fat proved a blessing and of great service. When fatigue and want were to be endured at the same time, he began to take the lead instead of the rear of the party. Several days before they reached home they would have perished, but for the fact that he alone had sufficient activity and strength to attempt to hunt for game, for they had seen none after leaving the buffalo.

They had reached a place called Council Grove—now a city of that name—in the State of Kansas, about one hundred and thirty miles from their homes. After so many weeks of hard marching they thought they could go no farther, and some dropped on the ground, thinking it useless to make the attempt. At this juncture Clark Davis said:

"Boys, I will go and kill a deer."

My father said the very word was tantalising to a lot of men who were almost dying of hunger. They did not know there was a deer in the country, or anything else that could be eaten, not even a snake, for cold weather was so near even they had disappeared. Davis, however, determined on his hunt, left his comrades, and had traveled only a few hundred yards until he saw two fine deer standing near. Directly the men in the camp heard the report of his gun, and as soon as he could reload they heard a second report, and then a shout, "Come here, boys! there is meat in plenty." You may imagine it was not long until everyone joined him. They drank every drop of blood that was in the two deer, ate the livers without cooking, and saved every particle, even taking the marrow out of their legs. This meat tided them over until they were able to reach other food.

Never before in the history of the past, nor since that time, did 150 pounds of surplus fat—so considered until starvation overtook them—prove to be of such great value, and was worth more to them than all the gold and silver in the Rocky Mountains. When the test came, it was found to be one of nature's reservoirs that could be drawn upon to save the lives of twenty-five brave men when all else failed them. Mr. Davis, as well as the rest of the party, no doubt often wished it could be dispensed with, as after losing his horse he carried it with great suffering and fatigue, before they learned its use, and that it was to be the salvation of the party. We often hear it said that truth is stranger than fiction, and this certainly was one of the cases where it proved to be so.

They finally reached home without losing one of their party; but they all gave the man whom they expected to leave to the wolves in the start the credit of saving their lives. When Mr. Davis reached his family the first thing his wife did was to set him a good meal. When he sat down to the table he said, "Jane, there is to be a new law for the future of our lives at our table."

She said, "What is it, Clark?"

He answered, "It is this. I never want to hear you or one of my children say bread again."

"What then must we call it?" asked his wife.

"Call it bready," said he, "for when I was starving on the plains it came to me that the word bread was too short and coarse a name to call such sweet, precious, and good a thing, and whoever eats it should use this pet name and be thankful to God who gives it, for I assure you, wife, the ordeal I have passed through will forever cause me to appreciate life and the good things that uphold it."

The outcome of this trip was drawing the party together, like one family, and they could not be kept long apart. It is a fact that mutual suffering begets an endearment stronger than ties of blood. It was interesting to me as a boy to hear them relate their experiences in reference to their hard trials and forebodings that were undergone, with no beneficial results. Some of them sent their specimens to St. Louis to be tested for silver, but received discouraging accounts of its value. If a very rich mine had been found at that time it would not have been of any practical value, for they were more than thirty years ahead of the time when silver-mining could be carried on, from an American standpoint, with success. There was no one west of the Alleghanies with capital and skill enough to carry on such an enterprise, and there were no means whatever for transporting machinery to the Rocky Mountains.

Chapter 4

The Mormons

Nothing of very great note occurred in the county of Jackson, after the cyclone of 1826, until the year 1830, when five Mormon elders made their appearance in the county and commenced preaching, stating to their audiences that they were chosen by the priesthood which had been organised by the prophet Joseph Smith, who had met an angel and received a revelation from God, who had also revealed to him and his adherents the whereabouts of a book written upon golden plates and deposited in the earth. This book was found in a hill called Cumorah, at Manchester, in the State of New York. They selected a place near Independence, Jackson County, Mo., in the early part of the year 1831, which they named Temple Lot, a beautiful spot of ground on a high eminence. They there stuck down their Jacob's staff, as they called it, and said:

> This spot is the centre of the earth. This is the place where the Garden of Eden, in which Adam and Eve resided, was located, and we are sent here according to the directions of the angel that appeared to our prophet, Joseph Smith, and told him this is the spot of ground on which the New Jerusalem is to be built, and, when finished, Christ Jesus is to make his reappearance and dwell in this city of New Jerusalem with the saints for a thousand years, at the end of which time there will be a new deal with reference to the nations of the earth, and the final wind-up of the career of the human family.

They claimed to have all the spiritual gifts and understanding of the works of the Almighty that belonged to the Apostles who were chosen by Christ when on his mission to this earth. They claim the gift of tongues and interpretation of tongues or languages spoken in an unknown tongue. In their silent meetings, the one who had received the gift of an unknown tongue knew nothing of its interpretation whatever, but after some silence someone in the audience would rise and claim to have the gift of interpretation, and would interpret what the brother or sister had previously spoken. They also claimed to have the gift of healing by anointing the sick with oil and laying on of hands, and some claimed that they could raise the dead; in fact, they laid claim to every gift that belonged to the Apostolic day or age.

They established their headquarters at Independence, where some of their leading elders were located. There they set up a printing office, the first that was established within 150 miles of Independence, and commenced printing their church literature, which was very distasteful to the members and leaders of other religious denominations, the community being composed of Methodists, Baptists of two different orders, Presbyterians of two different orders, and Catholics, and a denomination calling themselves Christians.

In that day and age, it was regarded as blasphemous or sacrilegious for anyone to claim that they had met angels and received from them new revelations, and the religious portion of the community, especially, was very much incensed and aroused at the audacity of any person claiming such interviews from the invisible world. Of course, the Mormon elders denounced the elders and preachers of the other denominations above mentioned, and said they were the blind leading the blind, and that they would all go into the ditch together. An elder by the name of Rigdon preached in the court house one Sunday in 1832, in which he said that he had been to the third heaven, and had talked face to face with God Almighty. The preachers in the community the next day went *en masse* to call upon him. He repeated what he had said the day before, telling them they had not the truth, and were the blind leading the blind.

The conduct of the Mormons for the three years that they remained there was that of good citizens, beyond their tantalising talks to outsiders. They, of course, were clannish, traded together, worked together, and carried with them a melancholy look that one acquainted with them could tell a Mormon when he met him by the look upon his face almost as well as if he had been of different colour. They claimed that God had given them that locality, and whoever joined the Mormons, and helped prepare for the next coming of the Lord

Jesus Christ, would be accepted and all right; but if they did not go into the fold of the Latter Day Saints, that it was only a matter of time when they would be crushed out, for that was the promised land and they had come to possess it. The Lord had sent them there and would protect them against any odds in the way of numbers.

Finally, the citizens, and particularly the religious portion of them, made up their minds that it was wrong to allow them to be printing their literature and preaching, as it might have a bad effect upon the rising generation; and on the 4th of July, 1833, there was quite a gathering of the citizens, and a mob was formed to tear down their printing office. While the mob was forming, many of the elders stood and looked on, predicting that the first man who touched the building would be paralyzed and fall dead upon the ground.

The mob, however, paid no attention to their predictions and prayers for God to come and slay them, but with one accord seized hold of the implements necessary to destroy the house, and within the quickest time imaginable had it torn to the ground, and scattered their type and literature to the four winds. This, of course, created an intense feeling of anger on the part of the Mormons against the citizens. At this time there were but a few hundred Mormons in the county against many times their number of other citizens. I presume there was not exceeding 600 Mormons in the county.

Immediately after they tore down the printing office they sent to the store of Elder Partridge and Mr. Allen, who was also an elder in the church, and took them by force to the public square, stripped them to their waists, and poured on them a sufficient amount of tar to cover their bodies well, and then took feathers and rubbed them well into the tar, making the two elders look like a fright. One of their names being Partridge, many began to whistle like a cock partridge, in derision. Now, be it remembered that the people who were doing this were not what is termed "rabble" of a community, but many among them were respectable citizens and law-abiding in every other respect, but who actually thought they were doing God's service to destroy, if possible, and obliterate Mormonism.

In all my experience I never saw a more law-abiding people than those who lived where this occurred. There is nothing, however, that they could have done that would have proved more effectual in building up and strengthening the faith of the people so treated as this and similar performances proved to do. For if there is anything under the sun that will strengthen people in their beliefs or faith, no matter whether it is error or truth, if they have adopted it as true, it is to abuse and punish them for their avowed belief in whatever they espouse as religion or politics.

A few months after the tearing down of the building, a dozen or two Mormons made their appearance one day on the county road west of the Big Blue and not far from the premises of Moses G. Wilson. Wilson's boy rode out to drive up the milk cows in the morning, and saw this group of Mormons and had some conversation with them, and they used some very violent language to the boy. He went back and told his father, and it happened that there were several of the neighbours in at the time, as he kept a little county store; and in those days men generally carried their guns with them, in case they should have a chance to shoot a deer or turkey as they went from one neighbour's to another.

It so happened that several of them had their guns with them; those who did not picked up a club of some kind, and they all followed the boy, who showed them where they were. When they got in close proximity to where the Mormons were grouped, seeing the men approaching with guns, the Mormons opened fire upon them, and the Gentiles, as they were called by the Mormons, returned the fire. There was a lawyer on the Gentile side by the name of Brazeel, who was shot dead; another man by the name of Lindsay was shot in the jaw and was thought to be fatally wounded, but recovered. Wilson's boy was also shot in the body, but not fatally. There were only one or two Mormons killed.

Of course, after this occurrence, it aroused an intense feeling of hate and revenge in the citizens, and the Mormons would not have been so bold had it not been for their elders claiming that under all circumstances and at all times they would be sustained by the Almighty's power, and that a few of them would be able to put their enemies to flight. The available Mormon men then formed themselves into an organisation for fighting the battles of the Lord, and started to Independence, about ten miles away, to take possession of the town. On their way, and when they were within about a mile of Independence, they marched with all the faith and fervour imaginable for fanatics to possess, encouraging each other with the words, "God will be with us and deliver our enemies into our hands."

At this point they met a gentleman whom I well knew, by the name

Nature's Tabernacle

of Rube Collins, a citizen of the place, who was leaving the town in a gallop to go home and get more help to defend the town from the Mormon invasion. He shouted out as he passed them, "You are a d——d set of fools to go there now; there are armed men enough there to exterminate you in a minute."

They were acquainted with Collins, and supposed he had told them the truth; however, at that time they could have taken the town had they pressed on, but his words intimidated them somewhat, and they filed off from the big road and hid themselves in the brush until they could hold a council, and I presume pray for light to be guided by. During this time there were runners going in all directions, notifying the citizens that the Mormons were coming to the town to take it, and every citizen, as soon as he could run bullets and fill his powder horn with powder, gathered his gun and made for the town; and in a few hours men enough had gathered to exterminate them had they approached.

In their council that they held they decided not to approach until they sent spies ahead to see whether Collins had told them the truth or not. They supposed he had, from the fact that they found the public square almost covered with men, and others arriving every minute. As quickly as the citizens had organised themselves into companies (my father, Benjamin Majors, being captain of one of them), they then sent a message by two or three citizens to the Mormons, where they were still secreted in the paw-paw brush, and told them that if they did not come and surrender immediately, the whole party that was waiting for them in the town would come out and exterminate them. This message sent terror to their hearts, with all their claims that God would go before them and fight their battles for them.

After holding another council, they decided the best thing they could do was to go and surrender themselves to their enemies, which they did. I never saw a more pale-faced, terror-stricken set of men banded together than these seventy-five Mormons, for it was all the officers could do to keep the citizens from shooting them down, even when they were surrendering. However, they succeeded in keeping the men quiet, and no one was hurt. They stacked all their arms around a big white-oak stump that was perhaps four feet in diameter, and at that time was standing in the public square.

Afterward the guns were put in the jail house for safe keeping, and were eaten up with rust, and never to my knowledge delivered to them. They then stipulated that every man, woman, and child should leave the county within three weeks. This was a tremendous hardship upon the Mormons, as it was late in the fall, and there were no markets for their crops or anything else that they had. The quickest way to get out of the county was to cross the river into Clay, as the river was the line between the two counties. They had to leave their homes, their crops, and in fact every visible thing they had to live upon. Many of their houses were burned, their fences thrown down, and the neighbours' stock would go in and eat and destroy the crop.

It has been claimed by people who were highly coloured in their prejudice against the Mormons that they were bad citizens; that they stole whatever they could get their hands on and were not law-abiding. This is not true with reference to their citizenship in Jackson County, where they got their first kick, and as severe a one as they ever received, if not the most severe. There was not an officer among them, all the offices of the county being in the hands of their enemies, and if one had stolen a chicken he could and would have been brought to grief for doing so; but it is my opinion there is nothing in the county records to show where a Mormon was ever charged with any misdemeanour in the way of violation of the laws for the protection of property.

The cause of all this trouble was solely from the claim that they had a new revelation direct from the Almighty, making them the chosen instruments to go forward, let it please or displease whom it might, to build the New Jerusalem on the spot above referred to, Temple Lot. And, as above stated, whoever did not join in this must sooner or later give way to those who would. I met a Presbyterian preacher, Rev. Mr. McNice, in Salt Lake City a number of years ago at the dinner table of a mutual friend, Doctor Douglas. It was on the Sabbath after hearing him preach a very bitter sermon against the Mormons, denouncing their doctrines and doings in a severe manner, and while we were at the dinner table, the subject of the Mormons came up, and I told him that I was thoroughly versed in their first troubles in Missouri, and he asked me what the trouble was.

I told him frankly that it grew out of the fact that they claimed to have seen an angel, and to have received a new revelation from God which was not in accord with the religious denominations that existed in the community at that time. He hooted at the idea and told me he had read the history of their troubles there, and that they were bad citizens with reference to being outlaws, thieves, etc., who would pick up their neighbours' property and the like. He insisted that he had read their history, and showed a disposition to discredit my statements. I then told him *I* was history, and knew as much about it as any living man could know, and that there were no charges of that kind against them; they were industrious, hard-working people, and worked for whatever they wanted to live upon, obtaining it by their industry, and not by stealing it from their neighbours.

He then scouted at the idea that people would receive such treatment as they did merely because they claimed to have seen angels and talked with God and claimed to have a new revelation. I then referred him to the fact that fifty or sixty years previous to that time the public mind in America lacked a great deal of being so tolerant as it was at the time of our conversation; that not more than one hundred years ago some of the American people were so superstitious that they could burn witches at the stake and drag Quakers through the streets of Boston on their backs, with a jack hitched to their heels; that the Mormons today could go to Jackson County, Mo., and preach the same doctrines that they did then, and the result would be that they would be laughed at instead of mobbed as they were sixty years ago.

I was sitting in a cabin with my father's miller, a Mr. Newman, a Mormon, at the time of this trouble. Mr. Newman's mother-in-law, who lived with him, was named Bentley; she had a son in the company that surrendered at Independence, and who walked six miles that evening and came home. The young man walked in and looked as sad as death, and when asked what the news was he stood there and related what had taken place that day at the surrender. They all sat in breathless silence and listened to the story, and when he was through with his statement and said the Mormons had agreed to leave the county within three weeks, the old lady, who sat by the table sewing, raised her hand and brought it down upon the table with a tremendous thud, and said:

"So sure, as this is a world there *will be* a New Jerusalem built."

I relate this little incident to show that even after they had met with such a galling defeat how zealous even the old women were with reference to their future success. But it is my opinion that the more often a fanatic is kicked and abused, the stronger is his faith in his cause, for then they would take up the Scriptures and read the sentences expressed by Christ:

But before all these they shall lay their hands on you and persecute you, delivering you up to the synagogues and into prisons, being brought before kings and rulers for my name's sake.
But take heed to yourselves, for they shall deliver you up to councils, and in the synagogues ye shall be beaten; and ye shall be brought before rulers and kings for my sake for a testimony against them.

From such passages they have always drawn the greatest consolation, and one would ask one another, "Where are the people the blessed Lord had reference to?"

Another brother, with all the sanctity and confidence imaginable for a fanatic to feel, would answer, "Well, brother, if you do not find them among the Latter Day Saints you cannot find them upon the face of this green earth, for we have suffered all the abuses the blessed Lord refers to in the Scripture you have just quoted."

I have said before that the Mormons all crossed the Missouri into Clay County, where they wintered in tents and log cabins hastily thrown together, and lived on mast, corn, and meat that they would procure from the citizens for whom they worked in clearing ground and splitting rails, and other work of a like character.

In the spring they were determined to return to their homes, although they were so badly destroyed, and claimed again as before that God would vindicate them and put to flight their enemies. The people of Jackson County, however, watched for their return, and gathered, at the appointed time, in a large body, on the opposite side of the river to where the Mormons were expected to congregate and cross back into the county.

Their spies came to the river, and seeing camps of the citizens, who had gathered to the number of four or five hundred strong (I being one of the number) to prevent their crossing, then changed their purpose and sent some of their leading men to locate in some other part of the State, for the time being, with the full understanding, however, that at the Lord's appointed time they would all be returned to Jackson County, and complete their mission in building the city of the New Jerusalem. The delegation they sent out selected Davis and Colwell counties as the portion of the State where they would make their temporary rally until they became strong enough for the Lord to restore them to their former location.

During that spring the citizens of Jackson County, feeling that there had been, in many cases, great outrages perpetrated upon the Mormons, held a public meeting at Independence and appointed five commissioners, whose duty it was to meet some of the leading elders of the Mormons at Liberty, the seat of Clay County, and make some reparation for the damages that had been done to their property the fall before in Jackson County. They met, but failed to agree, as the elders asked more and perhaps wanted to retain the titles they had to the lands, as they thought it would be sacrilege to part with them, for that was the chosen spot for the New Jerusalem.

During the time that elapsed between the commissioners crossing the river in the morning and returning in the evening, the ferryman (Bradbury), whom I have often met, a man with a very large and finely developed physique, a great swimmer, was supposed to be bribed by the Mormons to bore large auger-holes through the gunwales of his flatboat just at the water's edge. The boat having a floor in it some inches above the bottom, there could be no detection of the flow of the water until it was sufficiently deep to cover the inner floor. The commissioners went upon the boat with their horses, and had not proceeded very far from the shore until they found the water coming up in the second floor and the boat rapidly sinking. This, of course, produced great consternation, for the river was very high and turbulent. Bradbury, the owner of the ferry, said to his two men:

"Boys, we will jump off and swim back to the shore."

As above stated, he was a great swimmer, and had been known to swim the Missouri upon his back several times not long before this occurred. When the water rose in the boat so that it was necessary for the commissioners to leave it, three of them caught hold of their horses' tails, after throwing off as much clothing as they could before the boat went down with them. The other two men who could swim attempted to swim alone, but the current was so turbulent that they were overcome and were drowned. Those who hung on to the tails of their horses were brought safely to shore. One of the men drowned was a neighbour of my father's and as fine a gentleman and good fellow as ever lived. His name was David Lynch.

I remember well their names, and was well acquainted with two of the men who were pulled through by their horses, S. Noland and Sam C. Owens, the foremost merchant of the county, a man who stood high in every sense, and of marked ability.

This occurrence put the quietus on any further attempt to try to settle for the damages done the Mormons when driven from the county, for it caused in the whole population the most intense feeling against them, and they never were remunerated.

When Bradbury jumped off the boat he swam for the shore, but was afterward found dead, with one of his hands grasping the root of a cottonwood tree, so there was no opportunity for trying him for the crime, or finding out how it was brought about. It was supposed that he was bribed, as no one knew of any enmity he had against the commissioners.

The town the Mormons started, which they selected for their home in Paris County, they called Far West. This was the first experience that the people of Western Missouri had with the emigrants of the Eastern or New England States. Brigham Young, who afterward became the leader of the Mormons, was from Vermont, and many others composing the early pioneers of the Mormon church were from the New England States; some, however, from Ohio and Illinois, as well as some proselytes from Missouri. Up to the time of their appearance in Western Missouri the entire population was from some one of the four States—Virginia, North Carolina, Tennessee, or Kentucky.

It has been claimed by some that one of the causes of the dissatisfaction was that the Mormons were Abolitionists. This, however, played no part in the bitter feeling that grew up between them and their neighbours, for at the time of their coming to Jackson County there were but very few slaves, the people generally being poor farmers who lived from the labour of their own hands and that of their families. And then, when the Mormons were driven entirely from Missouri to Illinois, which was a free State, they soon got into difficulty with their neighbours there, as they had done in Missouri. It is claimed now, universally, by the people of this country that polygamy, or the plurality-wife system, is the only objection that good citizens can have to Mormonism.

This was not the cause of their difficulties or their trouble in Illinois and Missouri, as they had never, up to the time they left Nauvoo, Ill., proclaimed polygamy as being a church institution. And as I have previously stated, it was their clannishness, as is natural for a church to do, more or less, only they carried it to a greater degree than other denominations. Also, the new doctrine they were preaching, stating that they were the only and chosen people of God, and that they had the key of St. Peter, which was lost during the dark ages and was revealed again to Joseph Smith, their prophet; that the Lord would stand by them and enable them to prevail in their undertakings as against any array of opposition, no matter how much greater the numbers might be than their own.

They built up the city of Far West, of several thousand people, and while there increased very rapidly, having missionaries in many parts of the country preaching their doctrine. As quickly as an individual would accept their faith, they would at once rally to the headquarters, and in the course of a few years they had put a great deal of the prairie lands into cultivation and increased their numbers until they were so formidable that when they began to be odious to their neighbours by showing a hostile attitude toward any power that might interfere with them, they got into trouble much in the same way as they did in Jackson County.

A party of Gentiles and Mormons met at a point called Horn's Mill, and became involved in a quarrel, when there were some killed on both sides. This created such a feeling in the community that both Mormons and Gentiles felt insecure, living neighbours to each other as they were, and the trouble went on until it culminated in the Governor, Lilburn W. Boggs, calling out a portion of the militia of the State and ordering them to Far West, the Mormon centre. The Mormons were drilling continuously, and increasing their facilities for righting, when the militia reached the place designated, and organising, placed themselves in battle array.

The Mormons were also drawn up in long lines, and for a short time it looked as if a bloody battle was unavoidable, but before any engagement occurred the Mormons again surrendered. They then agreed to leave the State of Missouri, and in April, 1839, the last of the band left Far West, moved across the Mississippi into Illinois, where they afterward located and built the city of Nauvoo, but with no better results with the people in the free State than they experienced in Missouri. This shows that slavery had nothing to do with the hard feelings and prejudice they aroused in every community in which they lived.

The Mormons' new village was named Nauvoo, which means Peaceful Rest. While there, having increased to fifteen thousand souls, they built a temple to the Lord, which was, perhaps, the finest building that had ever been erected in the State up to that time. During the year 1844, trouble arose between them and the Gentiles, to suppress which the militia was called out, and in June of that year a writ was sworn out for the arrest of the Mormon prophet, Joseph Smith. His brother Hiram and Elder Taylor, who, after Brigham Young's death, became president of the church, accompanied him to Carthage, Ill., where he went to give himself up. Arriving at Carthage, all three were put in jail, where a mob succeeded in killing the two brothers and seriously wounding Taylor, who carried some of the bullets in his body during the remainder of his life. On the death of Joseph Smith, Brigham Young was chosen by the church as its prophet, president, and leader.

After three severe experiences in establishing settlements in Missouri and Illinois, they determined in their councils to emigrate farther west and start a colony which would be composed of Latter Day Saints, where they would be entirely distinct and separate from any antagonising elements. At that time Salt Lake Valley, being under Spanish dominion and a thousand miles from any white settlement, was ultimately chosen as the spot best suited for their purpose.

After leaving Nauvoo, Ill., they went to Council Bluffs, Iowa (called by them Kaneville), traveling through the State of Iowa, and undergoing the greatest hardships and sufferings any people were ever called upon to endure, being without money, some of them without the proper means of transportation, destitute of almost all the necessities of life, and a great many sick on account of exposure to the elements. Arriving at the place above named, on the Missouri River, they went into winter quarters, and the next spring planted and raised crops in that vicinity, the greater number of the emigrants remaining there for the next two years.

In the spring of 1847, at the time war was being carried on between the United States and Mexico, Brigham Young started west with a band of from seventy to seventy-five pioneers, having, I believe, an impression that in Salt Lake Valley might be found the Mecca of their hopes. They arrived in Salt Lake Valley on the 21st day of July of that year. Previous to this, in 1846, at the call of the President for troops for the Mexican War, Brigham Young raised a regiment of a thousand volunteers to go to Mexico, under a stipulation with the United States Government that, when the war was over, the survivors should receive their discharges in California. This agreement was made in view of the fact that they had already resolved to go west into

Spanish territory.

The treaty of peace between the United States and Old Mexico, at the close of the war, resulted in the Government of Mexico giving up to the United States all the territory possessed by it lying north of the present boundary line between the two countries, so that, after all the exertions the Mormons had made to effect a settlement on Spanish territory, in less than a year they found themselves still in the United States, where they have ever since remained, having built cities and towns on the colonising plan in every available portion of the Territory of Utah, and having quite a number of colonies in other Territories, with one at present established in Mexico, as I have lately been informed.

I have met in later years and become familiarly acquainted with many of the leading spirits of the Mormon church, and have had large business transactions with Brigham Young and many other prominent Mormons, among whom were Captain Hooper, General Eldridge, Ferrimore Little, William Jennings, John Sharp, Lew Hills, Gen. Daniel H. Wells, Wilford Woodruff (now president of the Mormon church), Joseph Smith, and George Q. Cannon, and a fairer, more upright set of gentlemen I never met.

I have heard all the leading elders of the Mormon Church preach, including Brigham Young, Heber Kimball, George Q. Cannon, George A. Smith (the historian), John Taylor, Orson Pratt, and Elder Woodruff, who is now president of the church.

Orson Pratt was the ablest expounder of the Scriptures, particularly of the prophecies, in the Mormon church. He was the man chosen by Brigham Young and his counsellors to discuss the subject of polygamy, from a Bible standpoint, with the Rev. John P. Newman, who was at that time pastor of one of the Methodist churches in Washington, D. C. I, among many other Gentiles, was present and heard the discussion, which took place in the Mormon Tabernacle.

President Young, as he was invariably called by his own people, was the boldest, most outspoken man I ever saw in the pulpit. I remember hearing him one Sabbath day when he was preaching in the Tabernacle, which seats 13,000 people, and on that day, was packed to its full capacity, there being probably one hundred and fifty or more strangers present—excursionists from the East on their way to California, who had stopped over Sunday to visit the Mormon church, and listen to the immense organ and singers, but whose greatest desire was to hear

Brigham Young expound the Mormon doctrine.

These strangers were given the most prominent seats by the ushers, and this is the only church in which I remember strangers having precedent over the regular church members in being seated. When Brigham Young was well along in his discussion, it occurred to him that the strangers present would want to know the size of his family, as that was a question often asked by visitors, so he ceased his discourse and said: "I suppose the strangers present would like to know how many wives and children I have," and then proceeded to say he had sixteen wives and forty-five living children, having lost eight or ten children, I believe. He then proceeded to finish his discourse.

I was present on another occasion when he was preaching to a very large congregation, and he said to them:

Brethren, we have thieves, scoundrels, perjurers, and villains in our church, but the day will come when the tares will be separated from the wheat and burned up with unquenchable fire; if this were not so, however, we could not claim to be the church of Jesus Christ, for he said that the kingdom of God was like a great net, which, being cast into the sea, brought all manner of fishes to the shore.

He was the only preacher I ever heard make such remarks to his own people, and recognise the church as being the true one because of the tares that grew among the wheat.

The Mormon church taught regeneration through baptism by immersion. In the commencement of their service a chapter from either the *Old* or *New Testament* was generally read, and during the discourse frequent reference was made to the *Book of Mormon* and to Joseph Smith, their prophet.

President Young was one of the smartest men, if not the ablest man, it was ever my fortune to meet. He was a man well posted on all subjects relating to the business interests of the country, especially to his own people. His bishops and himself settled all manner of difficulties arising out of business or church matters without the assistance of courts, and he always insisted that every difficulty should be settled by arbitration of the members of the community in which the disputants lived.

In the ten years I lived in Salt Lake City, which was from 1869 to 1879, I never heard any talk among the Mormons about the gift of speaking the unknown tongue, or the interpretation thereof, as they claimed to have in Missouri. They, however, claimed to possess all the gifts of the Apostolic age and, as I have stated in another place, the keys of St. Peter. They believed in church authority, as do the Catholics, and in a personal God; they differ widely, however, from their Catholic brethren when they come to the marriage relation, the Mormons believing their bishops and elders should each have many wives, the Catholics, on the other hand, denying marriage to their priests.

Mormon communities, like all others, are made up of those who are reliable and those who are not—in other words, the good and the bad. Polygamy, which was practiced among them for more than a quarter of a century, they claimed upon scriptural authority was practiced in the Apostolic days. Let that be as it may, perhaps there never was a time in the march of civilization when to adopt such a practice would have been in more direct opposition to the moral sense of the civilized world than the present one of the nineteenth century.

In by-gone days, when the people depended upon their own and home productions for their living, the larger a man's family, with everyone a worker, the easier it was for him to get along. Not so now, however, but it is just the reverse.

The Mormons believed that church and state should be one, and that the laws of God should be the laws of the land; therefore, many of them persisted in practicing polygamy after Congress passed laws prohibiting it, preferring, as they said, to practice the higher law in disobedience to the laws made by men, and many of them have gone, singing and dancing, to the penitentiary, consigned there by the courts for violating the statutes because of their belief.

Chapter 5

The Mormons' Mecca

The new Mormon temple marks the history of the Church of Jesus Christ of Latter Day Saints from the day when Brigham Young and his few followers first set foot in the new promised land. It is a work commenced in the wilderness, and completed forty years afterward.

The laying of the cap-stone of the temple recorded the culmination of a work the Mormon people have been eagerly anticipating for nearly two generations. It recalls, too, many chapters of history abounding in interest. It tells a tale of patience, industry, and unswerving devotion to an object and a religious principle.

It is forty years ago since the corner-stones of this temple were laid, and although there have been occasional lapses of time when nothing was done, and often only a few men employed, the work has practically been going on continuously.

Not more than a few days after the arrival of the Mormon pioneers in the Great Salt Lake Basin, the prophet, Brigham Young, was strolling about in the vicinity of his camping-place in company with some of the apostles of his church. The days previous had been employed in exploring the valley to the north and south. These explorations satisfied them that there was no more favourable location to commence the building of a new city in the wilderness than the one on which they had first pitched their tents. The night when Brigham took that stroll was at the end of a perfect day in July. Looking to the south the valley stretched awry into magnificent distances and beautiful *vistas* as lovely as eye ever beheld.

Over in the west was the Great Salt Lake, with its huge islands rising from the mirrored surface of its waters, and burying their mountainous heads in the white of the clouds and the blue of the sky. In the east were the cold and rugged ranges of the Wasatch. To the north were the brown hills that guarded the city in that direction. It was a scene to inspire beautiful and poetic thoughts, and Brigham gazed about him, apparently delighted with the sublimity of the glorious prospect.

Turning his eyes to the east he struck his cane into the earth and said, "Here is where the temple of our God shall rise." Not a word of dissent was heard to his proclamation. There were no suggestions that better sites might be had. Brigham had issued his edict, and when he had spoken it was law to his people, so solemn that all indorsed it. From that moment the Temple Square was looked upon as sacred to the purpose to which it had been dedicated.

Remembering with what matchless courage this great Mormon leader had conducted his insignificant army across the desert from the Missouri River, and through the mountain defiles into this then wilderness, it is impossible to still the thought, "Did his imagination's eye peer through the mist of years and see the grey and solemn pile which is now the temple?"

But that July night when Brigham Young struck his cane on the ground was in 1847, and nothing was done toward building the temple until six years afterward. Still it is doubtful if the original intention had ever been abandoned.

At first it was intended to build it of adobe, but when a mountain of granite, fine in its quality and most beautiful in colour, was found some miles from the city, that material was substituted. On a panel just above the second-storey window of the east end of the temple is this inscription:

HOLINESS TO THE LORD.

THE HOUSE OF THE LORD

BUILT BY

THE CHURCH OF JESUS CHRIST

OF

LATTER DAY SAINTS.

COMMENCED APRIL 6, 1853,

COMPLETED

——— ———

Below the word "completed" there is a blank line where, when the last piece of stone has been chiselled and the frescoer has applied the last touch of his brush, a date will be cut into the marble slab. That date may not be inscribed for two or three years yet, for there is still very much to do on the interior.

April 6, 1853, was a bright day in the history of Zion. Not only was the semi-annual conference of the Mormon church in session, but the corner-stone of the great temple was to be laid with imposing ceremonies. The first company of Mormon pioneers to enter the Salt Lake Valley only numbered 143, but six years afterward the city had a population of nearly 6,000 people. It was a city, too, peculiar and unique in its customs and the character of its residents. By that time Utah had many large settlements, and from the most remote of these the saints came to assemble at the centre stake of Zion. They came wearing their brightest and best garments and their happiest faces. Presumably, their souls were possessed of that sweet peace which passeth all understanding. A grand procession was formed in honour of the ceremony about to be celebrated.

An old program of that parade, and the exercises of the day, is yet in existence, and it is notable that the church dignitaries were the most conspicuous figures in the pageant. There were the presidents, apostles, and bishops, the high priests, the counsellors, the elders, and all the lesser degrees of Mormon ecclesiastical authorities.

Flags were flying, bands were playing—there were two bands in Utah, even then. Four corner-stones were laid, four dedicatory prayers offered, in which the Almighty was invoked to bless the building then begun, and four orations were delivered.

There are many conflicting stories in regard to the designer of the temple. A man by the name of Truman C. Angell was the first architect, and he drew the plans, but it was in the fertile genius of Brigham Young that the ideas of form and arrangement were conceived. These he submitted to Angell, who elaborated them. Doubtless Brigham had based his conceptions on the descriptions he had read of Solomon's temple, but however much of the plans he may have cribbed, to him belongs the credit. He claimed the design of the temple, even to the smallest detail, had been given him by a revelation from God.

Angell devoted his life to this building. After him two or three others directed the construction, but for the past four or five years Don Carlos Young, a son of Brigham's, has been the architect.

For many years the progress was exceedingly slow. The foundations were sunk sixteen feet below the surface. There was a great yawning hole to be filled with rock, every one of which had to be pulled by ox teams. Many people remember how slowly the building rose. They say it was several years before the walls could be seen above ground. But there was no hurry and nothing was slighted, for the temple when completed was intended to be as enduring as the mountains from which the stone it was built of was quarried.

No better illustration of the infinite patience, the ceaseless industry, and the religious zeal of the Mormon people could be given than they have manifested in this work. It was a stupendous undertaking. They possessed n6 modern mechanical appliances; everything had to be done by the crudest methods. Considering these difficulties, and the immense character of the work, it inspires wonder and admiration.

The temple quarries are in a mountain-walled canon called Little Cottonwood, twenty-two miles from the city. For many years, or until 1872, every stone had to be hauled that distance by ox teams. The wagons were especially constructed for that purpose, and some of the stones were so large that four or five yoke were required to pull the load. How slow and expensive a building of this magnitude must have been, when such methods were employed, can readily be appreciated. But in 1872 a branch railroad was built from the Temple Square to the quarries; since then the construction has been more rapid and less expensive.

Figures only give a suggestion of its gigantic proportions. It is only when seen from a distance that its massiveness manifests itself. Then it towers above the other tall buildings of the city like a mountain above the level plain—it stands out solemn, grand, majestic, and alone. It is 99 feet wide and 200 feet long. The four corner towers are 188 feet high; to the top of the central western tower is 204 feet. The main, or eastern tower, is 211 feet to the top of the great granite globe, and on that the statue of the angel Gabriel stands, the figure itself being 14 feet high. Above all these points are the supplementary spires, on which the electric lights will be fixed.

The lights on these sky-piercing spires will be interesting, for they will be so powerful as to penetrate the darkest corner of the valley, and will be like unto a beacon to a watching mariner. That on the main, or eastern spire, will be placed below the statue of the angel, and will be reflected upward, surrounding the figure with a brilliant halo.

In the designing of the temple, no startling architectural innovations seem to have been attempted. The exterior has a poverty of ornamentation, yet perhaps that is the most attractive feature. But the interior is exceedingly interesting. There are all manner of eccentricities and queer unexpected places. In the four corner towers are winding stone staircases reaching to the roof, each having 250 steps.

These were all cut by hand at a cost of $100 apiece, and they are anchored in walls of solid masonry. The largest room is in the top story, and is 80 x 120 feet and 36 feet high. This is to be used as an assembly hall, and will have a capacity to seat 1,000 people. The other rooms are much smaller. There is the fount-room, where baptisms are performed, for the Mormons, like the Baptists, believe in immersion. They baptise for the remission of sins, and the living, acting as proxies, are baptised for the dead.

As understood, if a person has some dear friend or relative who has passed into the beyond without having had the saving rite of baptism administered, the living can attend to that little formality so as to insure the dead a peaceful sojourn in the agreeable climate of the hereafter.

The uninitiated do not understand the purposes of Mormon temples. They are not intended to be used for public worship. Services of that character are never held in them. They are designed to be used for the meeting of the priesthood and for the performances of ordinances and ceremonies of marriage, baptisms, etc., and for the administering of ecclesiastical rites—the conferring of priestly degrees.

Thousands of people have seen this great monument which has been built by this peculiar people to their more peculiar religion, and have described the impressions it made on them. Some, in a too-pronounced enthusiasm, have declared it to be a wonder in architecture—a triumph in its way—as something grand, almost marvellous in its conception. It is not. There is little that is exceptionally remarkable about it. True, there is much to impress one, but it is rather its bigness and general appearance of solemnity than anything else. Then there is something in its historical associations, the great difficulties overcome, and the great zeal displayed in its construction that inspires admiration.

Rudyard Kipling, who once saw it, in a vein of his keenest satire characterized it as "architecturally atrocious, ugly, villainously discordant, contemptuously correct, altogether inartistic and un poetical," and other adjectives equally as forcible and uncomplimentary. But he was probably more severe than just in his criticism. There is nothing about it to shock the artistic eye, and there are a few things to please.

A word about the statue that is perched on the topmost pinnacle. Certainly, that is pleasing to the artistic soul. It is the work of a finished sculptor, who is even now not wholly unknown to fame. He is C. E. Dallin, and was born in Salt Lake City not much over thirty years ago. But the statue: It is not of marble, but of hammered copper, covered with gold. To the eye it looks as if it were made entirely of that metal. It is a very fascinating piece of work, and on its high pedestal it glistens in the sunlight as if made of fire. One prominent Mormon has said the statue is not intended to represent Gabriel, but the angel Moroni proclaiming the gospel to all the world. It was the angel Moroni, it will be remembered, who showed the golden plates to Joseph Smith from which the *Book of Mormon* was written.

From Dallin's boyhood he began to display the artistic bent and temperament of his nature. Before he ever had any instruction, he modelled in clay with such success as to attract attention to his work. Then he went abroad to study, and at the Paris Salon of 1888 he received the medal of "Honorable Merit" for his "Peace Signal," that being a full-sized figure of an Indian brave on horseback holding his lance in such a manner as to be a signal to his fellow warriors at a distance that all was well. He has also done other meritorious work, and is at present engaged on a statue to be built on one of the corners of the Temple Square in honour of Brigham Young and the Mormon pioneers.

There have been many extravagant statements made concerning the cost of this temple. Figures have been placed as high as $6,000,000, which is nearly double its actual cost. As it stands today, $3,000,000 have probably been expended, and not more than half a million will be required to complete it.

The laying of this cap-stone practically completes the temple. There is not another stone to be laid, all that remains to be done being confined to the interior, and that is mostly in a decorative way. In its fulfilment there is great rejoicing in the hearts of the Mormon people. It has been a work requiring the toil of years, the manifestation of much self-denial, and the display of religious earnestness and sincerity almost without a parallel.

CHAPTER 6

My First Venture

When I grew up and became a married man, with daughters who were to be clothed and educated, I found it impossible to make, with the labour of one man on a farm, sufficient money to meet my growing necessities. I was raised on a farm and had always been a farmer, but with increasing expenses I was compelled to go into business of some kind, where I could accumulate a sufficiency for such purposes.

As I was brought up to handle animals, and had been employed more or less in the teaming business, after looking the situation all over, it occurred to me there was nothing I was so well adapted for by my past experience as the freighting business that was then being conducted between Independence, Mo., and Santa Fé, New Mexico, a distance of 800 miles.

At that time almost the entire distance lay through Indian Territory, where we were likely, on a greater portion of the trail, to meet hostile Indians any moment.

Being a religious man and opposed to all kinds of profanity, and knowing the practice of teamsters, almost without an exception, was to use profane and vulgar language, and to travel upon the Sabbath day, another difficulty presented itself to my mind which had to be overcome.

After due reflection on this subject I resolved in my innermost nature, by the help of God, I would overcome all difficulties that presented themselves to my mind, let the hazard be whatever it might. This resolve I carried out, and it was the keynote to my great success in the management of men and animals.

Having reached this determination, and being ready to embark in

Nebraska City in overland freighting days

my new business, I formulated a code of rules for the behaviour of my employees, which read as follows:

> While I am in the employ of A. Majors, I agree not to use profane language, not to get drunk, not to gamble, not to treat animals cruelly, and not to do anything else that is incompatible with the conduct of a gentleman. And I agree, if I violate any of the above conditions, to accept my discharge without any pay for my services.

I do not remember a single instance of a man signing these "iron-clad rules," as they called them, being discharged without his pay. My employees seemed to understand in the beginning of their term of service that their good behaviour was part of the recompense they gave me for the money I paid them.

A few years later, when the Civil War had commenced, I bound my employees to pay true allegiance to the Government of the United States, while in my employ, in addition to the above.

I will say to my readers that, had I had the experience of a thousand years, I could not have formulated a better code of rules for the government of my business than those adopted, looking entirely from a moral standpoint. The result proved to be worth more to me in a money point of view than that resulting from any other course I could have pursued, for with the enforcement of these rules, which I had little trouble to do, a few years gave me control of the business of the plains and, of course, a widespread reputation for conducting business on a humane plan.

I can state with truthfulness that never in the history of freighting on the plains did such quiet, gentlemanly, fraternal feelings exist as among the men who were in my employ and governed by these rules.

It was the prevalent opinion, previous to the time I started across the plains, that none but daring, rough men were fit to contend with the Indians and manage teamsters upon those trips. I soon proved to the entire contrary this was a great mistake, for it was soon observable that both men and animals working under this system were superior, and got along better in every way than those working under the old idea of ruffianism.

It is my firm conviction that where men are born commanders or managers there is no need of the cruelty and punishment so often dealt out by so many in authority. With men who have the key of government in their natures there is little trouble in getting employees to conform strictly to their duty.

I have seen, to my great regret and dislike, such cruelty practiced by army officers in command, and managers upon steamships on the seas and steamboats on the rivers, as well as other places where men were in charge of their fellow beings and had command over them, as should receive the most outspoken protest, and ought not to be tolerated in Christendom.

If men in charge would first control themselves and carry out, in their management of others, the true principles of humanity and kindness, pursuing a firm and consistent course of conduct themselves, wearing at the same time an easy and becoming dignity, it would do away with all the cruelties that have so often shocked humanity and caused needless suffering to those who were compelled to endure them. I found that an ounce of dignity on the plains was worth more than a pound at home or in organised society.

With all the thousands of men I had in my employ it was never necessary to do more than give a manly rebuke, if anyone committed any misdemeanour, to avoid a repetition of the offense.

In all my vast business on the plains I adhered strictly as possible to keeping the Sabbath day, and avoided traveling or doing any unnecessary work. This fact enabled me to carry out perfectly the "iron-clad rules" with my employees. When they saw I was willing to pay them the same price as that paid for work including the Sabbath day, and let them rest on that day, it made them feel I was consistent in requiring them to conduct themselves as gentlemen.

In later years, when my business had so increased and the firm of Majors & Russell was formed, I insisted on carrying my system of government and management into the business of the new firm, and the same course was pursued by the firm of Russell, Majors & Waddell as I have above narrated.

Notwithstanding the disagreeable features mentioned, I selected this avocation, and on the 10th day of August, 1848, with my first little outfit of six wagons and teams, started in business.

At that time, it was considered hazardous to start on a trip of that kind so late in the season; but I made that trip with remarkable success, making the round run in ninety-two days, the quickest on record with ox teams, many of my oxen being in such good condition when I returned as to look as though they had not been on the road. This fact gave me quite a reputation among the freighters and merchants who were engaged in business between the two points above mentioned.

I was by no means the first to engage in the trade between Mexico and the United States, for as early as 1822 Captain Rockwell started in the trade, carrying goods in packs on mules.

The next notable era in the line of this trade was the introduction of wagons in the year 1824. This, of course, was an experiment, as there were no beaten roads, and the sand on some portions of the route was so deep (the worst part being in the valley of the Cimarron) that it was doubted whether wagons could be used with success. But the experiment proved to be so much superior to packing that it did away entirely with the former mode; and wagonmakers at St. Louis and Independence, MO., commenced to build wagons adapted solely to that trade.

It was not long after the adoption of wagon trains on that route until there was a wide and well-beaten road the entire distance, the country over which it passed being level plains, requiring no bridges; but little work of any kind was necessary to keep the thoroughfare in good traveling condition.

On a large portion of the route there was an abundance of grass and water for the work animals. In those early days a belt of at least 400 miles was covered with herds of buffalo.

This crossing with large and heavy trains so well established the route that, by the year 1846, the people on the west border of Missouri were equipped and prepared in every way for transporting the supplies for Colonel Doniphan's army, when he was ordered to cross from Fort Leavenworth, Kan., to Santa Fé, N. M., at the commencement of the war between the United States and Mexico.

To return to my own operations in the freighting business, it will be seen by the foregoing dates mentioned in this article that two years later I made my first start, and I met on my outward-bound trip many of the troops of Colonel Doniphan returning home, the war being over and peace having been made between the two countries.

I continued in the freighting business continuously from 1848 to 1866, most of the time in the employ of the United States Government, carrying stores to different forts and stations in the Western Territories, New Mexico, Colorado, and Utah. Having freighted on my own account for about seven years, in 1855 I went into partnership with Messrs. Russell & Waddell, residents of Lexington, Lafayette

County, Mo., my home being still in Jackson County, Mo. We did business three years under the firm name of Majors & Russell. In 1858, when we obtained a contract from the Government for transporting supplies to Utah, the name of the firm was changed to Russell, Majors & Waddell.

At this time freighting for the government had increased enormously on account of General Johnston, with an army, having been sent to Utah. All of the supplies for the soldiers and much of the grain for the animals had to be transported in wagons from the Missouri River. However, one of the conditions of the contract the firm made with the government, through the quartermaster-general at Washington, was that they should have another starting-point other than Fort Leavenworth, the established depot for supplies going west.

I made this proposition to General Jessup, knowing, from my long experience in handling that kind of business, that it would be next to impossible to handle the supplies from one depot, as there were not herding grounds within a reasonable distance to keep such a vast number of cattle as the business would require when conducted from one point.

My partner, Mr. Russell, remarked to me that if he had to make a station higher up the river I would have to go and attend to it, for he could not. My answer was I would willingly do so, for I knew that loading hundreds of thousands of pounds of supplies daily would create a confusion at one point as would retard the business.

It was then and there agreed between the quartermaster and ourselves that one-half the entire stores should be sent to another point to be selected by his clerk and myself.

Immediately after the contract was signed I went to Fort Leavenworth, and with Lieutenant Dubarry of the Quartermaster's Department set out to locate another point. We traveled up the Missouri River as far as Plattsmouth, when we concluded Nebraska City, Neb., was the most available point upon the river for our business. I at once arranged with the citizens of that town to build warehouses, preparatory to receiving the large quantities of supplies the government would soon begin to ship to that point.

The supplies sent to Utah in the year 1858 were enormous, being over sixteen million pounds, requiring over three thousand five hundred large wagons and teams to transport them. We found it was as much as we could do to meet the government requirements with the two points in full operation.

As agreed, I took charge of the new station and moved my family from my farm, nine miles south of Kansas City, Mo., to Nebraska City, where I bought a home for them and commenced to carry out my part of the agreement.

The firm of Russell, Majors & Waddell conducted the business for two years, and in the spring of 1860 I bought out my partners and continued the business in my own name that year.

In Nebraska City I found a very intelligent, enterprising, and clever people, among whom were S. F. Knuckle, J. Sterling Morton, Robert Hawk Dillon, Colonel Tewksberry, McCann, Metcalf, Rhodes, O. P. Mason, Judge Kinney, Rinkers, Seigle, and a great many others of integrity and enterprise. I never did business more pleasantly than with the gentlemen whom I met during my residence of nine years there.

CHAPTER 7

Faithful Friends

To one who has had to make friends of the brute creation, it is natural for him to claim companionship with those domestic animals with which he is constantly drawn by day and night, such as horses, oxen, mules, and dogs. The dog is most thoroughly the comrade of those who dwell upon the frontier, and a chapter regarding them will not, I feel, be uninteresting to the reader.

I have always been a great admirer of a good dog, but my knowledge of them is a general one, such as you and a great many other Western men have. I have never made him a scientific study, but I think he is the only domestic animal, and I don't know but the only animal that takes a joint ownership in all of his master's property so far as he can comprehend it, whether it be personal, portable, or realistic; in other words, the man owns the dog and his other property, and the dog seems to claim or own the man and all of his other effects, so far as he can comprehend them.

I had a Shepherd dog that would not allow a stranger to take hold of me or my horse, saddle, bridle, rope, spurs, gun, or anything else that he thought belonged to us, without making a fuss about it, and he seemed to think stepping upon a rope or blanket, or anything of that kind, was just the same as taking hold with the hands, and yet he was very good-natured with strangers otherwise.

He was very fond of playing with other dogs, especially young ones on the pup order, but if they ever took any freedom with our *joint* property, there was sure to be trouble. He would not allow them to take hold of, or sleep on, or lay down in the shade of a horse, wagon, buggy, or do anything that he thought was taking too much liberty with his peculiar rights. He would go almost any distance to hunt anything that I would lose, and was very quick to pick up anything that I would drop, and give it to me without mussing it, whether I was walking or on horseback.

He was a good retriever, either on land or water, and would cross a river to get a goose or duck if it fell on the opposite side after being shot. He would also take hold of one hind leg of a deer or antelope and help me all he could to drag it home or to where I would leave my horse, but he was more help in driving and handling stock than in any other way. He would also go after a horse that would get away, with a bridle or rope on, and catch him by the rein or rope and bring him back if he could lead him, or if not, he would try and hold on until I would come up. He had a great many other minor tricks to make sport for the boys in camp, such as speaking, jumping, waltzing, etc., and he would also carry in wood to make fires with, and thus save the men trouble.

I have also had experience with the Newfoundland and the Setter dogs, and found them fully as easy to train and as faithful as the Shepherd dog I have written about. A Newfoundland that I brought down from Montana with me would do almost anything that it was possible for a dog to do. When living in Salt Lake City I saw my daughter send him after an apple once when she was sitting in a room upstairs. He went down and found the doors all fastened, so he came back and went out at an upstairs window and onto a lower roof and from there down on a common rung ladder to the ground and out into some one's orchard, got an apple, and returned the same way, and did it quicker than any boy could possibly have performed the same thing.

But of course, he knew where the ladder was, and had climbed up and down it many times before that. I used to see the children in our neighbourhood sending this dog over in the orchards after apples, while they remained at the fence outside, and he would keep going and returning with the apples until they were satisfied. The people never objected that owned the fruit, as they thought it so smart in the dog to steal for the children that which he did not eat himself.

It came to my knowledge once of a dumb beast that showed the intelligence of a human being.

He was only a dog, but a remarkably clever one. He belonged to the class known as Shepherd dogs, which are noted for their sagacity and fidelity. His master was a little Italian boy called Beppo, who earned his living by selling flowers on the street.

River Scene at Nebraska City

Tony was very fond of Beppo, who had been his master ever since he was a puppy, and Beppo had never failed to share his crust with his good dog. Now, Tony had grown to be a large, strong dog, and took as much care of Beppo as Beppo took of him. Often while standing on the corner with his basket on his arm, waiting for a customer, Beppo would feel inclined to cry from very loneliness; but Tony seemed to know when the "blues" came, and would lick his master's hand, as much as to say: "You've got me for a friend. Cheer up! I'm better than nobody; I'll stand by you."

But one day it happened that when the other boys who shared the dark cellar home with Beppo went out early in the morning as usual, Beppo was so ill that he could hardly lift his head from the straw on which he slept. He felt that he would be unable to sell flowers that day. What to do he did not know. Tony did his best to comfort him, but the tears would gather in his eyes, and it was with the greatest difficulty that he at last forced himself to get up and go to the florist, who lived nearby, for the usual supply of buds.

Having filled his basket, the boy went home again and tied it around Tony's neck; then he looked at the dog and said: "Now, Tony, you're the only fellow I've got to depend on. Go and sell my flowers for me, and bring the money home safe; don't let anyone steal anything."

Then he kissed the dog and pointed to the door.

Tony trotted out to the street to Beppo's usual corner, where he took his stand. Beppo's customers soon saw how matters stood, and chose their flowers, and put their money into the tin cup in the centre of the basket. Now and then, when a rude boy would come along and try to snatch a flower from the basket, Tony would growl fiercely and drive him away.

So that day went safely by, and at nightfall Tony went home to his master, who was waiting anxiously for him, and gave him a hearty welcome. Beppo untied the basket and looked in the cup, and I should not wonder if he found more money in it than ever before. This is how Tony sold the rosebuds, and he did it so well that Beppo never tired of telling me about it.

A farmer's dog who had been found guilty of obtaining goods under false pretences is worthy of mention. He was extremely fond of sausages, and had been taught by his owner to go after them for him, carrying a written order in his mouth. Day after day he appeared at the butcher-shop, bringing his master's order, and by and by the butcher became careless about reading the document. Finally, when settlement day came, the farmer complained that he was charged with more sausage than he had ordered. The butcher was surprised, and the next time Lion came in with a slip of paper between his teeth he took the trouble to look at it. The paper was blank, and further investigation showed that whenever the dog felt a craving for sausage, he looked around for a piece of paper, and trotted off to the butcher's. The farmer is something out of pocket, but squares the account by boasting of the dog's intelligence, which enabled him to deliberately steal for him, and deceive the butcher to do so.

While in Edinburgh, Scotland, where my wife and I remained for a year, our apartments were cared for by an English maid, who owned a very fine Scotch terrier. Whenever she would come to our rooms the dog accompanied her, and soon became very much attached to me, and would come into our apartments whenever an opportunity offered, to pay his respects to me. My wife had a great aversion to dogs of all kinds, and particularly objected to having one in the room with her, as she declared she could feel fleas immediately upon the appearance of a canine, no matter how far away they were from her.

One morning, while I was quietly reading, my wife being busy in another part of the room, the dog slipped in and succeeded in establishing himself under my chair, without either of us being aware of his presence; but before many minutes had passed my wife discovered him, and remonstrated with me at once for allowing him to come in, when I knew so well how she detested him. I assured her of my ignorance as to his presence, but said nothing whatever to the dog. He arose with a crest-fallen air, and with his tail tucked between his legs, walked slowly across the room, stopping in the doorway to look once at Mrs. Majors, with the most reproachful, abused expression I have ever seen on any creature's face.

After that he always endeavoured to make his calls upon me when Mrs. Majors was absent, and would often come up and wait in one end of the hall until he would see her go into the adjoining room, when he would come to see me, but immediately upon hearing her opening the door of the other room, he would make a break for the door, making his escape before she would reach the room; and this, too, when she had never been unkind to him except in what she said of him.

One morning while the landlady and her servant were "doing up" our sleeping apartment, the dog as usual accompanying the servant, Mrs. Majors stepped into the room to speak to the landlady, and the servant, knowing the dog's fondness for me, said:

"Prince, ask Mrs. Majors if you can't go in to see Mr. Majors."

He turned around, went up to Mrs. Majors and commenced jumping up and down in front of her, asking as plain as dogs can speak for the coveted permission. My wife could not help laughing, and said, "Well, sir, you have won me over this time; you can go," whereupon he made a rush for the other room, leaped upon my lap, and seemed fairly wild with joy. I could not understand his unusual demonstrations until Mrs. Majors came in and explained.

A friend who owned a very fine dog was one morning accosted by a neighbour, who accused the dog of having killed several of his sheep in the night. The owner said he thought it was a mistake, as he had never known the dog to be guilty of such tricks, and after some discussion it was decided to examine the dog's mouth, and if wool was found sticking in his teeth, they would believe him guilty, and the man who had lost the sheep could kill him. They called the dog up while talking about it, and the master opened his mouth, and to his grief, found the evidence of his crime between his teeth. The neighbour knew the man's attachment for the dog, and not wishing to kill him in his presence, said he would defer the execution until a more convenient time.

The dog heard the conversation, appeared to understand the situation perfectly, and when the neighbour tried later to find him, he had disappeared, and neither the owner nor the neighbour ever heard of him again. He fled to parts unknown, thus showing his wisdom by putting himself out of harm's way.

It is hardly possible to say enough in the praise of the dog family, especially regarding their services to the pioneers in the settlement of the Mississippi Valley and frontier. At that time, bears, panthers, wolves, and small animals of prey were so thick that without the aid of dogs the stock, such as pigs, lambs, poultry, and such small animals, would have been completely destroyed in one single night. The dogs were constantly on guard, night and day, storm or sunshine, and upon the approach of an enemy, would warn the pioneers, giving them a sense of security against danger. They knew by the smell, often before hearing or seeing an enemy, and would give out the warning long before the pioneers themselves could have known of the proximity of the wild beasts.

As a rule, those faithful friends and protectors of our race have not been appreciated, more especially, as above stated, in the settlement of the frontier, for without them it would have been impossible for the pioneers to have saved their stock and poultry from the ravages of the wild beasts. I could write a volume upon the sagacity, faithfulness, and intelligence of these remarkable animals, as during my life in the Wild West I learned to fully appreciate them.

CHAPTER 8

Our War with Mexico

On the 18th of June, 1846, A. W. Doniphan was elected colonel of the regiment that he commanded in the Mexican War. In his speech at Independence, Jackson County, Mo., on July 29, 1837, he declared he had not been a candidate for office for seven years, and did not expect to be for the next seventy years to come. The passage by the American Congress of the resolutions of annexation, by which the republic of Texas was incorporated into the Union as one of the States, having merged her sovereignty into that of our own government, was the prime cause which led to the war with Mexico. However, the more immediate cause of the war may be traced to the occupation by the American Army of the strip of disputed territory lying between the Nueces and the Rio Grande.

Bigoted and insulting, Mexico was always prompt to manifest her hostility toward this government, and sought the earliest plausible pretext for declaring war against the United States. This declaration of war by the Mexican government, which bore date in April, 1846, was quickly and spiritedly followed by a manifesto from our Congress at Washington, announcing that a state of war existed between Mexico and the United States. Soon after this counter declaration, the Mexicans crossed the Rio Grande in strong force, headed by the famous generals, Arista and Ampudia. This force, as is well known, was defeated at Palo Also on the 18th, and at Resaca de la Palma on May 9, 1846, by the troops under command of Major-General Taylor, and repulsed with great slaughter.

The whole Union was in a state of intense excitement. General Taylor's recent and glorious victories were the constant theme of universal admiration. The war had actually begun; and that, too, in a manner which demanded immediate action. The United States Congress passed an act about the middle of May, 1846, authorising President Polk to call into the field 50,000 volunteers designed to operate against Mexico at three distinct points, namely: The southern wing, or the "Army of Occupation," commanded by Major-General Taylor, to penetrate directly into the heart of the country; the column under Brigadier-General Wool, or the "Army of the Centre," to operate against the city of Chihuahua; and the expedition under the command of Colonel (afterward Brigadier-General) Kearney, known as the "Army of the West," to direct its march upon the city of Santa Fé.

This was the original plan of operations against Mexico, but subsequently the plan was changed. Major-General Scott, with a well-appointed army, was sent to Vera Cruz, General Wool effected a junction with General Taylor at Saltillo, and General Kearney divided his force into three separate commands; the first he led in person to the distant shores of the Pacific. A detachment of nearly eleven hundred Missouri volunteers, under command of Col. A. W. Doniphan, was ordered to make a descent upon the State of Chihuahua, expecting to join General Wool's division at the capital, while the greater part was left as a garrison at Santa F, under command of Col. Sterling Price. The greatest eagerness was manifested' by the citizens of the United States to engage in the war, to redress our wrongs, to repel an insulting foe, and to vindicate our national honour and the honour of our oft-insulted flag.

The call of the President was promptly responded to, but of the 50,000 volunteers at first authorized to be raised, the service of about 17,000 only were required.

The cruel and inhuman butchery of Colonel Fannin and his men, all Americans, the subsequent and indiscriminate murder of all Texans who unfortunately fell into Mexican hands; the repeated acts of cruelty and injustice perpetrated upon the persons and property of American citizens residing in the northern Mexican provinces; the imprisonment of American merchants without the semblance of a trial by jury, and the forcible seizure and confiscation of their goods; the robbing of American travellers and tourists in the Mexican country of their passports and other means of safety, whereby they were in certain instances deprived of their liberty for a time; the forcible detention of American citizens, sometimes in prison and other times in free custody; the recent blockade of the Mexican ports against the United States trade; the repeated insults offered our national flag; the contemptuous ill treatment of our ministers, some of whom were spurned with their credentials; the supercilious and menacing air uniformly manifested toward the government, which with characteristic forbearance and courtesy had endeavoured to maintain a friendly understanding; Mexico's hasty and unprovoked declaration of war against the United States; the army's unceremonious passage of the Rio Grande in strong force and with hostile intentions; her refusal to pay indemnities, and a complication of lesser evils, all of which had been perpetrated by the Mexican authorities, or by unauthorized Mexican citizens, in a manner which clearly evinced the determination on the part of Mexico to terminate the amicable relations hitherto existing between the two countries, were the causes which justified the war.

On the 18th day of August, 1846, after a tiresome march of nearly 900 miles in less than fifty days, General Kearney with his whole command entered Santa Fé, the capital of the province of New Mexico, and took peaceable possession of the country, without the loss of a single man or shedding a drop of blood, in the name of the United States, and planted the American flag in the public square, where the stars and stripes and eagle streamed above the Palacio Grande, or stately residence of ex-Governor Armigo.

On the 29th of July, 1847, Captain Ruff was dispatched by General Smith with a squadron composed of one company of the Second Dragoons under Lieutenant Hawes and his own company of mounted riflemen, in all eighty-six men, to attack the town of San Juan de los Lianos. In this engagement the Mexicans lost forty-three killed and fifty wounded. Only one American was wounded and none killed. At the battle of San Pascual, on the morning of the 6th of December, General Kearney commanding, with Captains Johnson, Moore, and Hammond as principal aids, drove the enemy from the field. Loss not known. American loss, seventeen killed and fourteen wounded. On the 5th of November, 1846, a small detachment of forty-five volunteers, commanded by Captains Thompson and Burrows, met and totally defeated 200 Californians on the plains of Salinas, near Monterey. American loss, four killed and two wounded.

On the 8th of January General Kearney and Commodore Stockton, with 500 men, met the insurgents, 600 strong, to dispute the passage of the river San Gabriel. This action lasted one hour and a half. The next day the Mexicans were again repulsed. Their loss on both days estimated in killed and wounded not less than eighty-five; American, two killed and fifteen wounded. A battle commanded by Doniphan was fought on Christmas day at Brazito, twenty-five miles from El Paso. Mexican loss was seventy-one killed, five prisoners, and 150 wounded, among them their commanding general, Ponce de Leon. The Americans had none killed and eight wounded. On the 27th the city of El Paso was taken possession of without further opposition.

On the 13th a battle with the Indians occurred. Americans lost none; Indians had seventeen killed and not less than twenty-five wounded. On the 19th of January, Governor Bent was murdered with his retinue. On the 24th Colonel Rice encountered the enemy. Our loss was two killed and seven wounded. The Mexicans acknowledged a loss of thirty-six killed and forty-five prisoners. On the 3rd of February, met the enemy at Pueblo de Taos. The total loss of the Mexicans at the three engagements was 282 killed—wounded unknown. Our total was fifteen killed and forty-seven wounded. On the 24th, in an engagement at Las Vegas, the enemy had twenty-five killed, three wounded; our loss, one killed, three wounded.

At Red River Cañon we were vigorously attacked by a large body of Mexicans and Indians; Americans lost one killed and several wounded; Mexicans and Indians, seventeen killed, wounded not known. At Las Vegas Major Edmondson charged the town; there were ten Mexicans slain and fifty prisoners taken. On the 9th of July a detachment of Captain Morin's company was attacked; five of our men killed and nine wounded. On the 26th of June Lieutenant Love was attacked and surrounded by Indians; they cut their way through with a loss of eleven; the Indians lost twenty-five. On the 27th of October Captain Mann's train was attacked; American loss, one killed, four wounded; Indian loss not known.

Chapter 9
Doniphan's Expedition

On Sunday, the 28th of February, a bright and auspicious day, the American Army, under Colonel Doniphan, arrived in sight of the Mexican encampment at Sacramento, which could be distinctly seen at the distance of four miles. His command consisted of the following corps and detachments of troops:

The First Regiment, Colonel Doniphan, numbering about eight hundred men; Lieutenant-Colonel Mitchell's escort, ninety-seven men; artillery battalion, Major Clark and Captain Weightman, 117 men, with light field battery of six pieces of cannon; and two companies of teamsters, under Captains Skillman and Glasgow, forming an extra battalion of about one hundred and fifty men, commanded by Major Owens of Independence, making an aggregate force of 1,164 men, all Missouri volunteers. The march of the day was conducted in the following order: The wagons, near four hundred in all, were thrown in four parallel files, with spaces of thirty feet between each.

In the centre space marched the artillery battalion; in the space to the right the First Battalion, and in the space to the left the Second Battalion. Masking these, in front marched the three companies intending to act as cavalry—the Missouri Horse Guards, under Captain Reid, on the right; the Missouri Dragoons, under Captain Parsons, on the left; and the Chihuahua Rangers, under Captain Hudson, in the centre. Thus arranged, they approached the scene of action.

The enemy had occupied the brow of a rocky eminence rising upon a plateau between the River Sacramento and the Arroya Seca, and near the Sacramento Fort, eighteen miles from Chihuahua, and fortified its approaches by a line of field-works, consisting of twenty-eight strong redoubts and intrenchments. Here, in this apparently secure position, the Mexicans had determined to make a bold stand, for the pass was the key to the capital. So certain of the victory were the Mexicans, that they had prepared strings and handcuffs in which they meant to drive us prisoners to the City of Mexico, as they did the Texans in 1841. Thus fortified and intrenched, the Mexican army, consisting, according to a consolidated report "of the adjutant-general which came into Colonel Doniphan's possession after the battle, of 4,220 men, commanded by Major-General Jose A. Heredia, aided by Gen. Garcia Conde, former Minister of War in Mexico, as commander of cavalry; General Mauricia Ugarte, commander of infantry; General Justiniani, commander of artillery, and Gov. Angel Trias, brigadier-general, commanding the Chihuahua Volunteers, awaited the approach of the Americans.

When Colonel Doniphan arrived within one mile and a half of the enemy's fortifications (a reconnaissance of his position having been made by Major Clark), leaving the main road, which passed within the range of his batteries, he suddenly deflected to the right, crossed the rocky Arroya, expeditiously gained the plateau beyond, successfully deployed his men into line upon the highland, causing the enemy to change its first position, and made the assault from the west. This was the best point of attack that could possibly have been selected. The event of the day proves how well it was chosen.

In passing the Arroya the caravan and baggage trains followed close upon the rear of the army. Nothing could exceed in point of solemnity and grandeur the rumbling of the artillery, the firm moving of the caravan, the dashing to and fro of horsemen, and the waving of banners and gay fluttering of guidons, as both armies advanced to the attack on the rocky plain; for at this crisis General Conde, with a select body of 1,200 cavalry, rushed down from the fortified heights to commence the engagement. When within 950 yards of our alignment, Major Clark's battery of six-pounders and Weightman's section of howitzers opened upon them a well-directed and most destructive fire, producing fearful execution in their ranks. In some disorder they fell back a short distance, unmasking a battery of cannon, which immediately commenced its fire upon us.

A brisk cannonading was now kept up on both sides for the space of fifty minutes, during which time the enemy suffered great loss, our battery discharging twenty-four rounds to the minute. The balls from the enemy's cannon whistled through our ranks in quick succession.

Many horses and other animals were killed and the wagons much shattered. Sergeant A. Hughes of the Missouri Dragoons had both his legs broken by a cannon ball. In this action the enemy, who were drawn up in columns four deep, close order, lost about twenty-five killed, besides a great number of horses. The Americans, who stood dismounted in two ranks, open order, suffered but slight injury.

General Conde, with considerable disorder, now fell back and rallied his men behind the intrenchments and redoubts. Colonel Doniphan immediately ordered the buglers to sound the advance. Thereupon the American Army moved forward in the following manner, to storm the enemy's breastworks:

The artillery battalion, Major Clark in the centre, firing occasionally on the advance; the First Battalion, commanded by Lieutenant-Colonels Jackson and Mitchell, composing the right wing; the two select companies of cavalry under Captains Reid and Parsons, and Captain Hudson's mounted company, immediately on the left of the artillery; and the Second Battalion on the extreme left, commanded by Major Gilpin. The caravan and baggage trains, under command of Major Owens, followed close in the rear. Colonel Doniphan and his aids, Captain Thompson, United States Army, Adjutant De Courcy, and Sergeant-Major Crenshaw acted between the battalions.

At this crisis a body of 300 lancers and *lazadors* were discovered advancing upon our rear. These were exclusive of Heredia's main force, and were said to be criminals turned loose from the Chihuahua prisons, that by some gallant exploit they might expurgate themselves of crime. To this end they were posted in the rear to cut off stragglers, prevent retreat, and capture and plunder the merchants' wagons. The battalion of teamsters kept these at bay. Besides this force there were a thousand spectators—women, citizens, and *rancheros*—perched on the summits of adjacent hills and mountains, watching the event of the day.

As we neared the enemy's redoubts, still inclining to the right, a heavy fire was opened upon us from his different batteries, consisting in all of sixteen pieces of cannon. But owing to the facility with which our movements were performed, and to the fact that the Mexicans were compelled to fire plungingly upon our lines (their position being considerably elevated above the plateau, and particularly the battery placed on the brow of the Sacramento Mountain with the design of enfilading our column), we sustained but little damage.

When our column had approached within about 400 yards of the enemy's line of field-works, the three cavalry companies, under Captains Reid, Parsons, and Hudson, and Weightman's section of howitzers, were ordered to carry the main centre battery, which had considerably annoyed our lines, and which was protected by a strong bastion. The charge was not made simultaneously, as intended by the colonel; for this troop having spurred forward a little way, was halted for a moment under a heavy crossfire from the enemy, by the adjutant's misapprehending the order. However, Captain Reid, either not hearing or disregarding the adjutant's order to halt, leading the way, waved his sword, and rising in his stirrups exclaimed: "Will my men follow me?"

Hereupon Lieutenants Barnett, Hinton, and Moss, with about twenty-five men, bravely sprang 'forward, rose the hill with the captain, carried the battery, and for a moment silenced the guns, but were too weak to hold possession of it. By the overwhelming force of the enemy, we were beaten back, and many of us wounded. Here Maj. Samuel C. Owens, who had voluntarily charged upon the redoubt, received a cannon or musket shot, which instantly killed both him and his horse. Captain Reid's horse was shot under him, and a gallant young man of the same name immediately dismounted and generously offered the captain his.

By this time the remainder of Captain Reid's company, under Lieutenant Hocklin, and the section of howitzers under Captain Weightman and Lieutenants Choteau and Evans, rose the hill, and supported Captain Reid. A deadly volley of grape and canister shot, mingled with *yager* balls, quickly cleared the intrenchments and redoubt. The battery was retaken and held. Almost at the same instant Captains Parsons and Hudson, with the two remaining companies of cavalry, crossed the intrenchments to Reid's left and successfully engaged with the enemy. They resolutely drove him back and held the ground.

All the companies were now pressing forward, and pouring over the intrenchments and into the redoubts, eagerly vying with each other in the noble struggle for victory. Each company, as well as each soldier, was ambitious to excel. Companies A, B, C, and a part of Company D, composing the right wing, all dismounted, respectively under command of Captains Waldo, Walton, Moss, and Lieutenant Miller, led on by Lieutenant-Colonels Jackson and Mitchell, stormed a formidable line of redoubts on the enemy's left, defended by several pieces of cannon and a great number of well-armed and resolute men. A part of this wing took possession of the strong battery on Sacramento Hill, which had kept a continued cross-firing upon our right during the whole engagement. Colonels Jackson and Mitchell and their captains, lieutenants, non-commissioned officers, and the men generally, behaved with commendable gallantry. Many instances of individual prowess were exhibited. But it is invidious to distinguish between men, where all performed their duty so nobly.

Meanwhile the left wing, also dismounted, commanded by Major Gilpin, a gallant and skilful officer, boldly scaled the heights, passed the intrenchments, cleared the redoubts, and, with considerable slaughter, forced the enemy to retreat from its position on the right. Company G, under Captain Hughes, and a part of Company F, under Lieutenant Gordon, stormed the battery of three brass four-pounders strongly defended by embankments and ditches filled by resolute and well-armed Mexican infantry. Some of the artillerists were made prisoners while endeavouring to touch off the cannon. Companies H and E, under Captains Rodgers and Stephenson, and a part of Hudson's company, under Lieutenant Todd, on the extreme left, behaved nobly, and fought with great courage. They beat the Mexicans from their strong places, and chased them like bloodhounds. Major Gilpin was not behind his men in bravery—he encouraged them to fight by example.

Major Clark, with his six-pounders, and Captain Weightman, with his howitzers, during the whole action rendered the most signal and essential service, and contributed much toward the success of the day. The gallant charge led by Captain Reid, and sustained by Captain Weightman, in point of daring and brilliancy of execution, has not been excelled by any similar exploit during the war.

General Heredia made several unsuccessful attempts to rally his retreating forces, to infuse into their minds new courage, and to close up the breaches already made in his lines. General Conde, with his troop of horse, also vainly endeavoured to check the advance of the Missourians. They were dislodged from their strong places, and forced from the hill in confusion.

The rout of the Mexican army now became general, and the slaughter continued until night put an end to the chase. The battle lasted three hours and a half. The men returned to the battlefield after dark, completely worn out and exhausted with fatigue. The Mexicans lost 304 men killed on the field, and a large number wounded, perhaps not less than five hundred, and seventy prisoners, among whom was Brigadier-General Cuilta, together with a vast quantity of provisions, $6,000 in specie, 50,000 head of sheep, 1,500 head of cattle, 100 mules, twenty wagons, twenty-five or thirty *caretas*, 25,000 pounds of ammunition, ten pieces of cannon of different calibre, varying from four to nine pounders; six culverins, or wall pieces; 100 stand of small colours, seven fine carriages, the general's *escritoire*, and many other things of less note. Our loss was Major Samuel C. Owens, killed, and eleven wounded, three of whom have subsequently died.

Thus, was the army of Central Mexico totally defeated, and completely disorganised, by a column of Missouri volunteers. The Mexicans retreated precipitately to Durango, and dispersed among the *ranchos* and villages. Their leaders were never able to rally them.

In this engagement Colonel Doniphan was personally much exposed, and by reason of his stature was a conspicuous mark for the fire of the enemy's guns. He was all the while at the proper place, whether to dispense his orders, encourage his men, or use his sabre in thinning the enemy's ranks. His courage and gallant conduct were only equalled by his clear foresight and great judgment. His effective force actually engaged was about nine hundred and fifty men, including a considerable number of amateur fighters, among whom James L. Collins, James Kirker, Messrs. Henderson and Anderson, interpreters, Major Campbell, and James Stewart, deserve to be favourably mentioned. They fought bravely. It was impossible for Captains Skillman and Glasgow to bring their companies of teamsters into the action. They deserve great honour for their gallantry in defending the trains. The soldiers encamped on the battlefield, within the enemy's entrenchments, and feasted sumptuously upon his viands, wines, and pound-cake.

There they rested.

Colonel Doniphan, not like Hannibal loitering on the plains of Italy after the Battle of Cannae when he might have entered Rome in triumph, immediately followed up his success and improved the advantage which his victory gave him. Early the next morning (March 1st) he dispatched Lieutenant-Colonel Mitchell, with 150 men under command of Captains Reid and Weightman, and a section of artillery, to take formal possession of the capital, and occupy it in the name of his Government. This detachment, before arriving in the city, was met by several American gentlemen escaping from confinement, who represented that the Mexicans had left the place undefended, and fled with the utmost precipitation to Durango.

The Spanish consul, also, came out with the flag of his country to salute and acknowledge the conqueror. This small body of troops entered and took military possession of Chihuahua without the slightest resistance, and the following night occupied the Cuartel, near Hidalgo's monument, which stands on the Alameda.

Meanwhile Colonel Doniphan and his men collected the booty, tended the captured animals, refitted the trains, remounted those who had lost their steeds in the action, arranged the preliminaries of the procession, and having marched a few miles encamped for the night. On the morning of March 2nd Colonel Doniphan, with all his military trains, the merchant caravan, gay fluttering colours, and the whole spolia opima, triumphantly entered the city to the tunes of "Yankee Doodle" and "Hail Columbia," and fired in the public square a national salute of twenty-eight guns. This was a proud moment for the American troops. The Battle of Sacramento gave them the capital, and now the stars and stripes and serpent eagle of the model republic were streaming victoriously over the stronghold of Central Mexico.

CHAPTER 10

The Pioneer of Frontier Telegraphy

It is thirteen years, (as at 1892), since Edward Creighton, the pioneer of frontier telegraphy, died, and that he is so well and honourably remembered in the Omaha of today—aye, his memory respected by the thousands who have gone there since he was no more—but illustrates how great was his service to the community, how broad and enduring a mark he made upon his time. No man did so much to sustain Omaha in its early and trying days as Edward Creighton.

His career was a notable one in its humble beginning and splendid triumph in the flush of manhood. He was born in Belmont County, Ohio, August 31, 1820, of Irish parentage. His early days were passed upon a farm, but at the age of twenty he took the contract for building part of the national stage road from Wheeling, W. Va., to Springfield, Ohio. He continued in the contracting business, but it was not until 1847 that he entered upon that branch of it in which he achieved his greatest success and laid the foundation of his after fortunes.

In that year he received the contract for and constructed a telegraph line between Springfield and Cincinnati. To this business he devoted his time and energies for five years, being successfully engaged in the construction of telegraph lines in all parts of the country, completing the line from Cleveland to Chicago in 1852. In 1856, while engaged in telegraph construction in Missouri, Mr. Creighton visited Omaha, and his brothers, John A., James, and Joseph, and his cousin James, locating there, he returned to Ohio, where he wedded Mary Lucretia Wareham of Dayton, and in 1857 he also went to Omaha and located. He continued in the telegraph construction business, completing, in 1860, the first line which gave Omaha connection with the outer world *via* St. Louis.

For years Mr. Creighton entertained a pet project the building of a line to the Pacific Coast—and in the winter of 1860, after many conferences with the wealthy stockholders of the Western Union Company, a preliminary survey was agreed upon. In those days the stagecoach was the only means of overland travel, and that was beset with great danger from Indians and road agents. In the stagecoach Mr. Creighton made his way to Salt Lake City, where he enlisted the interest and support of Brigham Young, the great head of the Mormon church, in his project. It had been arranged to associate the California State Telegraph Company in the enterprise, and on to Sacramento, in midwinter, Mr. Creighton pressed on horseback.

It was a terrible journey, but the man who made it was of stout heart, and he braved the rigors of the mountains and accomplished his mission, and in the spring of 1861 he returned to Omaha to begin his great work. Congress, meanwhile, had granted a subsidy of $40,000 a year for ten years to the company which should build the line. Then a great race was inaugurated, for heavy wagers, between Mr. Creighton's construction force and the California contractors who were building eastward, to see which should reach Salt Lake City first. Mr. Creighton had 1,100 miles to construct and the Californians only 450, but he reached Salt Lake City on the 24th of October, one week ahead of his competitors.

On October 24th, but little more than six months after the enterprise was begun, Mr. Creighton had established telegraphic communication from ocean to ocean. He had taken $100,000 worth of the stock of the new enterprise at about eighteen cents on the dollar, and when the project was completed the company trebled its stock, Mr. Creighton's $100,000 becoming $300,000. The stock rose to 85 cents, and he sold out $100,000 worth for $850,000, still retaining $200,000 of the stock. He continued in the telegraphic construction business until 1867, when his great cattle interests, in which he had embarked in 1864, and his great plains freighting business, established before the building of the Union Pacific and continued even after its completion, to the mining regions of Montana and Idaho, exacted his attention.

During all these years of great business success, Mr. Creighton was firm in his allegiance to Omaha. He was the first president of the first national bank in the city, and was ever ready to aid, by his means, and counsel, and enterprise, the furthering of Omaha's interests. He commanded the confidence of all the people, his sterling integrity and unwavering fidelity combining with his generous and charitable nature to make him a very lovable man. No man has an unkind word to say of Edward Creighton, and his memory is revered to this day as an upright, just, and kind man, who, out of his own sterling qualities, had wrought a successful and honourable career. He was stricken with paralysis and died November 5, 1874. To his memory Creighton College was erected and endowed by his widow, in response to his own wish, expressed during his lifetime, to found a free institution for the non-sectarian education of youth—the institution to be under Catholic control

CHAPTER 11

An Overland Outfit

The organisation of a full-fledged train for crossing the plains consisted of from twenty-five to twenty-six large wagons that would carry from three to three and a half tons each, the merchandise or contents of each wagon being protected by three sheets of thin ducking, such as is used for army tents. The number of cattle necessary to draw each wagon was twelve, making six yokes or pairs, and a prudent freighter would always have from twenty to thirty head of extra oxen, in case of accident to or lameness of some of the animals.

In camping or stopping to allow the cattle to graze, a corral or pen of oblong shape is formed by the wagons, the tongues being turned out, and a log chain extended from the hind wheel of each wagon to the fore wheel of the next behind, etc., thus making a solid pen except for a wide gap at each end, through which gaps the cattle are driven when they are to be yoked and made ready for travel, the gaps then being filled by the wagon-master, his assistant, and the extra men, to prevent the cattle from getting out. When the cattle are driven into this corral or pen, each driver yokes his oxen, drives them out to his wagon, and gets ready to start. The entire train of cattle, including extras, generally numbered from 320 to 330 head and usually from four to five mules for riding and herding.

The force of men for each train consisted of a wagon-master, his assistant, the teamsters, a man to look after the extra cattle, and two or three extra men as a reserve to take the places of any men who might be disabled or sick, the latter case being a rare exception, for as a rule there was no sickness. I think perhaps there was never a set of labouring men in the world who enjoyed more uninterrupted good health than the teamsters upon the plains. They walked by the side of their teams, as it was impossible for them to ride and keep them moving with regularity. The average distance travelled with loaded wagons was from twelve to fifteen miles per day, although in some instances, when roads were fine and there was a necessity for rapid movement, I have known them to travel twenty miles. But this was faster traveling than they could keep up for any length of time. Returning with empty wagons they could average twenty miles a day without injury to the animals.

Oxen proved to be the cheapest and most reliable teams for long trips, where they had to live upon the grass. This was invariably the case. They did good daily work, gathered their own living, and if properly driven would travel 2,000 miles in a season, or during the months from April to November; traveling from 1,000 to 1,200 miles with the loaded wagons, and with plenty of good grass and water, would make the return trip with the empty wagons in the same season. However, the distance travelled depended much upon the skill of the wagon-masters who had them in charge. For if the master was not skilled in handling the animals and men, they could not make anything like good headway and success. To make everything work expeditiously, thorough discipline was required, each man performing his duty and being in the place assigned him without confusion or delay.

I remember once of timing my teamsters when they commenced to yoke their teams after the cattle had been driven into their corral and avowed to stand long enough to become quiet. I gave the word to the men to commence yoking, and held my watch in my hand while they did so, and in sixteen minutes from the time they commenced, each man had yoked six pairs of oxen and had them hitched to their wagons ready to move. I state this that the reader may see how quickly the men who are thoroughly disciplined could be ready to "pop the whip" and move out, when unskilled men were often more than an hour doing the same work.

The discipline and rules by which my trains were governed were perfect, and as quick as the men learned each one his place and duty, it became a very pleasant and easy thing for him to do. Good moral conduct was required of them, and no offense from man to man was allowed, thus keeping them good-natured and working together harmoniously. They were formed into what they called "messes," there being from six to eight men in a mess, each mess selecting the man best fitted to serve as cook, and the others carrying the water, fuel, and standing guard, so that the cook's sole business when in camp was to get his utensils ready and cook the meals.

We never left the cattle day or night without a guard of two men, the teamsters taking turns, and arranging it so that each man was on guard two hours out of the twenty-four, and sometimes they were only obliged to go on guard two hours every other night. This matter they arranged among themselves and with the wagon-master. The duty of the wagon-master was about the same as that of a captain of a steamboat or ship, his commands being implicitly obeyed, for in the early stages of travel upon the plains the men were at all times liable to be attacked by the Indians; therefore, the necessity for a perfect harmony of action throughout the entire band.

The assistant wagon-master's duty was to carry out the wagon-master's instructions, and he would often be at one end of the train while the master was at the other, as the train was moving. It was arranged, when possible, that no two trains should ever camp together, as there was not grass and water sufficient for the animals of both, and thus all confusion was avoided.

The average salary paid the men was $1 a day and expenses. Most of the traveling in the early days of freighting was done upon what was called the Santa Fé road, starting from Independence, Mo., and unloading at Santa Fé, N. M. The rattlesnakes on that road, in the beginning of the travel, were a great annoyance, often biting the mules and oxen when they were grazing.

At first, mules were used altogether for traveling, but they would either die or become useless from the bite of a rattlesnake, and the men would sometimes be sent ahead of the caravan with whips to frighten the snakes out of the pathway, but later on, the ox-teamsters, with their large whips, destroyed them so fast that they ceased to trouble them to any great extent. It has been claimed by men that the snakes and prairie-dogs, who were also found in great numbers upon the plains, lived in the same houses, the dog digging the hole and allowing the snake to inhabit it with him; but I do not think this is correct.

Men came to this conclusion from seeing the snakes when frightened run into the dog-holes, but I think they did it to get out of the way of danger, and they lived, too, in the houses that had been abandoned by the dogs. It is a fact that the prairie dogs would only live in one hole for about a year, when they would abandon it and dig a new one, leaving the old ones to be taken possession of by the rattlesnakes and prairie owls. As far as I have been able to find out, there is no creature on earth that will live with a rattlesnake. They are hated and feared by all living animals.

The following are the names of the men who were employed on our trains, in one capacity and another, and a number of them are still alive, (1892):

Dr. J. Hobbs, Jim Lobb, Alex Lobb, Aquila Lobb, Joel Dunn, Mitchell Wilson, Hank Bassett, George W. Marion N. H. Fitzwater, George Bryant, Tom A. Brawley, Peter Bean, James L. Davis, William Hickman, A. W. Street, Joel Hedgespeth, Charles Byers, Nathan Simpson, R. D. Simpson, Ben Tunley, Hiram Cummings, John Ewing, Rev. Ben Baxter, A. and P. Byram, Frank McKinney, John T. Renick, John D. Clayton, William Wier, Frank Hoberg, Gillis of Pennsylvania, David Street, Joel Lyal, Albert Bangs, Elijah Majors, Aquila Davis, Samuel Poteete, William Hayes, George A. Baker, James Brown, William Dodd, Mr. Badger, Green Davis, John Scudder, Jackson Cooper, Samuel Foster, Robert Foster, Chat. Renick, John Renick, Mr. Levisy, Dick Lipscomb, James Aiken, Johnson Aiken, Stephen De Wolfe, Linville Hayes, Sam McKinny, Ben Rice, Ferd Smith, Henry Carlisle, Alexander Carlisle, Robert Ford, Joseph Erwin, Daniel D. White, Johnny Fry, Alexander Benham, Luke Benham, Benjamin Ficklin, John Kerr.

CHAPTER 12

Kit Carson

Kit Carson, as he was familiarly known and called, was born in Madison County, Ky., on the 24th of December, 1809.

During the early days of Carson's childhood his father moved from Kentucky to Missouri, which State was then called Upper Louisiana, where Kit Carson passed a number of years, early becoming accustomed to the stirring dangers with which his whole life was so familiar.

At the age of fifteen years he was apprenticed to a Mr. Workman, a saddler. At the end of two years, when his apprenticeship was ended, young Carson voluntarily abandoned the further pursuit of a trade which had no attractions for him, and from that time on pursued the life of a trapper, hunter, and Indian fighter, distinguishing himself in many ways and rendering invaluable service to the Government of the United States, in whose employ he spent a large part of his life, in which service he had risen to the rank of colonel and was brevetted brigadier-general before his death, which occurred at Fort Lyon, Colo., on the 23rd of May, 1868, from the effects of the rupture of an artery, or probably an aneurism of an artery in the neck.

Carson as a trapper, hunter, and guide had no superior, and as a soldier was the peer of any man.

The following from the life of Kit Carson will be found most interesting reading regarding this great scout:

> With fresh animals and men well fed and rested, McCoy and Carson and all their party soon started from Fort Hall for the rendezvous again, upon Green River, where they were detained some weeks for the arrival of other parties, enjoying as they best might the occasion, and preparing for future operations.

A party of a hundred was here organised, with Mr. Fontenelle and Carson for their leaders, to trap upon the Yellowstone and the headwaters of the Missouri. It was known that they would probably meet the Blackfeet, in whose grounds they were going, and it was therefore arranged, that while fifty were to trap and furnish the food for the party, the remainder should be assigned to guard the camp and cook. There was no disinclination on the part of any to another meeting with the Blackfeet, so often had they troubled them, especially Carson, who, while he could be magnanimous toward an enemy, would not turn aside from his course if able to cope with him; and now that he was in a company which justly felt itself strong enough to punish the 'thieving Blackfeet,' as they spoke of them, he was anxious to pay off some old scores.

They saw nothing, however, of these Indians; but afterward learned that the smallpox had raged terribly among them, and that they had kept themselves retired in mountain valleys, oppressed with fear and severe disease.

The winter's encampment was made in this region, and a party of Crow Indians which was with them camped at a little distance on the same stream. Here they secured an abundance of meat, and passed the severe weather with a variety of amusements, in which the Indians joined them in their lodges, made of buffalo hides. These lodges, very good substitutes for houses, were made in the form of a cone, spread by means of poles spreading from a common centre, where there was a hole at the top for the passage of smoke. These were often twenty feet in height and as many feet in diameter, where they were pinned to the ground with stakes.

In a large village the Indians often had one lodge large enough to hold fifty persons, and within were performed their war dances around a fire made in the centre. During the palmy days of the British Fur Company, in a lodge like this, only made instead of birch bark, Irving says the Indians of the North held their 'primitive fairs' outside the city of Montreal, where they disposed of their furs.

There was one drawback upon conviviality for this party, in the extreme difficulty of getting food for their animals; for the food and fuel so abundant for themselves did not suffice for their horses. Snow covered the ground, and the trappers were obliged to gather willow twigs, and strip the bark from cottonwood trees, in order to keep them alive. The inner bark of the cottonwood is eaten by the Indians when reduced to extreme want. Besides, the cold brought the buffalo down upon them in great herds, to share the nourishment they had provided for their horses.

Spring at length opened, and gladly they again commenced trapping; first on the Yellowstone and soon on the headwaters of the Missouri, where they learned that the Blackfeet were recovered from the sickness of last year, which had not been so severe as it was reported, and that they were still anxious and in condition for a fight, and were encamped not far from their present trapping grounds.

Carson and five men went forward in advance 'to reconnoitre,' and found the village preparing to remove, having learned of the presence of the trappers. Hurrying back, a party of forty-three was selected from the whole, and they unanimously selected Carson to lead them, and leaving the rest to move on with the baggage, and aid them if it should be necessary when they should come up with the Indians, they started forward eager for a battle.

Carson and his command were not long in overtaking the Indians; and dashing among them, at the first fire killed ten of their braves; but the Indians rallied and retreated in good order. The white men were in good spirits, and followed up their first attack with deadly results for three full hours, the Indians making scarce any resistance. Now their firing became less animated, as their ammunition was getting low, and they had to use it with extreme caution. The Indians, suspecting this from the slackness of their fire, rallied, and with a tremendous whoop turned upon their enemies.

Now Carson and his company could use their small arms, which produced a terrible effect, and which enabled them to again drive back the Indians. They rallied yet again, and charged with so much power and in such numbers, they forced the trappers to retreat.

During this engagement the horse of one of the mountaineers was killed, and fell with his whole weight upon his rider. Carson saw the condition of the man, with six warriors rushing to take his scalp, and reached the spot in time to save his friend. Leaping from the saddle he placed himself before his fallen companion, shouting at the same time for his men to rally around him, and with deadly aim from his rifle, shot down the foremost warrior.

The trappers now rallied around Carson and the remaining five warriors retired, without the scalp of their fallen foe. Only two of them reached a place of safety, for the well-aimed fire of the trappers levelled them with the earth.

Carson's horse was loose, and as his comrade was safe, he mounted behind one of his men and rode back to the ranks, while by general impulse the firing on both sides ceased. His horse was captured and restored to him, but each party, now thoroughly exhausted, seemed to wait for the other to renew the attack.

While resting in this attitude, the other division of the trappers came in sight, but the Indians, showing no fear, posted themselves among the rocks at some distance from the scene of the last skirmish, and coolly waited for their adversaries. Exhausted ammunition had been the cause of the retreat of Carson and his force, but now, with a renewed supply, and an addition of fresh men to the force, they advanced on foot to drive the Indians from their hiding places.

The contest was desperate and severe, but powder and ball eventually conquered, and the Indians, once dislodged, scattered in every direction. The trappers considered this a complete victory over the Blackfeet, for a large number of their warriors were killed, and many more were wounded, while they had but three men killed and a few severely wounded.

Fontenelle and his party now camped at the scene of the engagement, to recruit their men and here bury their dead. Afterward they trapped through the whole Blackfeet country, and with great success, going where they pleased without fear or molestation. The Indians kept off their route, evidently having acquaintance with Carson and his company enough to last them their lifetime.

With the smallpox and the white man's rifles the warriors were much reduced, and the tribe, which had formerly numbered 30,000, was already decimated, and a few more blows like the one dealt by this dauntless band would suffice to break its spirit and destroy its power for future and evil.

KIT CARSON'S GRAVE

During the battle with the trappers the women and children of the Blackfeet village were sent on in advance, and when the engagement was over and the braves returned to them so much reduced in numbers, and without a single scalp, the big lodge that had been erected for the war dance was given up for the wounded, and in hundreds of Indian hearts grew a bitter hatred for the white man.

An express, dispatched for the purpose, announced the place of the rendezvous to Fontenelle and Carson, who were now on Green River, and with their whole party and a large stock of furs, they at once set out for the place upon Mud River, to find the sales commenced before their arrival, so that in twenty days they were ready to break up camp.

Carson now organised a party of seven and proceeded to a trading post called Brown's Hole, where he joined a company of traders to go to the Navajo Indians. He found this tribe more assimilated to the white man than any Indians he had yet seen, having many fine horses and large flocks of sheep and cattle. They also possessed the art of weaving, and their blankets were in great demand through Mexico, bringing high prices on account of their great beauty, being woven in flowers with much taste. They were evidently a remnant of the Aztec race.

They traded here for a large drove of fine mules, which, taken to the fort on the South Platte, realised good prices, when Carson went again to Brown's Hole, a narrow but pretty valley, about sixteen miles long, upon the Colorado River.

After many offers for his services from other parties, Carson at length engaged himself for the winter to hunt for the men at this fort, and, as the game was abundant in this beautiful valley, and in the *cañon* country farther down the Colorado, in its deer, elk, and antelope reminding him of his hunts upon the Sacramento, the task was a delightful one to him.

In the spring Carson trapped with Bridger and Owens, with passable success, and went to the rendezvous upon Wind River, at the head of the Yellowstone, and from thence, with a large party of the trappers at the rendezvous, to the Yellowstone, where they camped in the vicinity for the winter without seeing their old enemy, the Blackfeet Indians, until midwinter, when they discovered they were near their stronghold.

A party of forty was selected to give them battle, with Carson, of course, for their captain. They found the Indians already in the field to the number of several hundred, who made a brave resistance until night, and darkness admonished both parties to retire. In the morning, when Carson and his men went to the spot whither the Indians had retired, they were not to be found. They had given them a 'wide berth,' taking their all away with them, even their dead.

Carson and his command returned to camp, where a council of war decided that, as the Indians would report at the principal encampment the terrible loss they had sustained, and others would be sent to renew the fight, it was wise to prepare to act on the defensive, and use every precaution immediately; and accordingly, a sentinel was stationed on a lofty hill nearby, who soon reported that the Indians were upon the move.

Their plans matured, they at once threw up a breastwork, under Carson's directions, and waited the approach of the Indians, who came in slowly, the first parties waiting for those behind. After three days a full thousand had reached the camp about half a mile from the breastwork of the trappers. In their war paint, stripes of red across the forehead and down either cheek, with their bows and arrows, tomahawks and lances, this army of Indians presented a formidable appearance to the small body of trappers who were opposed to them.

The war dance was enacted in sight and hearing of the trappers, and at early dawn the Indians advanced, having made every preparation for the attack. Carson commanded his men to reserve their fire till the Indians were near enough to have every shot tell; but, seeing the strength of the white men's position, after a few ineffectual shots, the Indians retired, camped a mile from them, and finally separated into two parties, and went away, leaving the trappers to breathe more freely, for, at the best, the encounter must have been of a desperate character.

They evidently recognized the leader who had before dealt so severely with them, in the skill with which the defence was arranged, and if the name of Kit Carson was on their lips, they knew him for both bravery and magnanimity, and had not the courage to offer him battle.

Another winter gone, with saddlery, *moccasin*-making, lodge-building, to complete the repairs of the summer's wars and the winter's fight all completed, Carson, with fifteen men, went past Fort Hall again to the Salmon River, and trapped part of the season there, and upon Big Snake and Goose creeks, and selling his furs at Fort Hall, again joined Bridger in another trapping excursion into the Blackfeet country.

The Blackfeet had molested the traps of another party who had arrived there before them, and had driven them away. The Indian assailants were still near, and Carson led his party against them, taking care to station himself and men in the edge of a thicket, where they kept the savages at bay all day, taking a man from their number with nearly every shot of their well-directed rifles. In vain the Indians now attempted to fire the thicket; it would not burn, and suddenly they retired, forced again to acknowledge defeat at the hands of Kit Carson, the 'Monarch of the Prairies.'

Carson's party now joined with the others, but concluding that they could not trap successfully with the annoyance the Indians were likely to give them, as their force was too small to hope to conquer, they left this part of the country for the north fork of the Missouri.

Now they were with the friendly Flatheads, one of whose chiefs joined them in the hunt, and went into camp near them with a party of his braves. This tribe of Indians, like several other tribes which extend along this latitude of the Pacific, have the custom which gives them their name, thus described by Irving, in speaking of the Indians upon the Lower Columbia, about its mouth, he says.

> A most singular custom prevails not only among the Chinooks, but among most of the tribes about this part of the coast, which is the flattening of the forehead. The process by which this deformity is effected commences immediately after birth. The infant is laid in a wooden trough by way of cradle; the end on which the head reposes is higher than the rest. A padding is placed on the forehead of the infant, with a piece of bark above it, and is pressed down by cords which pass through holes upon the sides of the trough.
>
> As the tightening of the padding and the pressure of the head to the board is gradual, the process is said not to be attended with pain. The appearance of the infant, however, while in this state of compression, is whimsically

hideous, and its little black eyes, we are told, being forced out by the tightness of the bandages, resemble those of a mouse choked in a trap.

About a year's pressure is sufficient to produce the desired effect, at the end of which time the child emerges from its bandages a complete flathead, and continues so through life. It must be noted, however, that this flattening of the head has something in it of aristocratic significance, like the crippling of the feet among the Chinese ladies of quality. At any rate it is the sign of freedom. No slave is permitted to bestow this deformity upon the head of his children. All the slaves, therefore, are roundheads.

In December, 1846, after a severe battle with the Mexicans and the condition of General Kearney and his men had become desperate, a council of war was called. After discussing a variety of measures, Carson showed himself "the right man in the right place." He said:

Our case is a desperate one, but there is yet hope. If we stay here we are all dead men; our animals can not last long, and the soldiers and marines at San Diego do not know of our coming, but if they receive information of our condition, they will hasten to our rescue. I will attempt to go through the Mexican lines, then to San Diego, and send relief from Commodore Stockton.

Lieutenant Beale of the United States Navy at once seconded Carson, and volunteered to accompany him. General Kearney immediately accepted the proposal as his only hope, and they started at once, as soon as the cover of darkness hung around them. Their mission was to be one of success or of death to themselves and the whole force. Carson was familiar with the customs of the Mexicans, as well as the Indians, of putting their ears to the ground to detect any sound, and therefore knew the necessity of avoiding the slightest noise. As it was impossible to avoid making some noise wearing their shoes, they removed them, and putting them under their belts crept over bushes and rocks with the greatest caution and silence.

They discovered that the Mexicans had three rows of sentinels, whose beats extended past each other, embracing the hill where Kearney and his men were held in siege. They were doubtless satisfied these could not be eluded, but they crept on, often so near a sentinel as to see his figure and equipment in the darkness, and once, when within a few yards of them, discovered one of the sentinels, who had dismounted and lighted his cigarette with his flint and steel.

Discovering this sentinel, Kit Carson, as he lay flat on the ground, put his foot back and touched Lieutenant Beale, as a signal for him to be still, as he was doing. The minutes the Mexican was occupied in this way seemed hours to our heroes, who momentarily feared they would be discovered. Carson asserted they were so still he could hear Lieutenant Beale's heart beat, and, in the agony of the time, he lived a year. But the Mexican finally mounted his horse and rode off in a contrary direction, as if guided by Providence to give safety to these courageous adventurers.

For full two miles Kit Carson and Lieutenant Beale thus worked their way along upon their hands and knees, turning their eyes in every direction to detect anything which might lead to their discovery; and, having passed the last sentinel and left the lines sufficiently far behind, they felt an immeasurable relief in once more gaining their feet. But their shoes were gone. In the excitement of this perilous journey neither had thought of his shoes since he first put them in his belt, but they could speak again and congratulate themselves and each other that the great danger was passed, and thank heaven that they had been aided thus far.

But there were still many difficulties in their path, which was rough with bushes, from the necessity of having to avoid the well-trodden trail, lest they be discovered. The prickly pear covered the ground, its thorns penetrated their feet at every step, and their road was lengthened by going out of the direct path, though the latter would have shortened their journey many a weary mile.

All the day following they pursued their journey onward without cessation, and into the night following, for they could not stop until they were assured relief was to be furnished their anxious and perilous conditioned fellow soldiers.

Carson pursued so straight a course and aimed so correctly for his mark that they entered the town by the most direct route, and answering "friends" to the challenge of the sentinel, it was known from whence they came, and they were at once conducted to Commodore Stockton, to whom they related their errand, and the further particulars we have already narrated.

Commodore Stockton immediately detailed a force of nearly two hundred men, and, with his usual promptness, ordered them to go to the relief of their besieged countrymen by forced marches. They took with them a piece of ordnance, which the men were obliged themselves to draw, as there were no animals to be had for this work.

Carson's feet were in a terrible condition, and he did not return with the soldiers; he needed rest and the best of care or he might lose his feet; but he described the position of General Kearney so accurately that the party sent to his relief could find him without difficulty, and yet had the commodore expressed the wish, Carson would have undertaken to guide the relief party upon its march.

Lieutenant Beale was partially deranged for several days from the effects of the severe service, and was sent on board a frigate lying in port for medical attendance, and he did not fully recover his former health for more than two years.

The relief party from Commodore Stockton reached General Kearney without encountering any Mexicans, and very soon all marched to San Diego, where the wounded soldiers received medical assistance.

CHAPTER 13

An Adventure with Indians

In the early part of June, 1850, I loaded my train, consisting of ten wagons drawn by 130 oxen, at Kansas City, Mo., with merchandise destined for Santa Fé, N. M., a distance of about eight hundred miles from Kansas City, and started for that point. After being out some eight or ten days and traveling through what was then called Indian Territory, but was not organised until four years later, and was then styled Kansas. Arriving one evening at a stream called One Hundred and Ten, I camped for the night. I unyoked my oxen and turned them upon the grass. Finding the grass so good and the animals weary with the day's work, I thought they would not stroll away, and therefore did not put any guard, as was my custom.

At early dawn on the following morning I arose, saddled my horse, which, by the way, was a good one, and told my assistant to arouse the teamsters, so they could be ready to yoke their teams as soon as I drove them into the corral, which was formed by the wagons. I rode around what I supposed to be all the herd, but in rounding them up before reaching the wagons, I discovered that there were a number of them missing. I then made a circle, leaving the ones I had herded together. I had not travelled very far when I struck the trail of the missing oxen; it being very plain, I could ride my horse on a gallop and keep track of it.

I had not travelled more than a mile when I discovered the tracks of Indian ponies. I then knew the Indians had driven off my oxen. I thought of the fact that I was unarmed, not thinking it necessary to take my gun when I left the wagons, as I only expected to go a few hundred yards. We had not yet reached the portion of the territory where we would expect to meet hostile Indians, so I went ahead on

An Adventure with Indians

the trail, thinking it was some half-friendly ones that had driven my oxen away, as they sometimes did, in order to get a fee for finding and bringing them back again.

I expected to overtake them at any moment, for the trail looked very fresh, as though they were only a short distance ahead of me. So, on and on I went, galloping my horse most of the time, until I had gone about twelve miles from my camp. I passed through a skirt of timber that divided one portion of the open prairie from the other, and there overtook thirty-four head of my oxen resting from their travel.

About sixty yards to the east of the cattle were six painted Indian braves, who had dismounted from their horses, each one leaning against his horse, with his right hand resting upon his saddle, their guns being in their left. I came upon them suddenly, the timber preventing them from seeing me until I was within a few rods of them. I threw up my hand, went in a lope around my oxen, giving some hideous yells, and told the cattle they could go back to the wagons on the trail they had come. They at once heeded me and started. I never saw six meaner or more surprised looking men than those six braves were, for I think they thought I had an armed party just behind me, or I would not have acted so courageously as I did.

So, I followed my cattle, who were ready to take their way back, and left the six savages standing in dismay. The oxen and myself were soon out of sight in the forest, and that is the last I saw of the six braves who had been sent out by their chief the night before to steal the oxen. Very soon after I got through the timber and into the prairie again I met, from time to time, one or two Indians trotting along on their ponies, following the trail that the cattle made when their comrades drove them off. When within a short distance of the herd they would leave the trail, and leave plenty of space to the cattle, fall in behind me, and trot on toward the six braves I had left. I will say here that I began to feel very much elated over my success in capturing my cattle from six armed savages, and being given the right-of-way by other parties also armed.

But I did not have to travel very far under the pleasant reflection that I was a hero; when I was about half-way back to the wagons I looked ahead about half-a-mile and saw a large body of Indians, comprising some twenty-five warriors, who proved to be under the command of their chief, armed and coming toward me. I then began to feel a little smaller than I had a few minutes previous, for I was entirely unarmed, and even had I been armed what could I have done with twenty-five armed savages?

My fears were very soon realised, for when they arrived within a few hundred yards of me and the chief saw me returning with the cattle he had sent his braves to drive off, he commanded his men to make a descent upon me, and he undertook the job of leading them. They raised a hideous yell and started toward me at the top of their horses' speed. If my oxen had not been driven so far and become to some extent tired, I would have had a royal stampede. The animals only ran a few hundred yards until I succeeded in holding them up. By this time the Indians had reached me and my cattle. The braves surrounded the cattle, and the chief came at the top of his horse's speed directly toward me, with his gun drawn up in striking attitude. Of course, I did not allow him to get in reaching distance. I turned my horse and put spurs to him; he was a splendid animal and it was a comparatively easy matter for me to keep out of the reach of the vicious chief, who did not want to kill me, but desired to scare me, or cause me to run away and leave my herd, or disable me so I could not follow him and his band if they attempted to take the cattle.

This chasing me off for some distance was repeated three times, I returning in close proximity to where his braves surrounded the cattle on every side, some on foot holding their ponies, others on horseback. Those who had alighted were dancing and yelling at the tops of their voices. The third time I returned to where the chief and one of his braves, armed with bow and arrows, were sitting on their horses, some distance from the cattle and in line between me and the group of braves. When I got within thirty or forty yards of him he beckoned me to come to him, for all the communication we had was carried on by means of signs; I did not speak their language nor they mine. I rode cautiously up side by side, a short distance from the chief, with our horses' heads in the same direction.

When I had fairly stopped to see what he was going to do, his brave who was on the opposite side from me slid off his horse, ran under the neck of the chief's, and made a lunge to catch the bridle of my horse. His sudden appearance caused the animal to jump so quick and far that he had just missed getting hold of the rein. Had he succeeded in the attempt they would have taken my horse and oxen and cleared out, leaving me standing on the prairie. When he found he had failed in his attempt, he returned to his horse, mounted, and he and the chief rode slowly toward me, for I had reined up my horse when I found I was out of reach. I sat still to see what their next manoeuvre would be. The brave changed from the left of the chief to the right as they came slowly toward me.

When they got within a few feet of me, with the heads of our horses in the same direction, they reined up their ponies and the brave suddenly drew his bow at full bend, with a sharp-pointed steel in the end of the arrow. He aimed at my heart with the most murderous, vindictive, and devilish look on his face and from his eyes that I ever saw portrayed on any living face before or since. Of course, there was no time for doing anything but to keep my eye steadfast on his. To show the influence of the mind over the body, while he was pointing the arrow at me I felt a place as large as the palm of my hand cramping where the arrow would have struck me had he shot.

While in this position he pronounced the word "say" with all the force he could summon. I did not at that time understand what he meant. The chief relieved my suspense by holding up his ten fingers and pointing to the oxen. I then understood that if I gave him ten of my animals he would not put the dart through me. I felt that I could not spare that number and move on with my train to its destination, and in a country where I had not the opportunity of obtaining others, so I refused. He then threw up five fingers and motioned to the cattle. Again, I shook my head.

He then motioned me to say how many I would give, and I held up one finger. The moment I did so he gave the word of command to his braves, who were still dancing and screaming round the cattle, and they, whirling into line, selected one of the animals so quickly that one had hardly time to think, and left thirty-three of the oxen and myself standing in the prairie. I had held them there so long, refusing to let them go without following them, I think they were afraid some of my party would overtake me. There was no danger of that had they only known it, for on my return I found all my men at the wagons wondering what had become of me. I had left the camp at daylight and it was after noon when I returned.

In conclusion, I will say that never at any time in my life, and I have encountered a great many dangers, have I felt so small and helpless as upon this occasion, being surrounded by twenty-five or thirty armed savages and with whom I could communicate only by signs. To surrender the animals to them was financial ruin, and to stay with them was hazarding my life and receiving the grossest abuse and insults. The effect of passing through this ordeal, on my mind, was that I became so reduced in stature, I felt as if I was no larger than my thumb, a hummingbird or a mouse; all three passed through my mind, and I actually looked at myself to see if it was possible I was so small.

No one can tell, until he has been overpowered by hostile savages, how small he will become in his own estimation. However, when they left me, I at once came back to my natural size and felt as if a great weight had been lifted from me.

Although the Indians were nothing more nor less than specimens of nature's sons, without any education whatever of a literary nature, they were very shrewd and quick to see and take up an insult. They were remarkable for reading faces, and although they were not able to understand one word of English, they could tell when looking at a white man and his comrades when in conversation about them, almost precisely what they were saying by the shadows that would pass over their faces, and by the nodding of heads and movement of hands or shoulders, for the reason that they talked with each other and the different tribes that they would meet by signs, and it was done generally by the movement of the hands.

They had but few vices, in fact might say almost none outside of their religious teachings, which allowed them to steal horses and fur skins, and sometimes take the lives of enemies or opposing tribes. Persons who were not thoroughly acquainted with Indian character and life might wonder why there were so many different tribes—or bands, as they were sometimes called—and if it could be there were so many nationalities among them. This is accounted for solely and truly upon the fact that when a tribe grew to a certain number it became a necessity in nature for them to divide, which would form two bands or tribes and at that point of time and condition it became necessary for the one leaving the main tribe to have a name to designate themselves from the family that they had of necessity parted from, for as soon as a tribe reached such a proportion in numbers that it was inconvenient for them to rendezvous at some given point easy of access, their necessities in such cases demanded a new deal or different arrangements; hence the different names by which tribes were called.

These tribes differed in their methods of living according to the conditions with which they were surrounded. Indians who lived along the Atlantic Coast and made their living from fishing, as well as from hunting, were very different from the Indians of the plains and Rocky Mountain regions, who live almost solely upon buffalo and other varieties of game that they were able to secure.

The Indians from the Atlantic and Mississippi valleys were more dangerous, as a rule, when they came into a combat with white soldiers, than were the Indians of the plains and Rockies. The Shawnee and Delaware Indian braves a hundred years ago, when my grandfather was an Indian fighter in Kentucky, were considered equal to any white soldiers and proved themselves in battle to be so. Their mode of warfare, however, was not on horseback, as was the mode of warfare with the Indians of the plains. They were "still" hunters, as they might be called, and when they met with white men in battle array, would get behind trees, if possible, as a protection, and remain and fight to the bitter end.

When these tribes became overpowered, it was easy, compared with the Indians of the plains, to bring them under some of the conditions of civilization; therefore the Cherokees, Seminoles, Chickasaws, Choctaws, Shawnees, Delawares, Wyandottes, Kickapoos, Sacs, Foxes, the Creeks, and many others whose names I cannot now recall, have become somewhat civilized, and many of them semicivilized tribes, but the Indians of the plains and Rocky Mountain regions have been very slow to accept what we term civilization. They seem somewhat like the buffalo and other wild animals that we have never been able to domesticate. It looks to one like myself that has known them for so many years, that before they are civilized they will become almost exterminated; that is to say that civilized life does not agree with them, and they die from causes and conditions that such life compels them to exist under, and in my opinion the day will come when there will be few, if any, in the near future, left of the tribes that were known to belong to the territory west of the Mississippi River and extending to the Pacific Coast.

There was often among the wildest tribes of America many good traits. If they found you hungry and alone and in distress, as a rule they would take care of you, giving you the very best they had, and never with a view of charging you for their kindness. If they had a grudge against the white race for some misdemeanour some white man may have committed, they might kill you in retaliation. For this reason, white men always felt, when they were among them, that their safety depended largely upon how the tribe had been treated by some other white man, or party of white men. As far as I know, throughout the entire savage tribes, retaliation is one of the laws by which they are governed.

The women, as a rule, were very generous and kind-hearted, and I know of one case where a friend of mine, Judge Brown of Pettis County, Mo., had his life saved and his property restored to him through the instrumentality of an Indian woman. The Indians were at that time quite hostile toward the whites, and had held council and determined to kill him, as they had him a prisoner and at their mercy. This woman seemed to be one of great influence in the tribe, and when the braves held their council and decided to take his life and property, she rose to her feet and plead for the life of my friend.

Of course, he could not understand a word she said, but he saw in her face a benevolence and kindness that gave him heart, for he had about despaired of ever living another hour. From the way in which she looked, talked, and gestured, he felt certain that she was assuming his cause, and he in relating the circumstances to me and others said he never saw a greater heroine in the appearance and conduct of any woman in his life. Of course, this he had to judge largely of from appearances, as the Indians judge of the white people that I before alluded to.

CHAPTER 14

Crossing the Plains

Everything worked along smoothly on my westward way, after my adventure with the Indians, until I reached Walnut Creek, at the Big Bend of the Arkansas River. At that point the buffalo, running past my herd of oxen in the night, scattered them, part running with the buffalo and crossing the river where it was very high, it being the season of the year when the channel was full of water, from the melting of the snow in the mountains from which it received its waters.

The next morning, as before, at the One Hundred and Ten, I found a portion of my herd missing, but not so many this time as to prevent me from traveling. I had the teams hitched up, some of them being a yoke of oxen minus, but sufficient remained to move the wagons, and I started my assistant, Mr. Samuel Poteet, one of the most faithful of my men, on the road with the teams, and I took my extra man to hunt for the missing oxen. We crossed the river where it was almost at swimming point and at the place where the buffalo had crossed the night before, for we had followed their trail for several miles. After losing the trail, for they had so scattered we could not tell which trail to take, we wandered around for a time in the open prairie, expecting Indians to appear at any moment; but in that we were happily disappointed.

I finally found my cattle all standing in a huddle near a pond. We soon surrounded them and started driving them to the river, crossed them and reached the road, following the train, until we overtook it a little before sundown that evening. From that point there was nothing to trouble or disturb our movements until we reached the Wagon Mounds, beyond the borders of New Mexico, now a station upon the Atchison, Topeka & Santa Fé Railroad. There we came upon the ruins of a stage-coach which had been burned; the bones and skeletons of some of the horses that drew it, as well as the bones of the party of ten men who were murdered outright by the Indians. Not one escaped to tell the story, and they were, I think, a party of ten as brave men as could be found anywhere. Whether there were any Indians killed while they were massacring this party is not known, for it was some few days before the news of the affair was known, as there was little travel over the road at that season of the year.

This party had passed me on the road some weeks before, and being able to travel three times as far per day as I could, had reached the point of their fate several weeks before, so we could see nothing but the bones the wolves had scratched out of the ground where they had been buried. In fact, there was nothing to bury when we found them. The wolves would not even let them lie at rest. It seemed there was no flesh the wolves could get hold of they were so fond of as the flesh of an American or white man, and, strange to say, they would not eat a Mexican at all. It frequently happened that when the Indians killed a party on the Santa Fé Road there were both Mexicans and Americans left dead upon the same spot. When found the bodies of the Americans would invariably be eaten, and the bodies of the Mexicans lying intact without any interference at all.

There were various speculations with travellers along that road as to why this was so. Some thought it was because the Mexicans were so saturated with red pepper, they making that a part of their diet. Others thought it was because they were such inveterate smokers and were always smoking cigarettes. I have no suggestions to make on the subject any further than to say such was a fact, and there are many American boys today who would not be eaten by wolves, so impregnated are they with nicotine.

After passing this gloomy spot at the Wagon Mounds, which almost struck terror to our hearts to see the bones of our fellow-men who had been swept away by the hand of the savages, without a moment's warning, we pursued our way to Santa Fé, N. M., and delivered my freight to the merchants. They paid me the cash, $13,000 in silver— Mexican dollars—for freighting their goods to that point, a distance of 800 miles from the place of loading at Kansas City, Mo. I returned home without any further drawbacks or molestations on that trip.

On arriving home, I found that Maj. E. A. Ogden of Fort Leavenworth desired to send a load of Government freight to Fort Mann,

400 miles west on the same road I had just travelled over, at about the point on the Arkansas River where Fort Dodge now stands. I agreed with him on terms at once, and loaded my wagons for that point. Lieutenant Heath of the United States Army was in command of the little post at Fort Mann. I arrived in good time, with everything in good order, and when the Government freights were unloaded he expressed a desire that I should take my entire train and go south about twenty-five miles, where there was some large timber growing near a stream called Cottonwood, for the purpose of bringing him a lot of saw-logs to make lumber for the building of his post.

A more gentlemanly or clever man I never met in the United States Army or out of it—thoroughly correct in his dealings, and kind and courteous as could be. I made the trip and brought him a fine lot of cottonwood and walnut saw-logs, for these were the only kinds of timber that grew along the without losing any men or animals. The men were all in fine health and good spirits, as men generally are when everything moves successfully in their business, and particularly a business which hangs upon so many contingencies as our trips across the plains did.

In the year 1851 I again crossed the plains with a full outfit of twenty-five wagons and teams. This trip was a complete success; we met with no molestations, and returned home without the loss of any animals, but, owing to the cholera prevailing to some extent among the men who were on the plains, I lost two men by that disease. Several would have died, perhaps, but for the fact that I had provided myself with the proper remedies before leaving Kansas City.

In 1852 I corralled my wagons, sold my oxen to California emigrants, and did no more work upon the plains that year. In 1853 I bought a new supply of work-cattle and again loaded my wagons at Kansas City for Santa Fé, N. M., as I had previously been doing. I was very successful in my operations that year, meeting with no loss of men and no animals worth mentioning.

I also made a second trip that year from Fort Leavenworth to Fort Union, in New Mexico, returning to my home near Westport, Mo., late in November. During the year 1854 I also went upon the plains as a freighter, changing my business from freighting for the merchants in New Mexico to carrying United States Government freights. At this time, I added to my transportation, making 100 wagons and teams for that year, divided into four trains. Everything moved along this year in a most prosperous way, without loss of life among my men, but I lost a great many of my work-cattle on account of the Texas fever. The loss was not so great, however, as to impede my traveling. The Government officers with whom I came in contact at either end of the route were well pleased with my way of doing business as a freighter, for everything was done in the most prompt and business-like manner.

In 1855 W. H. Russell of Lexington, Mo., and I formed a partnership under the name and style of Majors & Russell. That year we carried all the Government freight that had to be sent from Fort Leavenworth to the different posts or forts. The cholera prevailed among our men that year. Not more than two or three died, however, but quite a delay and additional expense were caused on account of this dire disease among our teamsters, with a train load of freight for Fort Riley. This was in June, and the train was almost deserted.

Another train was entirely deserted, the sick men being taken to some of the farmers in the neighbourhood, the well ones leaving for their homes, our oxen scattering and going toward almost every point of the compass. It was not long, however, until we got straightened again, and the train started for its destination.

Not long after this Maj. A. E. Ogden, the United States quartermaster at Fort Leavenworth, was taken with the cholera, and died at Fort Riley. A more honest, straightforward, and Christian gentleman could not be found in any army, or out of it. He had more excellent qualities than are generally allotted to man, and his death was much mourned by all who had the pleasure of his acquaintance. He left a very estimable wife and several children to mourn his death.

After the cholera disappeared that year, the freighting business moved along nicely and resulted in a prosperous year's work, after all the drawbacks in the early part of the season.

We also did a large business in freighting in 1856. I think that year we had about three hundred to three hundred and fifty wagons and teams at work, and our profits for 1855 and 1856 footed up about three hundred thousand dollars. This sum included our wagons, oxen, and other freighting and transportation outfits, valuing them at what we thought they would bring the beginning of the freighting season the next year.

In 1857 the government extended the contract to Majors & Russell for one year longer, and it was during this year the United States Government determined to send an army to Utah to curtail the power that Brigham Young was extending over the destiny of that country; many complaints having reached Washington through the government officials who had been sent to the Territory to preside as judges in the United States Courts. This resulted in a very great increase of transportation that year, and great difficulties were encountered, to begin with, which required quite an increase in the facilities for transportation, which had to be very hurriedly brought together.

Before all the Government freight reached Fort Leavenworth, it became too late for trains to reach the headquarters of the army before cold weather set in, in the high altitude of Fort Bridger and that portion of the country where the army was in winter quarters; therefore, many of the animals perished on account of having to be kept, under army orders, where grass and water were sometimes scarce, and they suffered more or less from severe cold weather. The result was great loss of the work-animals and an entire loss of the previous two years' profits.

A party of Mormons, under command of Col. Lott Smith, had been sent out by the Mormon authorities in the rear of Johnston's army to cut off his supplies. They captured and burned three of our trains, two on the Sandy, just east of Green River, and one on the west bank of Green River. They gave the captain of each train the privilege of taking one of his best wagons and teams and loading it with supplies, to return home or back to the starting point. They committed no outrage whatever toward the men, and, as soon as the captain of each train told them he had all the food necessary to supply him to get back to the starting point, they told him to abandon the train, and they were set on fire and everything burned that was consumable.

The captains of the trains, with their teamsters, returned to the States in safety. The cattle were driven off by the Mormons, and those that were not used for beef by the hungry men were returned in the summer to the company after peace had been made between the Mormons and the government. The loss to the army was about five hundred thousand pounds of government supplies. This loss put the army upon short rations for that winter and spring, until they could be reached with supplies in the spring of 1858.

That spring, our firm, under the name of Russell, Majors & Waddell, obtained a new contract from the United States Government to carry government freight to Utah for the years 1858-59. That year the government ordered an immense lot of freight, aggregating

16,000,000 pounds, most of which had to be taken to Utah. We had to increase the transportation from three or four hundred wagons and teams we had previously owned to 3,500 wagons and teams, and it required more than forty thousand oxen to draw the supplies; we also employed over four thousand men and about one thousand mules.

Our greatest drawback that year was occasioned by floods and heavy rains upon the plains, which made our trains move tardily in the outset. We succeeded admirably, however, considering the vast amount of material we had to get together and organise, which we could not have done had we not had so many years' experience, previous to this great event, in the freighting enterprise; and especially was. this so with me, for I had had, previous to this, a great many years' experience in handling men and teams, even before I crossed the plains ten years before. We succeeded this year in carrying everything to the army in Utah, fifty miles south of Salt Lake City, to Camp Floyd, the headquarters of Sidney Johnston's command, a distance of 1,250 miles.

After unloading the wagons at Camp Floyd, they were taken to Salt Lake City and placed as near as they could stand to each other in the suburbs of the city, and covered many acres of ground, where they remained for one year or more, when our agent sold them to the Mormon authorities for $10 apiece, they having cost us at the manufacturers' $150 to $175 apiece. The Mormons used the iron about them for the manufacture of nails. The oxen we sent to Skull Valley and other valleys near Camp Floyd, known to be good winter quarters for cattle and mules. During the year 1859, while our teams were at Camp Floyd we selected 3,500 head as suitable to drive to California and put on the market, and they were driven to Ruby Valley, in Nevada, where it was intended they should remain, that being considered a favourable winter locality; and in the spring of 1860 they were to be driven to California, the intention being to let them graze on the wild oats and clover in the valleys of the Sacramento, and convert them into beef-cattle when fully ready for the market.

A very few days after the herders reached the valley with them, which was late in November, a snow-storm set in and continued more or less severe, at intervals, until it covered the ground to such a depth that it was impossible for the cattle to get a particle of subsistence, and in less than forty days after the animals were turned out in the valley they were lying in great heaps frozen and starved to death. Only 200 out of the 3,500 survived the storm. They were worth at the time

A Rough Trail

they were turned into the valley about $150,000, as they were a very superior and select lot of oxen. This was the largest disaster we met with during the years 1858 and 1859.

In 1857 the Indians attacked the herders who had charge of about one thousand head on the Platte River, west of Fort Kearney, which is now called Kearney City, in Nebraska, killing one of the herders and scattering the cattle to the four winds. These were also a complete loss.

We had very little trouble with the Indians in 1857, 1858, and 1859 in any way, owing to the fact that Johnston's army, consisting of about five thousand regulars, besides the teamsters, making in all about seven thousand well-armed men, had passed through the country in 1857, and they had seen such a vast army, with their artillery, that they were completely intimidated, and stayed at a very respectful distance from the road on which this vast number of wagons and teams travelled.

Each one of our wagons was drawn by six yoke, or twelve oxen, and contained from five to six thousand pounds of freight, and there was but one wagon to each team. The time had not yet come when, what was afterward adopted, trail wagons were in use. This means two or three wagons lashed together and drawn by one team. Twenty-five of our wagons and teams formed what was called a train, and these trains were scattered along the road at intervals of anywhere from two to three miles, and sometimes eight to ten miles, and even greater distances, so as to keep out of the way of each other.

The road, until we reached the South Pass, was over the finest line of level country for traveling by wagons, with plenty of water and grass at almost every step of the way. Crossing the South Platte at what was then called Julesburg, and going across the divide to North Platte, at Ash Hollow, we continued in the valley of the North Platte to the mouth of the Sweetwater, and up that stream until we passed through the South Pass. After passing that point it was somewhat more difficult to find grass and water, but we were fortunate enough all along the road to get sufficient subsistence out of nature for the sustenance of our animals, and were not obliged to feed our oxen. They did the work allotted to them, and gathered their own living at nights and noon-times.

In the fall of 1857 a report was sent by the engineers who were with General Johnston's army at Fort Bridger, and who had crossed the plains that year, to the Quartermaster's Department at Washington, stating it was impossible to find subsistence along the road for the number of animals it would require to transport the freight necessary for the support of the army. General Jessup, who was then Quartermaster of the United States Army at Washington, and as fine a gentleman as I ever met, gave me this information, and asked me if it would deter me from undertaking the transportation. I told him it would not, and that I would be willing to give him my head for a foot-ball to have kicked in Pennsylvania Avenue if I did not supply the army with every pound that was necessary for its subsistence, provided the government would pay me to do it. We satisfied him after the first year's work had been done that we could do even more than I assured him could be done.

There is no other road in the United States, nor in my opinion elsewhere, of the same length, where such numbers of men and animals could travel during the summer season as could over the thoroughfare from the Missouri River up the Platte and its tributaries to the Rocky Mountains. In fact, had it been necessary to go east from the Missouri River, instead of west, it would have been impossible in the nature of things to have done so, owing to the uneven surface of the country, the water being in little deep ravines and, as a rule, in small quantities, often muddy creeks to cross, at other times underbrush and timber that the animals could have roamed into and disappeared, all of which would have prevented progress had we started with such an enterprise east instead of west.

But the country west of the Missouri River for hundreds of miles, so far as making roads for travel of large numbers of animals is concerned, is as different from the east as it is possible for two landscapes to be. The whole country from the west border of the Missouri, Iowa, and Arkansas was thoroughly practical, before inhabited by farmers, for carrying the very largest herds and organisations of people on what one might term perfectly natural ground, often being able to travel hundreds of miles toward the sunset without a man having to do one hour's work in order to prepare the road for the heaviest wagons and teams.

The road from Missouri to Santa Fé, N. M., up the Arkansas River, a distance of 800 miles, was very much like the one up the Platte River, and over which millions of pounds of merchandise were carried, and where oxen almost invariably, but sometimes mules, did the work and subsisted without a bite of any other food than that obtained from the grasses that grew by the roadside.

The roads all running west from the Missouri River came up the valleys of the Platte, Kansas, or Arkansas Rivers, running directly from the mountains to the Missouri River. These rivers had wide channels, low banks, and sandy bottoms, into which a thousand animals could go at one time, if necessary, for drink, and spread over the surface, so as not to be in each other's way, and whatever disturbance they made in the water, in the way of offal or anything of that kind, was soon overcome by the filtering of the water through the sand, which kept it pure, and thousands of men and animals could find purer water on account of these conditions.

Then again, the first expedient in the way of fuel was what was called buffalo chips, which was the offal from the buffalo after lying and being dried by the sun; and, strange to say, the economy of nature was such, in this particular, that the large number of work-animals left at every camping-place fuel sufficient, after being dried by the sun, to supply the necessities of the next caravan or party that travelled along. In this way the fuel supply was inexhaustible while animals travelled and fed upon the grasses.

This, however, did not apply to travel east of the Missouri River, as the offal from the animals there soon became decomposed and was entirely worthless for fuel purposes. This was altogether owing to the difference in the grasses that grew west of the Missouri River on the plains and in the Rocky Mountains and that which grew in the States east of the Missouri. Thus, the fuel supply was sufficient for the largest organisations of people who, in those days, were traveling on the plains. Armies, small and great, that found it necessary to cross the plains, found sufficient supply of this fuel, and it seemed to be a necessity supplied by nature on the vast open and untimbered plains lying between the Missouri River and the Rocky Mountains, far beyond the Canadian line to the north, without which it would have been practically impossible to have crossed the plains with any degree of comfort, and in cold weather would have been absolutely impossible.

The small groups of timber growing along the streams would soon have been exhausted if used for fuel, and there would have been nothing to supply those who came later.

History records no other instance of like nature, where an immense area of country had the same necessity and where that necessity was supplied in such a manner as on the vast plains west of the Missouri River. These chips would lay for several years in perfect condition for fuel.

CHAPTER 17

"The Jayhawkers of 1849"

In this year a number of gentlemen made up a party and started for the far West. During that fearful journey they were lost for three months in the "Great American Desert," the region marked on the map as the "unexplored region." General Fremont, with all the patronage of the Government at his command, tried to cross this desert at several points, but failed in every attempt. This desert is bounded by the Rocky Mountains and Wasatch range on the east and the Sierra Nevada on the west. From either side running streams sink near the base of the mountains, and no water exists except alkali and the hot springs impregnated with nitre.

The party arrived at Salt Lake late in the season of '49. It was thought by the older members of the company to be too late to cross the Sierra Nevada by the northern routes. No wagon had ever made the trip to the Pacific Coast by way of the Spanish Trail from Santa Fé to the Pacific, but it was determined to undertake this perilous journey. Captain Hunt, commander of the Mormon Battalion in the Mexican War, agreed to pilot the train through to Pueblo de los Angeles for the sum of $1,200.

The weather south being too warm for comfortable travel, the party remained in Salt Lake City two months, leaving that place October 3, 1849. Upon their arrival at Little Salt Lake, a few restless comrades, angry that the party did not go through by the northern route, formed a band and determined to cross the desert at all hazards, and thus save hundreds of miles' travel *via* Los Angeles route. The sufferings they endured cannot be described.

The survivors have since been scattered through the country, and have never come together since they separated at Santa Barbara, on the Pacific, February 4, 1850, until the twenty-third anniversary of their arrival was celebrated at the residence of Col. John B. Colton. The following letter will explain:

> Galesburg, Ill.,
> January 12, 1872.
>
> Dear Sir: You are invited to attend a reunion of the "Jayhawkers of '49," on the 5th day of February next at 10 o'clock in the forenoon, at my house, to talk over old times and compare notes, after the lapse of twenty-three years from the time when the "Jayhawkers" crossed the "Great American Desert."
>
> In the event that you cannot be present, will you write a letter immediately on receipt of this, to be read on that occasion, giving all the news and reminiscences that will be of interest to the old crowd?
>
> Yours fraternally,
>
> John B. Colton.

A short sketch of the party's wanderings may not be amiss. On the 5th of April, 1849, a large party of men, with oxen and wagons, started from Galesburg, Ill., and vicinity for the then newly discovered gold-fields of California. To distinguish their party from other parties who went the same year, they jestingly took the name of "Jayhawkers," and that name has clung to them through all the years that have come and gone.

They encountered no trouble until after leaving Little Salt Lake, when taking the directions given them by Indian Walker and Ward—old mountaineers, who gave them a diagram and told them they could save 500 miles to the mines in California by taking the route directed—the Jayhawkers branched off from the main body. They found nothing as represented, and became lost in the desert, wandering for months, traversing the whole length of the Great American Desert, which Fremont, with all the aid of the government at his call, could not cross the shortest way, and laid it down on the map as the "unexplored region."

They cut up their wagons on Silver Mountain and made of them pack-saddles for their cattle. Here thirteen of their number branched off, on New Year's Day, taking what jerked beef they could carry, and started due west over the mountains, which the main party could not do on account of their cattle, but when they came to a mountain they took a southerly course around it. Of these thirteen, but two lived to get through, and they were found by ranch Indians in a helpless condition, and brought in and cared for. They had cast lots and lived on each other until but two remained. When questioned afterward in regard to their trip, they burst into tears and could not talk of it.

The main body of Jayhawkers kept their cattle, for they were their only hope; on these they lived, and the cattle lived on the bitter sagebrush and grease-wood, except when they occasionally found an oasis with water and a little grass upon it. The feet of the cattle were worn down until the blood marked their every step. Then the boys wrapped their feet in raw hides, as they did their own. Many died from exposure, hunger, and thirst, and were buried in the drifting sands where they fell, while those who were left moved on, weak and tottering, not knowing whose turn would be next.

But for their cattle, not a man could have lived through that awful journey. They ate the hide, the blood, the refuse, and picked the bones in camp, making jerked beef of the balance to take along with them. People who are well fed, who have an abundance of the good things of life, say: "I would not eat this; I would not eat that; I'd starve first." They are not in a position to judge. Hunger swallows up every other feeling, and man in a starving condition is as savage as a wild beast.

After many desert wanderings and untold suffering, they at last struck a low pass in the Sierra Nevada Mountains, and emerged suddenly into the Santa Clara Valley, which was covered with grass and wild oats and flowers, with thousands of fat cattle feeding, a perfect paradise to those famished skeletons of men. There were thirty-four of the party who lived to reach that valley, and every one shed tears of joy at the sight of the glorious vision spread before them and the suddenness of their deliverance.

The boys shot five head of the cattle, and were eating the raw flesh and fat when the ranch Indians, hearing the firing, came down with all the shooting irons they could muster, but seeing the helpless condition of the party, they rode back to headquarters and reported to Francisco, the Spaniard who owned the ranch and cattle. He came down and invited them to camp in a grove near his home, bade them welcome, and furnished the party with meat, milk, grain, and everything they needed, and kept them until they were recruited and able to go on their way. Verily, he was a good Samaritan. They were strangers, and he took them in; hungry, and he fed them; thirsty, and he gave them drink. In the grand summing up of all things, may the

ALEXANDER MAJORS.
R. H. HASLAM ("Pony Bob").   PRENTISS INGRAHAM.
JOHN B. COLTON.   W. F. CODY ("Buffalo Bill").

noble Francisco be rewarded a thousandfold.

They reached the Santa Clara Valley the 4th of February, 1850, and on that day each year they celebrate their deliverance by a reunion, where in pleasant companionship and around the festive board they recount reminiscences of the past, and live over again those scenes, when young and hopeful, they lived and suffered together.

There are but eleven of the survivors of that party alive today, (1892), and these are widely scattered east of the Rocky Mountains and on the Pacific Slope. Some are old men, too feeble to travel, and can only be present in spirit and by letter at the annual reunions. Gladly would every Jayhawker welcome one and all of that band, bound together by ties of suffering in a bond of brotherhood which naught but death can sever.

The names and residences of the original party are as follows:

John B. Colton, Kansas City, Mo.
Alonzo C. Clay, Galesburg, Ill.
Capt. Asa Haines, Belong, Knox County, Ill., died March 29, 1889.
Luther A. Richards, Beaver City, Neb.
Charles B. Mecum, Perry, Greene County, Iowa.
John W. Plummer, Toulon, Ill., died June 22, 1892.
Sidney P. Edgerton, Blair, Neb., died January 31, 1880.
Edward F. Bartholomew, Pueblo, Colo., died February 13, 1891.
Urban P. Davidson, Derby P. O., Fremont County, Wyo.
John Groscup, Cahto, Mendocino County, Cal.
Thomas McGrew, died in 1866, in Willamette Valley, Ore.
John Cole, died in Sonora, Cal., in 1852.
John L. West, Coloma, Cal., since died.
William B. Rude, drowned in the Colorado River, New Mexico, in 1862.
L. Dow Stevens, San José, Cal.
William Robinson, Maquon, Ill., died in the desert.
—— Harrison, unknown.
Alexander Palmer, Knoxville, Ill., died at Slate Creek, Sierra County, Cal., in 1853.
Aaron Larkin, Knoxville, Ill., died at Humboldt, Cal., in 1853
Marshall G. Edgerton, Galesburg, Ill., died in Montana Territory in 1855.
William Isham, Rochester, N.Y., died in the desert.

———— Fish, Oscaloosa, Iowa, died in the desert.
———— Carter, Wisconsin, unknown.
Harrison Frans, Baker City, Baker County, Ore.
Capt. Edwin Doty, Naples, Santa Barbara County, Cal., died June 14, 1891.
Bruin Byram, Knoxville, Ill., died in 1863.
Thomas Shannon, Los Gatos, Santa Clara County, Cal.
Rev. J. W. Brier, wife, and three small children, Lodi City, San Joaquin County, Cal.
George Allen, Chico, Cal., died in 1876.
Leander Woolsey, Oakland, Cal., died in 1884.
Man from Oscaloosa, Iowa, name not remembered, died in California.
Charles Clark, Henderson, Ill., died in 1863.
———— Gretzinger, Oscaloosa, Iowa, unknown.

A Frenchman, name unknown, became insane from starvation, wandered from camp near the Sierra Nevada Mountains, captured by the Digger Indians, and was rescued by a United States surveying party fifteen years after.

The following are today, (1892), the sole survivors of the Jayhawk party of 1849:

John B. Colton, Kansas City, Mo.
Alonzo G. Clay, Galesburg, Ill.
Luther A. Richards, Beaver City, Neb.
Charles B. Mecum, Perry, Iowa.
Urban P. Davidson, Derby, Wyo.
John Groscup, Cahto, Cal.
L. Dow Stevens, San José, Cal.
Rev. J. W. Brier and Mrs. J. W. Brier, Lodi City, Cal.
Harrison Frans, Baker City, Ore.
Thomas Shannon, Los Gatos, Cal.

The last reunion of the Jayhawkers was held at the home of Col. John B. Colton of Kansas City, Mo., just forty-four years after the arrival of the party upon the Pacific Slope.

Of the eleven survivors there were but four able to be present, but the absent ones responded to their invitations with their photographs and letters of good will.

Among the invited guests to meet these old heroes were Col. W. F.

Cody (Buffalo Bill), Col. Frank Hatton of the Washington *Post*, General Van Vliet, Capt. E. D. Millet (an old ranger), and the writer, who wishes the remnant of the little hero band may yet live to enjoy a score more of such delightful meetings.

CHAPTER 16

Mirages

About September 1, 1848, on my way from Independence, Mo., to Santa Fé, N. M., I met some of the soldiers of General Donaldson's regiment returning from the Mexican War on the Hornather or dry route, lying between the crossing of the Arkansas and Cimarron. It was about noon when we met. I saw them a considerable distance away. They were on horseback, and when they first appeared, the horses' legs looked to be from fifteen to eighteen feet long, and the body of the horses and the riders upon them presented a remarkable picture, apparently extending into the air, rider and horse, forty-five to sixty feet high. This was my first experience with mirage, and it was a marvel to me.

At the same time, I could see beautiful clear lakes of water, apparently not more than a mile away, with all the surroundings in the way of bulrushes and other water vegetation common to the margin of lakes. I would have been willing, at that time, to have staked almost anything upon the fact that I was looking upon lakes of pure water. This was my last experience of the kind until I was returning later on in the season, when one forenoon, as my train was on the march, I beheld just ahead the largest buffalo bull that I ever saw.

I stopped the train to keep from frightening the animal away, took the gun out of my wagon, which was in front, and started off to get a shot at the immense fellow, but when I had walked about eighty yards in his direction, I discovered that it was nothing more nor less than a little coyote, which would not have weighed more than thirty pounds upon the scales.

The person who imagines for a minute that there is nothing in the great desert wastes of the Southwest but sand, cacti, and villainous reptiles is deluded. It is one of the most common fallacies to write down these barren places as devoid of beauty and usefulness. The rhymester who made Robinson Crusoe exclaim, "Oh, solitude, where are the charms that sages have seen in thy face?" never stood on a sand-dune or a pile of volcanic rock in this Southwestern country just at the break of day or as the sun went down, else the rhyme would never have been made to jingle.

To one who has never seen the famous mirages which Dame Nature paints with a lavish hand upon the horizon that bounds an Arizona desert, it is difficult to convey an intelligent portrait of these magnificent phenomena. And one who has looked upon these incomparable transformation scenes, the Titanic paintings formed by nature's curious slight-of-hand, can never forget them. They form the memories of a lifetime.

Arizona is rich in mirage phenomena, which, owing to the peculiar dryness of the atmosphere, are more vivid and of longer duration than in other parts. The variety of subjects which from time to time have been presented likewise gives them an unusual interest. Almost everyone who has lived in the Territory any length of time, and one who has merely passed through, especially on the Southern Pacific Route, is familiar with the common water mirage which appears at divers places along the railroad. The most common section in which this phenomenon may be seen is between Tucson and Red Rock, and through the entire stretch of the Salton Basin from Ogilby to Indio.

Here in the early morning or in the late afternoon, if the atmospheric conditions be right, lakes, river, and lagoons of water can be seen from the train windows. Ofttimes the shimmering surface is dotted with tiny islands, and the shadows of umbrageous foliage are plainly seen reflected in the supposed water; yet an investigation shows nothing but long rods of sand-drifts or saline deposits.

Animals as well as men are deceived by these freaks of the atmosphere. Many instances are recorded where whole bands of cattle have rushed from the grazing grounds across the hot parched plains in pursuit of the constantly retreating water phantom, until they perish from exhaustion, still in sight of running brooks and surging springs. Prior to the advent of the railroad through this region, when overland passengers passed by on the old Yuma road to San Diego, scores of adventurous spirits perished in chasing this illusive phantom. It is said that one entire company of soldiers was thus inveigled 'from the highway and perished to a man.

One of the most interesting sights of this class is to be seen almost any time of the year in Mohave County, down in the region of the Big Sandy. Here for leagues upon leagues the ground is strewn with volcanic matter and basalt. It is one of the hottest portions of the continent, and except in the winter months it is almost unendurable by man or beast

At a point were the main road from the settlements on the Colorado to Kingman turns toward the east, there are a number of volcanic buttes. At these buttes just before sunrise the famous cantilever bridge which spans the Colorado River near the Needles, seventy miles distant, is plainly visible, together with the moving trains and crew. The train has the appearance of being perhaps an eighth of a mile distant, and every motion on board, the smoke, the escaping steam, are as natural and vivid as though not a hundred yards away.

At this same point huge mountains are seen to lift themselves up bodily and squat down again in the highway. Near these buttes, which are known as the Evil Ones, away back in the sixties a small force of cavalry was making its way from Fort Yuma to Fort Whipple. Owing to the extreme heat during the day, and as a further precaution against the hostile Indians, they were obliged to march at night, finding shelter in some mountain canon during the day.

Shortly after daybreak, as they were preparing to go into camp, a whole legion of painted devils appeared on their front and hardly a quarter of a mile distant. The troops were thrown into confusion, and an order was immediately given to break ranks, and every man concealed himself behind the rocks, awaiting the attack which all felt must necessarily end in massacre.

For some minutes the Indians were seen to parley and gesticulate with each other, but they gave no signs of having noticed their hereditary foe. The unhappy troopers, however, were not kept in suspense long. As the great red disk of the day began to mount slowly up over the adjoining mountains, the redskins vanished as noiselessly and as suddenly as they had appeared.

Used as they were to treachery, and fearing some uncanny trick, the soldiers maintained their position throughout the long hot day, nor did they attempt to move until late in the night. Some weeks later it was learned from captives that on that very morning a band of nearly one thousand Chinhuevas and Wallapais were lying in wait for this same command but ninety miles up the river, expecting the soldiers by that route.

The most remarkable of all the mirages which have been witnessed in Arizona, at least by white man's eyes, was seen some years ago by an entire train-load of passengers on the Southern Pacific Railroad, near the small eating station of Maricopa, thirty-five miles below Phoenix. The train was due at the eating station at 6.30 a. m.

At 6.15 o'clock it stopped at a small water-tank a few miles east. During this stop the trainmen and such of the passengers as were awake were amazed to see spring out of the ground on the sky a magnificent city. The buildings were of the old Spanish and Morisco architecture, and were mostly *adobe*. Spacious court-yards lay before the astonished lookers-on, filled with all varieties of tropical fruits and vegetation.

Men and women clothed in the picturesque garbs of Old Spain were seen hurrying along the narrow, irregular streets to the principal edifice, which had the appearance of a church. Had the astonished spectators been picked up bodily and landed in one of the provincial towns of Seville or Andalusia, they would not have seen a more dazzling array of stately *senoras* and laughing black-eyed *muchachas* of the land of forever *manana*.

But the vision lasted much less time than it takes to write of the strange occurrence. It vanished as mysteriously as it came. Of course, all of the hysterical women fainted. That is one of woman's prerogatives, in lieu of an explanation.

This phenomenon remained unsolved for two or three years. About that time, after the mirage was seen, a young civil engineer who was among the witnesses was engaged on the Gulf coast survey from the headwaters below Yuma to Guaymas. In the course of his labours he found himself at the old Mexican *pueblo* of Altar, and there he saw the original of the picture in the sky seen three years before near Maricopa Station. The distance, as a buzzard flies, from Maricopa to Altar is more than a hundred miles.

The native tribes are very superstitious concerning the mirage, and when one is once observed, that locality receives a wide berth in the future.

In the secluded Jim-Jam Valley of the San Bernardino Mountains there are the most marvellous mirages known to the world. The wonderful mirages of the Mojave Desert have been talked about a great deal, and they are entitled to all the prominence they have had. But those of the Jim-Jam Valley are far more wonderful than these.

It is called Jim-Jam Valley because of the strange things seen there, and I defy any man, however sound of mind he maybe, to go in there and not think he has "got 'em" before he gets out.

This valley is about twenty-five miles long by fifteen miles wide. It is uninhabited. It is bordered by the main San Bernardino range on the east, and by a spur of the Sierra Magdalenas on the west. There is no well-defined trail through the heart of it. The valley is a desert. The surrounding mountains are terribly serrated and cut up. The peaks are jagged. Altogether the surroundings are weird and forbidding.

Leaving Fisk's ranch on the trail at the foot of the Sierra Magdalenas, you climb an easy grade to Dead Man's Pass, the entrance to the valley.

Go in, and pretty soon you see lakes, and running rivers, and green borders, and flying water-fowl. Willows spring up here and there, and in the distance, you see waterlilies.

What you behold contrasts finely with the rugged mountains, and you are charmed with it, and go on thinking you have struck an earthly paradise. Indian camps appear in view, and little oarsmen propel fantastic crafts upon the waters. Advancing still farther, dimly outlined forms may be seen, and the pantomime reminds you of a strange hobgoblin dance.

Sometimes a storm brews in the valley, and then the scene is all the more terrible. Forked lightning blazes about, and strange, uncouth animals, differing from any you have ever read about, are to be seen there.

These phenomena are seen for a stretch of about fifteen miles, up and down the middle of the valley principally, and they have been viewed by a great many people. They cannot understand why the forms of the mirage, if such it may be called, are so much more strange there than on the Mojave Desert.

Everybody is in 'awe of the valley, and there are mighty few men, however nervy they may be ordinarily, who care to go there a second time.

CHAPTER 17

The First Stage into Denver

In the winter of 1858, while my partner, Mr. W. H. Russell, John S. Jones, a citizen of Pettis County, Mo., and myself were all in Washington, D. C., which was about the time that the Pike's Peak excitement was at its highest pitch, Messrs. Jones and Russell conceived the idea (I do not know from which one it emanated), and concluded to put a line of daily coaches in operation between the Missouri River and Denver City, when Denver was but a few months old. They came to me with the proposition to take hold of the enterprise with them.

I told them I could not consent to do so, for it would be impossible to make such a venture, at such an early period of development of this country, a paying institution, and urgently advised them to let the enterprise alone, for the above stated reasons. They, however, paid no attention to my protest, and went forward with their plans, bought 1,000 fine Kentucky mules and a sufficient number of Concord coaches to supply a daily coach each way between the Missouri River and Denver. At that time Leavenworth was the starting point on the Missouri. A few months later, however, they made Atchison the eastern terminus of the line and Denver the western.

They bought their mules and coaches on credit, giving their notes, payable in ninety days; sent men out to establish a station every ten to fifteen miles from Leavenworth due west, going up the Smoky Hill fork of the Kansas River, through the Territory of Kansas, and direct to Denver. The line was organised, stations built and put in running shape in remarkably quick time.

They made their daily trips in six days, traveling about one hundred miles every twenty-four hours. The first stage ran into Denver on May 17, 1859. It was looked upon as a great success, so far as putting the enterprise in good shape was concerned, but when the ninety days expired and the notes fell due they were unable to meet them. And in spite of my protests in the commencement of the. organisation as against having anything to do with it, it became necessary for Russell, Majors & Waddell to meet the obligation that Jones & Russell had entered into in organising and putting the stock on the line. To save our partner we had to pay the debts of the concern and take the mules and coaches, or, in other words, all the paraphernalia of the line, to secure us for the money we had advanced.

The institution then having become the property of Russell, Majors & Waddell, we continued to run it daily. A few months after that, we bought out the semi-monthly line of Hockaday & Liggett, that was running from St. Joseph, Mo., to Salt Lake City, thinking that by blending the two lines we might bring the business up to where it would pay expenses, if nothing more.

This we failed in, for the lines, even after being blended, did not nearly meet expenses. Messrs. Hockaday & Liggett had a few stages, light, cheap vehicles, and but a few mules, and no stations along the route. They travelled the same team for several hundreds of miles before changing, stopping every few hours and turning them loose to graze, and then hitching them up again and going along.

I made a trip in the fall of 1858 from St. Joseph, Mo., to Salt Lake City in their coaches. It was twenty-one days from the time I left St. Joseph until I reached Salt Lake, traveling at short intervals day and night. As soon as we bought them out we built good stations and stables every ten to fifteen miles all the way from Missouri to Salt Lake, and supplied them with hay and grain for the horses and provisions for the men, so they would only have to drive a team from one station to the next, changing at every station.

Instead of our schedule time being twenty-two days, as it was with Hockaday & Liggett, and running two per month, we ran a stage each way every day and made the schedule time ten days, a distance of 1,200 miles. We continued running this line from the summer of 1859 until March, 1862, when it fell into the hands of Ben Holliday. From the summer of 1859 to 1862 the line was run from Atchison to Fort Kearney and from Fort Kearney to Fort Laramie, up the Sweet Water route and South Pass, and on to Salt Lake City.

This is the route also run by the Pony Express, each pony starting from St. Joseph instead of Atchison, Kan., from which the stages started. We had on this line about one thousand Kentucky mules and 300 smaller-sized mules to run on through the mountain portion of the line, and a large number of Concord coaches. It was as fine a line, considering the mules, coaches, drivers, and general outfitting, perhaps, as was ever organised in this or any other country, from the beginning.

And it was very fortunate for the government and the people that such a line was organised and in perfect running condition on the middle route when the late war commenced, as it would have been impossible to carry mails on the route previously patronised by the government, which ran from San Francisco *via* Los Angeles, El Paso, Fort Smith, and St. Louis, for the Southern people would have interfered with it, and would not have allowed it to run through that portion of the country during the war.

It turned out that Senator Gwin's original idea with reference to running a pony express from the Missouri River to Sacramento to prove the practicability of that route at all seasons of the year was well taken, and the stage line as well as the pony proved to be of vital importance in carrying the mails and government dispatches.

It so transpired that the firm of Russell, Majors & Waddell had to pay the fiddler, or the entire expense of organising both the stage line and the pony express, at a loss, as it turned out, of hundreds of thousands of dollars. After the United States mail was given to this line it became a paying institution, but it went into the hands of Holliday just before the first quarterly payment of $100,000 was made. The government paid $800,000 a year for carrying the mails from San Francisco to Missouri, made in quarterly payments.

The part of the line that Russell, Majors & Waddell handled received $400,000, and Butterfield & Co. received $400,000 for carrying the mails from Salt Lake to California. During the war there was a vast amount of business, both in express and passenger traveling, and it was the only available practicable line of communication between California and the States east of the Rocky Mountains.

CHAPTER 18

The Gold Fever

During the winter of 1858-59 the public generally, throughout the United States, began to give publicity to a great gold discovery reported to have been made in the Pike's Peak region of the Rocky Mountains.

From week to week, as time passed, more extended accounts were given, until the reports became fabulous.

The discovery was reported to have been made in Cherry Creek, at or near its junction with the South Platte River, and one of the newspapers at the time, published in Cleveland, Ohio, came out, giving a cut which was claimed to be a map of the country. Pike's Peak was given as the central figure. The South Fork of the Platte River was represented as flowing out from the mountain near its base, and Cherry Creek as coming out of a gorge in the mountain's side, and forming a junction with the Platte in the low lands, at which point Denver was designated.

Reports went so far as to state that gold was visible in the sands of the creek-bed, and that the banks would pay from grass roots to bed rock.

People became wild with excitement, and a stampede to Pike's Peak appeared inevitable.

The great question with the excited people was as to the shortest, cheapest, and quickest way to get to the country, with little thought of personal safety or comfort, or as to how they should get back in the event of failure. But the problem was soon believed to have been solved to the satisfaction of all concerned.

A brilliant idea took possession of the fertile brain of an energetic Buckeye citizen, and a plan was conceived and to an extent put in execution. A canal-boat which had been converted into a steam tug was secured, not only for the purpose of transporting the multitudes from Cleveland to Denver, but to transport the millions of treasures back to civilization, or, as it was then put, "to God's country." Passengers were advertised for at $100 per head; the route given as follows: From Cleveland, Ohio, *via* the lake to Chicago, thence via Illinois Canal and River to the Mississippi River, then to the mouth of the Missouri River and up the Missouri to the mouth of the Platte River, and, thence up the Platte to Denver, and it was with pride that this boat was advertised as the first to form a line of steamers to regularly navigate the last-named stream.

Of course, this trip was never made, for in fact, at certain seasons of the year, it would be difficult to float a two-inch plank down the river from Denver to the Missouri, and yet this is but illustrative of the hundreds of visionary, crude and novel plans conceived and adopted by the thousands of so-called Pike's Peakers who swarmed the plains between Denver and the border during the early part of 1859.

Having caught the fever, and there being no remedy for the disease equal to the gold hunter's experience, horses and wagon were secured and, with traveling companions, the trip was made by land. Many novel experiences to the participants occurred during that trip.

At Leavenworth one of my companions concluded to economize, which he did by piloting six yoke of oxen across the plains for me. He drove into Denver in the morning and drove out of it in the evening of the same day, fully convinced (as he himself stated) that all reports of the country were either humbugs or greatly exaggerated, and that he had seen and knew all that was worth seeing and knowing of that land. I suggested the advisability of further investigation before moving on, but not being favourable to delay, and suiting himself to his means, he secured an ox and cart that had been brought in from the Red River of the North, and loading it with all necessary supplies headed for Denver, with a determination so aptly and forcibly expressed in the usual motto, "Pike's Peak or bust." All went well until he reached the Little Blue River in Kansas, when he "busted," or at least the cart did, and the result was the location of a ranch on that stream and an end to his westward career.

Thus, Kansas is largely indebted for her early and rapid settlement to the discovery of gold in Colorado, and to the misfortunes of many of the Pike's Peakers who, for some cause, failed to reach the end desired, and who were thus compelled to stop and become settlers of that now great State.

Shortly before the time of which I write, June, 1859, Horace Greeley passed through Leavenworth *en route* for Denver, and thousands of people were to be found in every principal town and city, from St. Louis to Council Bluffs (there was no Omaha at that time), who were awaiting his report, which was daily expected, and for once, at least, the New York *Tribune* was in demand on the borders. I may say here that Horace Greeley was *dead-headed* through to California.

In the early part of July came a favourable report in the *Tribune*, and at that time a shipment of gold was made from Denver and put on exhibition in one of the banks at Leavenworth.

Thus, new life was given to the immigration movement, and soon the towns along the border were largely relieved of their floating population, and the plains at once became alive with a moving, struggling mass of humanity, moving westward in the mad rush for the goldfields of Pike's Peak.

Among my friends an association was formed and the following party organised, *viz*.: Alfred H. Miles and his wife, their son George T., and two daughters, Fannie D. and Emma C. Miles, with William McLelland and P. A. Simmons.

They outfitted with two wagons, four yoke of oxen, two saddle-mules, one cow, and all supplies presumed to be sufficient for at least one year. On the first day of August, 1859, they moved out from Leavenworth, happy and full of "great expectations" for the future. Forty-nine days were spent in making the drive, and then they landed in Denver on the eighteenth day of the following month. And here let me say, that I believe this party of seven proved an exception to the rule, in this, that every member of it became a permanent settler, and for the last thirty-three years they have been actively connected with, and identified in, the various departments of life and business, both public and private.

All are yet living and residents of the State, except Mrs. Miles, who recently passed to a higher life, respected and loved by all who knew her; and I here venture the opinion that no other party of emigrants in this country, of equal number, can show a better record.

Many novel events occurred on this trip also, but to mention all the new and novel experiences incident to an expedition of that kind would require more than the allotted space for a chapter. I will, therefore, confine the account to one incident alone which will make manifest the radical changes that are sometimes wrought in the individual lives of people, in a sometimes radically short space of time.

Two of the ladies of the party before mentioned arrived in Leavenworth about one month previous to their departure on this trip. They were just graduated from a three years' course of study in a female seminary, and in thirty days from that time they were transported from their boarding-school surroundings to the wilds of the Great American Desert, and after passing into the timberless portion of the great desert, the great query with them was as to how and where they were to secure fuel necessary for culinary purposes; and when informed that it would be necessary to gather and use buffalo chips for that purpose, their incredulity became manifest, and their curiosity was rather increased than satisfied.

When called upon to go, gunny-sack in hand, out from the line of travel to gather the necessary fuel, it was difficult to persuade them they were not being made the victims of a joke; but when finally led into the field of "chips," and the discovery made of their character, the expression upon the face of each would have been a delight to an artist and amusing to the beholder; and to say that the distance between the chip-field and the camp was covered by them in the time rarely, if ever, covered by the native antelope, is to speak without exaggeration.

As before stated, all of the seven members of this party, on their arrival in Denver, became residents and actively identified in the various departments of life and business, and to each and every one there is no spot on the face of this globe that is quite so good, so grand, and so dear as the Centennial State, of which Denver is the centre of their love.

CHAPTER 19

The Overland Mail

Over thirty-two years ago, when a bachelor occupied the President's mansion at Washington, and there was no Pacific Railroad and no transcontinental telegraph line in operation over the Great American Desert of the old schoolbooks, and the wild Indian was lord of the manor—a true native American sovereign—St. Joseph, Mo., was the western terminus of railway transportation. Beyond that point the traveller bound for the regions of the Occident had his choice of a stage-coach, an ox-team, a pack-mule, or some equally stirring method of reaching San Francisco.

Just at that interesting period in our history—when the gold and silver excitement, and other local advantages of the Pacific Coast, had concentrated an enterprising population and business at San Francisco and the adjacent districts the difficulty of communication with the East was greatly deplored, and the rapid overland mail service became an object of general solicitude. In the year 1859 several magnates in Wall Street formed a formidable lobby at Washington in the interests of an overland mail route to California, and asked Congress for a subsidy for carrying the mails overland for one year between New York and San Francisco.

The distance was 1,950 miles. Mr. Russell proposed to cover this distance with a mail line between St. Joseph, Mo., and San Francisco, that would deliver letters at either end of the route within ten days.

Five hundred of the fleetest horses to be procured were immediately purchased, and the services of over two hundred competent men were secured. Eighty of these men were selected for express riders. Light-weights were deemed the most eligible for the purpose; the lighter the man the better for the horse, as some portions of the route had to be traversed at a speed of twenty miles an hour. Relays were established at stations, the distance between which was, in each instance, determined by the character of the country.

These stations dotted a wild, uninhabited expanse of country 2,000 miles wide, infested with road-agents and warlike Indians, who roamed in formidable hunting parties, ready to sacrifice human life with as little unconcern as they would slaughter a buffalo. The Pony Express, therefore, was not only an important, but a daring and romantic enterprise. At each station a sufficient number of horses were kept, and at every third station the thin, wiry, and hardy pony-riders held themselves in readiness to press forward with the mails. These were filled with important business letters and press dispatches from Eastern cities and San Francisco, printed upon tissue paper, and thus especially adapted by their weight for this mode of transportation.

The schedule time for the trip was fixed at ten days. In this manner they supplied the place of the electric telegraph and the lightning express train of the gigantic railway enterprise that subsequently superseded it.

The men were faithful, daring fellows, and their service was full of novelty and adventure. The facility and energy with which they journeyed was a marvel. The news of Abraham Lincoln's 'election was carried through from St. Joseph to Denver, Colo., 665 miles, in two days and twenty-one hours, the last ten miles having been covered in thirty-one minutes, The last route on the occasion was traversed by Robert H. Haslam, better known as "Pony Bob," who carried the news 120 miles in eight hours and ten minutes, riding from Smith's Creek to Fort Churchill, on the Carson River, Nevada, the first telegraph station on the Pacific Coast.

On another occasion, it is recorded, one of these riders journeyed a single stretch of 300 miles—the other men who should have relieved him being either disabled or indisposed—and reached the terminal station on schedule time.

The distance between relay riders' stations varied from sixty-five to one hundred miles, and often more. The weight to be carried by each was fixed at ten pounds or under, and the charge for transportation was $5 in gold for each half of an ounce. The entire distance between New York City and San Francisco occupied but fourteen days. The riders received from $120 to $125 per month for their arduous services. The pony express enterprise continued for about two years, at the end of which time telegraph service between the Atlantic and Pacific oceans was established. Few men remember those days of excitement and interest. The danger surrounding the riders cannot be told. Not only were they remarkable for lightness of weight and energy, but their service required continual vigilance, bravery, and agility.

Among their number were skilful guides, scouts, and couriers, accustomed to adventures and hardships on the plains—men of strong wills and wonderful powers of endurance. The horses were mostly half-breed California mustangs, as alert and energetic as their riders, and their part in the service—sure-footed and fleet—was invaluable. Only two minutes were allowed at stations for changing mails and horses. Everybody was on the *qui vive*. The adventures with which the service was rife are numerous and exciting.

The day of *the first start*, the 3rd of April, 1860, at noon, Harry Roff, mounted on a spirited half-breed *broncho*, started from Sacramento on his perilous ride, and covered the first twenty miles, including one change, in fifty-nine minutes. On reaching Folson, he changed again and started for Placerville, at the foot of the Sierra Nevada Mountain, fifty-five miles distant. There he connected with "Boston," who took the route to Friday's Station, crossing the eastern summit of the Sierra Nevada. Sam Hamilton next fell into line, and pursued his way to Genoa, Carson City, Dayton, Reed's Station, and Fort Churchill—seventy-five miles. The entire run, 185 miles, was made in fifteen hours and twenty minutes, and included the crossing of the western summits of the Sierras, through thirty feet of snow.

This seems almost impossible, and would have been, had not pack trains of mules and horses kept the trail open. Here "Pony Bob"—Robert H. Haslam—took the road from Fort Churchill to Smith's Creek, 120 miles distant, through a hostile Indian country. From this point Jay G. Kelley rode from Smith's Creek to Ruby Valley, Utah, 116 miles; from Ruby Valley to Deep Creek, H. Richardson, 105 miles; from Deep Creek to Rush Valley, old Camp Floyd, eighty miles; from Camp Floyd to Salt Lake City, fifty miles; George Thacher the last end. This ended the Western Division, under the management of Bolivar Roberts, now in Salt Lake City.

Among the most noted and daring riders of the Pony Express was Hon. William F. Cody, better known as Buffalo Bill, whose reputation is now established the world over. While engaged in the express service, his route lay between Red Buttes and Three Crossings, a distance

A FRONTIER VILLAGE

of 116 miles. It was a most dangerous, long, and lonely trail, including the perilous crossing of the North Platte River, one-half mile wide, and though generally shallow, in some places twelve feet deep, often much swollen and turbulent. An average of fifteen miles an hour had to be made, including changes of horses, detours for safety, and time for meals.

Once, upon reaching Three Crossings, he found that the rider on the next division, who had a route of seventy-six miles, had been killed during the night before, and he was called on to make the extra trip until another rider could be employed. This was a request the compliance with which would involve the most taxing labours and an endurance few persons are capable of; nevertheless, young Cody was promptly on hand for the additional journey, and reached Rocky Ridge, the limit of the second route, on time. This round trip of 384 miles was made without a stop, except for meals and to change horses, and every station on the route was entered on time. This is one of the longest and best ridden pony express journeys ever made.

Pony Bob also had a series of stirring adventures while performing his great equestrian feat, which he thus describes:

> About eight months after the Pony Express commenced operations, the Piute war began in Nevada, and as no regular troops were then at hand, a volunteer corps, raised in California, with Col. Jack Hayes and Henry Meredith the latter being killed in the first battle at Plymouth Lake—in command, came over the mountains to defend the whites. Virginia City, Nev., then the principal point of interest, and hourly expecting an attack from the hostile Indians, was only in its infancy. A stone hotel on C Street was in course of erection, and had reached an elevation of two stories. This was hastily transformed into a fort for the protection of the women and children.
>
> From the city the signal fires of the Indians could be seen on every mountain peak, and all available men and horses were pressed into service to repel the impending assault of the savages. When I reached Reed's Station, on the Carson River, I found no change of horses, as all those at the station had been seized by the whites to take part in the approaching battle. I fed the animal that I rode, and started for the next station, called Buckland's, afterward known as Fort Churchill, fifteen miles farther down the river.

This point was to have been the termination of my journey (as I had been changed from my old route to this one, in which I had had many narrow escapes and been twice wounded by Indians), as I had ridden seventy-five miles, but to my great astonishment, the other rider refused to go on. The superintendent, W. C. Marley, was at the station, but all his persuasion could not prevail on the rider, Johnnie Richardson, to take the road. Turning then to me, Marley said:

'Bob, I will give you $50 if you make this ride.'

I replied:

'I will go you once.'

Within ten minutes, when I had adjusted my Spencer rifle—a seven-shooter—and my Colt's revolver, with two cylinders ready for use in case of an emergency, I started. From the station onward was a lonely and dangerous ride of thirty-five miles, without a change, to the Sink of the Carson. I arrived there all right, however, and pushed on to Sand's Spring, through an alkali bottom and sand-hills, thirty miles farther, without a drop of water all along the route. At Sand's Springs I changed horses, and continued on to Cold Springs, a distance of thirty-seven miles. Another change, and a ride of thirty miles more, brought me to Smith's Creek. Here I was relieved by J. G. Kelley. I had ridden 185 miles, stopping only to eat and change horses.

After remaining at Smith's Creek about nine hours, I started to retrace my journey with the return express. When I arrived at Cold Springs, to my horror I found that the station had been attacked by Indians, and the keeper killed and all the horses taken away. What course to pursue I decided in a moment—I would go on. I watered my horse—having ridden him thirty miles on time, he was pretty tired—and started for Sand Springs, thirty-seven miles away. It was growing dark, and my road lay through heavy sage-brush, high enough in some places to conceal a horse. I kept a bright lookout, and closely watched every motion of my poor horse's ears, which is a signal for danger in an Indian country.

I was prepared for a fight, but the stillness of the night and the howling of the wolves and coyotes made cold chills run through me at times, but I reached Sand Springs in safety and reported what had happened. Before leaving I advised the station-keeper to come with me to the Sink of the Carson, for

I was sure the Indians would be upon him the next day. He took my advice, and so probably saved his life, for the following morning Smith's Creek was attacked. The whites, however, were well protected in the shelter of a stone house, from which they fought the Indians for four days. At the end of that time they were relieved by the appearance of about fifty volunteers from Cold Springs. These men reported that they had buried John Williams, the brave station-keeper of that station, but not before he had been nearly devoured by wolves.

When I arrived at the Sink of the Carson, I found the station men badly frightened, for they had seen some fifty warriors, decked out in their war-paint and reconnoitring the station. There were fifteen white men. here, well-armed and ready for a fight. The station was built of *adobe*, and was large enough for the men and ten or fifteen horses, with a fine spring of water within ten feet of it. I rested here an hour, and after dark started for Buckland's, where I arrived without a mishap and only three and a half hours behind the schedule time. I found Mr. Marley at Buckland's, and when I related to him the story of the Cold Springs tragedy and my success, he raised his previous offer of $50 for my ride to $100.

I was rather tired, but the excitement of the trip had braced me up to withstand the fatigue of the journey. After the rest of one and one-half hours, I proceeded over my own route, from Buckland's to Friday's Station, crossing the western summit of the Sierra Nevada. I had travelled 380 miles within a few hours of schedule time, and surrounded by perils on every hand.

"Pony Bob."

After the "Overland Pony Express" was discontinued, "Pony Bob" was employed by Wells, Fargo & Co., as a pony express rider, in the prosecution of their transportation business. His route was between Virginia City, Nev., and Friday's Station, and return, about one hundred miles, every twenty-four hours, schedule time ten hours. This engagement continued for more than a year; but as the Central Pacific Railway gradually extended its line and operations, the pony express business as gradually diminished. Finally, the track was completed to Reno, Nev., twenty-three miles from Virginia City, and over this route "Pony Bob" rode for over six months, making the run every day, with fifteen horses, inside of one hour.

When the telegraph line was completed, the pony express over this route was withdrawn, and "Pony Bob" was sent to Idaho, to ride the company's express route of 100 miles, with one horse, from Queen's River to the Owhyee River. He was at the former station when Major McDermott was killed, at the breaking out of the Modoc war. On one of his rides he passed the remains of ninety Chinamen who had been killed by the Indians, only one escaping to tell the tale, and whose bodies lay bleaching in the sun for a distance of more than ten miles from the mouth of Ive's Cañon to Crooked Creek.

This was "Pony Bob's" last experience as a pony express rider. His successor, Sye Macaulas, was killed the first trip he tried to make. Bob bought a Flathead Indian pony at Boisé City, Idaho, and started for Salt Lake City, 400 miles away, where his brother-in-law, Joshua Hosmer, was United States Marshal. Here "Pony Bob" was appointed a deputy, but not liking the business, was again employed by Theodore Tracy—Wells-Fargo's agent—as first messenger from that city to Denver after Ben Holliday had sold out to Wells, Fargo & Co.—a distance of 720 miles by stage—which position Bob filled a long time.

"Pony Bob" is now, (1892), a resident of Chicago, where he is engaged in business.

Chapter 20

The Pony Express and Its Brave Riders

During the winter of 1859, Mr. W. H. Russell, of our firm, while in Washington, D. C., met and became acquainted with Senator Gwin of California. The Senator was very anxious to establish a line of communication between California and the States east of the Rocky Mountains, which would be more direct than that known as the Butterfield route, running at that time from San Francisco *via* Los Angeles, Cal.; thence across the Colorado River and up the valley of the Gila; thence *via* El Paso and through Texas, crossing the Arkansas River at Fort Gibson, and thence to St. Louis, Mo.

This route, the Senator claimed, was entirely too long; that the requirements of California demanded a more direct route, which would make quicker passage than could be made on such a circuitous route as the Butterfield line.

Knowing that Russell, Majors & Waddell were running a daily stage between the Missouri River and Salt Lake City, and that they were also heavily engaged in the transportation of Government stores on the same line, he asked Mr. Russell if his company could not be induced to start a pony express, to run over its stage line to Salt Lake City, and from thence to Sacramento; his object being to test the practicability of crossing the Sierra Nevadas, as well as the Rocky Mountains, with a daily line of communication.

After various consultations between these gentlemen, from time to time, the Senator urging the great necessity of such an experiment, Mr. Russell consented to take hold of the enterprise, provided he could get his partners, Mr. Waddell and myself, to join him.

With this understanding, he left Washington and came west to Fort Leavenworth, Kan., to consult us. After he explained the object of the enterprise, and we had well considered it, we both decided that it could not be made to pay expenses. This decision threw quite a damper upon the ardour of Mr. Russell, and he strenuously insisted we should stand by him, as he had committed himself to Senator Gwin before leaving Washington, assuring him he could get his partners to join him, and that he might rely on the project being carried through, and saying it would be very humiliating to his pride to return to Washington and be compelled to say the scheme had fallen through from lack of his partners' confidence.

He urged us to reconsider, stating the importance attached to such an undertaking, and relating the facts Senator Gwin had laid before him, which were that all his attempts to get a direct thoroughfare opened between the State of California and the Eastern States had proved abortive, for the reason that when the question of establishing a permanent central route came up, his colleagues, or fellow senators, raised the question of the impassability of the mountains on such a route during the winter months; that the members from the Northern States were opposed to giving the whole prestige of such a thoroughfare to the extreme southern route; that this being the case, it had actually become a necessity to demonstrate, if it were possible to do so, that a central or middle route could be made practicable during the winter as well as summer months.

That as soon as we demonstrated the feasibility of such a scheme he (Senator Gwin) would use all his influence with Congress to get a subsidy to help pay the expenses of such a line on the thirty-ninth to forty-first parallel of latitude, which would be central between the extreme north and south; that he could not ask for the subsidy at the start with any hope of success, as the public mind had already accepted the idea that such a route open at all seasons of the year was an impossibility; that as soon as we proved to the contrary, he would come to our aid with a subsidy.

After listening to all Mr. Russell had to say upon the subject, we concluded to sustain him in the undertaking, and immediately went to work to organise what has since been known as "The Pony Express."

As above stated, we were already running a daily stage between the Missouri River and Salt Lake City, and along this line stations were located every ten or twelve miles, which we utilised for the Pony Express, but were obliged to build stations between Salt Lake City and Sacramento, Cal.

Within sixty days or thereabouts from the time we agreed to undertake the enterprise, we were ready to start ponies, one from St. Joseph, Mo., and the other from Sacramento, Cal., on the same day. At that time there was telegraphic communication between the East and St. Joseph, Mo., and between San Francisco and Sacramento, Cal.

The quickest time that had ever been made with any message between San Francisco and New York, over the Butterfield line, which was the southern route, was twenty-one days. Our Pony Express shortened the time to ten days, which was our schedule time, without a single failure, being a difference of eleven days.

To do the work of the Pony Express required between four hundred and five hundred horses, about one hundred and ninety stations, two hundred men for station-keepers, and eighty riders; riders made an average ride of thirty-three and one-third miles. In doing this each man rode three ponies on his part of the route; some of the riders, however, rode much greater distances in times of emergency.

The Pony Express carried messages written on tissue paper, weighing one-half ounce, a charge of $5 being made for each dispatch carried.

As anticipated, the amount of business transacted over this line was not sufficient to pay one-tenth of the expenses, to say nothing about the amount of capital invested. In this, however, we were not disappointed, for we knew, as stated in the outset, that it could not be made a paying institution, and was undertaken solely to prove that the route over which it ran could be made a permanent thoroughfare for travel at all seasons of the year, proving, as far as the paramount object was concerned, a complete success.

Two important events transpired during the term of the Pony's existence; one was the carrying of President Buchanan's last message to Congress, in December, 1860, from the Missouri River to Sacramento, a distance of two thousand miles, in eight days and some hours. The other was the carrying of President Lincoln's inaugural address of March 4, 1861, over the same route in seven days and, I think, seventeen hours, being the quickest time, taking the distance into consideration, on record in this or any other country, as far as I know.

One of the most remarkable feats ever accomplished was made by

F. X. Aubery, who travelled the distance of 800 miles, between Santa F, N. M., and Independence, Mo., in five days and thirteen hours. This ride, in my opinion, in one respect was the most remarkable one ever made by any man. The entire distance was ridden without stopping to rest, and having a change of horses only once in every one hundred or two hundred miles. He kept a lead horse by his side most of the time, so that when the one he was riding gave out entirely, he changed the saddle to the extra horse, left the horse he had been riding and went on again at full speed.

At the time he made this ride, in much of the territory he passed through he was liable to meet hostile Indians, so that his adventure was daring in more ways than one. In the first place, the man who attempted to ride 800 miles in the time he did took his life in his hands. There is perhaps not one man in a million who could have lived to finish such a journey.

Mr. Aubery was a Canadian Frenchman, of low stature, short limbs, built, to use a homely simile, like a jack-screw, and was in the very zenith of his manhood, full of pluck and daring.

It was said he made this ride upon a bet of $1,000 that he could cover the distance in eight days.

One year previous to this, in 1852, he made a bet he could do the same distance in ten days. The result was he travelled it in a little over eight days, hence his bet he could make the ride in 1853 in eight days, the result of that trip showing he consumed little more than half that time.

I was well acquainted with and did considerable business with Aubery daring his years of freighting. I met him when he was making his famous ride, at a point on the Santa Fé Road called Rabbit Ear. He passed my train at a full gallop without asking a single question as to the danger of Indians ahead of him.

After his business between St. Louis and Santa Fé ceased, his love for adventure and his daring enterprise prompted him to make a trip from New Mexico to California with sheep, which he disposed of at good prices, and returned to New Mexico.

Immediately upon his return he met a friend, a Major Weightman of the United States Army, who was a great admirer of his pluck and daring. Weightman was at that time editor of a small paper called the Santa Fé *Herald*. At their meeting, as was the custom of the time, they called for drinks. Their glasses were filled and they were ready to drink, when Aubery asked Weightman why he had published a damned lie about his trip to California. Instead of taking his drink, Weightman tossed the contents of his glass in Aubery's face. Aubery made a motion to draw his pistol and shoot, when Weightman, knowing the danger, drew his knife and stabbed Aubery through the heart, from which blow he dropped dead upon the floor.

The whole affair was enacted in one or two seconds. From the time they started to take a friendly drink till Aubery was lying dead on the floor less time elapsed than it takes to tell the story.

This tragedy was the result of rash words hastily spoken, and proves that friends, as well as enemies, should be careful and considerate in the language they use toward others.

In the spring of 1860 Bolivar Roberts, superintendent of the Western Division of the Pony Express, came to Carson City, Nev., which was then in St. Mary's County, Utah, to engage riders and station men for a pony express route about to be established across the great plains by Russell, Majors & Waddell. In a few days fifty or sixty men were engaged, and started out across the Great American Desert to establish stations, etc.

Among that number the writer can recall to memory the following: Bob Haslam ("Pony Bob"), Jay G. Kelley, Sam Gilson, Jim Gilson, Jim McNaughton, Bill McNaughton, Jose Zowgaltz, Mike Kelley, Jimmy Buckton, and "Irish Tom." At present, (1892), "Pony Bob" is living on "the fat of the land" in Chicago. Sam and Jim Gilson are mining in Utah, and all the old "Pony" boys will rejoice to know they are now millionaires. The new mineral, gilsonite, was discovered by Sam Gilson. Mike Kelley is mining in Austin, Nev.; Jimmy Bucklin, "Black Sam," and the McNaughton boys are dead. William Carr was hanged in Carson City, for the murder of Bernard Cherry, his unfortunate death being the culmination of a quarrel begun months before, at Smith Creek Station. His was the first legal hanging in the Territory, the sentence being passed by Judge Cradlebaugh.

J. G. Kelley has had a varied experience, and is now fifty-four years of age, an eminent mining engineer and mineralogist, residing in Denver, Colo. In recalling many reminiscences of the plains in the early days, I will let him tell the story in his own language:

Yes, I was a pony express rider in 1860, and went out with Bol Roberts (one of the best men that ever lived), and I tell you it was no picnic. No amount of money could tempt me to repeat my experience of those days. To begin with, we had to build willow roads (corduroy fashion) across many places along the Carson River, carrying bundles of willows two and three hundred yards in our arms, while the mosquitoes were so thick it was difficult to discern whether the man was white or black, so thickly were they piled on his neck, face, and hands.

Arriving at the Sink of the Carson River, we began the erection of a fort to protect us from the Indians. As there were no rocks or logs in that vicinity, the fort was built of *adobes*, made from the mud on the shores of the lake. To mix this mud and get it the proper consistency to mould into *adobes* (dried brick), we tramped around all day in it in our bare feet. This we did for a week or more, and the mud being strongly impregnated with alkali (carbonate of soda), you can imagine the condition of our feet. They were much swollen, and resembled hams. Before that time, I wore No. 6 boots, but ever since then No. 9s fit me snugly.

This may, in a measure, account for Bob Haslam's selection of a residence in Chicago, as he helped us make the *adobes*, and the size of his feet would thereafter be less noticeable there than elsewhere.

We next built a fort of stone at Sand Springs, twenty-five miles from Carson Lake, and another at Cold Springs, thirty-seven miles east of Sand Springs.

At the latter station I was assigned to duty as assistant station-keeper, under Jim McNaughton. The war against the Piute Indians was then at its height, and we were in the middle of the Piute country, which made it necessary for us to keep a standing guard night and day. The Indians were often seen skulking around, but none of them ever came near enough for us to get a shot at them, till one dark night, when I was on guard, I noticed one of our horses prick up his ears and stare. I looked in the direction indicated and saw an Indian's head projecting above the wall.

My instructions were to shoot if I saw an Indian within shooting distance, as that would wake the boys quicker than anything else; so, I fired and missed my man.

Later on, we saw the Indian camp-fires on the mountain, and in the morning, saw many tracks. They evidently intended to stampede our horses, and if necessary kill us. The next day one of our riders, a Mexican, rode into camp with a bullet hole through him from the left to the right side, having been shot by Indians while coming down Edwards Creek, in the Quakenasp bottom. This he told us as we assisted him off his horse. He was tenderly cared for, but died before surgical aid could reach him. "As I was the lightest man at the station, I was ordered to take the Mexican's place on the route. My weight was then 100 pounds, while now I weigh 230. Two days after taking the route, on my return trip, I had to ride through the forest of quakenasp trees where the Mexican had been shot. A trail had been cut through these little trees, just wide enough to allow horse and rider to pass. As the road was crooked and the branches came together from either side, just above my head when mounted, it was impossible to see ahead more than ten or fifteen yards, and it was two miles through the forest.

I expected to have trouble, and prepared for it by dropping my bridle reins on the neck of the horse, put my Sharp's rifle at full cock, kept both spurs into the flanks, and he went through that forest like a 'streak of greased lightning.'

At the top of the hill I dismounted to rest my horse, and looking back, saw the bushes moving in several places. As there were no cattle or game in that vicinity, I knew the movements must be caused by Indians, and was more positive of it when, after firing several shots at the spot where I saw the bushes moving, all agitation ceased. Several days after that, two United States soldiers, who were on their way to their command, were shot and killed from the ambush of those bushes, and stripped of their clothing, by the red devils.

One of my rides was the longest on the route. I refer to the road between Cold Springs and Sand Springs, thirty-seven miles, and not a drop of water. It was on this ride that I made a trip which possibly gave to our company the contract for carrying the mail by stage-coach across the plains, a contract that was largely subsidised by Congress.

One day I trotted into Sand Springs covered with dust and perspiration. Before reaching the station, I saw a number of men running toward me, all carrying rifles, and as I supposed they took me for an Indian, I stopped and threw up my hands. It seemed they had a spy-glass in camp, and recognising me had come to the conclusion I was being run in by Piutes and were coming to my rescue.

Bob Haslam was at the station, and in less than one minute relieved me of my mail-pouch and was flying westward over the plains. Some of the boys had several fights with Indians, but they did not trouble us as much as we expected; personally, I only met them once face to face. I was rounding a bend in the mountains, and before I knew it, was in a camp of Piute Indians. Buffalo Jim, the chief, came toward me alone. He spoke good English, and when within ten yards of me I told him to stop, which he did, and told me he wanted '*tobac*' (tobacco).

I gave him half I had, but the old fellow wanted it all, and I finally refused to give him any more; he then made another step toward me, saying that he wanted to look at my gun. I pulled the gun out of the saddle-hock and again told him to stop. He evidently saw that I meant business, for, with a wave of his hand, he said: 'All right, you pooty good boy;' you go.' I did not need a second order, and quickly as possible rode out of their presence, looking back, however, as long as they were in sight, and keeping my rifle handy.

As I look back on those times I often wonder that we were not all killed. A short time before, Major Ormsby of Carson City, in command of seventy-five or eighty men, went to Pyramid Lake to give battle to the Piutes, who had been killing emigrants and prospectors by the wholesale. Nearly all the command were killed in a running fight of sixteen miles. In the fight Major Ormsby and the lamented Harry Meredith were killed. Another regiment of about seven hundred men, under the command of Col. Daniel E. Hungerford and Jack Hayes, the noted Texas ranger, was raised.

Hungerford was the *beau ideal* of a soldier, the hero of three wars, and one of the best tacticians of his time. This command drove the Indians pell-mell for three miles to Mud Lake, killing and wounding them at every jump. Colonel Hungerford and Jack Hayes received, and were entitled to, great praise, for at the close of the war terms were made which have kept the Indians peaceable ever since. Jack Hayes died several years since in Alameda, Cal. Colonel Hungerford, at the ripe age of seventy years, is hale and hearty, enjoying life and resting on his laurels in Italy, where he resides with his granddaughter, the Princess Colona.

As previously stated, it is marvellous that the pony boys were not all killed. There were only four men at each station, and the Indians, who were then hostile, roamed all over the country in bands of 30 to 100.

What I consider my most narrow escape from death was being shot at one night by a lot of fool emigrants, who, when I took them to task about it on my return trip, excused themselves by saying, 'We thought you was an Indian.'

I want to say one good word for our bosses, Messrs. Russell, Majors & Waddell. The boys had the greatest veneration for them because of their general good treatment at their hands. They were different in many respects from all other freighters on the plains, who, as a class, were boisterous, blasphemous, and good patrons of the bottle, while Russell, Majors & Waddell were God-fearing, religious, and temperate themselves, and were careful to engage none in their employ who did not come up to their standard of morality.

Calf-bound Bibles were distributed by them to every employ. The one given to me was kept till 1881, and was then presented to Ionic Lodge No. 35, A. F. & A. M., at Leadville, Colo.

The Pony Express was a great undertaking at the time, and was the foundation of the mail-coach and railroad that quickly followed.

During the war J. G. Kelley was commissioned by Gov. James W. Nye as captain of Company C, Nevada Infantry, and served till the end of the war, after which he resumed his old business of mining, and is still engaged in it.

CHAPTER 21

The Battle of the Buffaloes

It was the afternoon of a day in early summer, along in 1859, when we found ourselves drifting in a boat down the Missouri. The morning broke with a drizzling rain, out of a night that had been tempestuous, with a fierce gale, heavy thunder, and unusually terrific lightning. Gradually the rain stopped, and we had gone but a short distance when the clouds broke away, the sun shone forth, and the earth appeared glistening with a new beauty. Ahead of us appeared, high up on the bluffs, a clump of trees and bushes.

As we drew near, a sudden caprice seized us, and shooting our boat up on the shelving bank, we secured it, and then climbed the steep embankment. We intended to knock around in the brush a little while, and then resume our trip. A fine specimen of an eagle caught our eye, perched high up on the dead bough of a tree.

Moving around to get a good position to pick him off with my rifle, so that his body would not be torn, I caught sight through an opening of the trees of an immense herd of buffaloes, browsing and moving slowly in our direction. We moved forward a little to get a better view of the herd, when the eagle, unaware to us, spread his pinions, and when we looked again for him he was soaring at a safe distance from our rifles.

We were on the leeward side of the herd, and so safe from discovery, if we took ordinary precaution, among the trees. It was a fine spectacle which they presented, and, what was more, we were in just the mood to watch them. The land undulated, but was covered for many acres with minute undulations of dark-brown shoulders slowly drifting toward us. We could hear the rasping sound which innumerable mouths made chopping the crisp grass. As we looked, our ears caught a low, faint, rhythmical sound, borne to us from afar.

We listened intently. The sound grew more distinct, until we could recognise the tread of another herd of buffaloes coming from an opposite direction.

We skulked low through the undergrowth, and came to the edge of the wooded patch just in time to see the van of this new herd surmounting a hill. The herd was evidently spending its force, having already run for miles. It came with a lessening speed, until it settled down to a comfortable walk.

About the same time the two herds discovered each other. Our herd was at first a little startled, but after a brief inspection of the approaching mass, the work of clipping the grass of the prairies was resumed. The fresh arrivals came to a standstill, and gazed at the thousands of their fellows, who evidently had pre-empted their grazing grounds. Apparently, they reached the conclusion that that region was common property, for they soon lowered their heads and began to shave the face of the earth of its green growths.

The space separating the herds slowly lessened. The outermost fringes touched but a short distance from our point of observation. It was not like the' fringes of a lady's dress coming in contact with the lace drapery of a window, I can assure you. Nothing so soft and sibilant as that. It was more like the fringes of freight engines coming in contact with each other when they approach with some momentum on the same track.

The powerful bulls had unwittingly found themselves in close proximity to each other, coming from either herd. Suddenly shooting up from the sides of the one whose herd was on the ground first, flumes of dirt made graceful curves in the air. They were the signals for hostilities to commence. The hoofs of the powerful beast were assisted by his small horns, which dug the sod and tossed bunches that settled out of the air in his shaggy mane.

These belligerent demonstrations were responded to in quite as defiant a fashion by the late arrival. He, too, was an enormous affair. We noticed his unusual proportions of head. But his shoulders, with their great manes, were worth displaying to excite admiration and awe at their possibilities, if they could do nothing more.

Unquestionably the two fellows regarded themselves as representative of their different herds, the one first on the ground viewing the other as an interloper, and he in his turn looking upon the former as reigning, because no one had the spirit to contest his supremacy and show him where he belonged. They sidled up near each other, their heads all the while kept low to the ground, and their eyes red with anger and rolling in fiery fury. This display of the preliminaries of battle drew the attention of an increasing number from either herd. At first, they would look up, then recommence their eating, and then direct their attention more intensely as the combatants began to measure their strength more closely. And when the fight was on they became quite absorbed in the varying fortunes of the struggle.

At last the two huge fellows, after a good deal of circumlocution, made the grand rush. I reckon it would be your everlasting fortune if one of you college fellows who play football had the force to make the great rush which either one of these animals presented. The collision was straight and square. A crash of horns, a heavy, dull thud of heads. We thought surely the skull of one or the other, or possibly both, was crushed in. But evidently, they were not even hurt.

Didn't they push then? Well, I guess they did. The force would have shoved an old-fashioned barn from its foundations. The muscles swelled up on the thighs, the hoofs sank into the earth, but they were evenly matched.

For a moment there was a mutual cessation of hostilities to get breath. Then they came together with a more resounding crash than before. Instantly we perceived that the meeting of the heads was not square. The new champion had the best position. Like a flash he recognized it and redoubled his efforts to take its full advantage. The other appeared to quadruple his efforts to maintain himself in position, and his muscles bulged out, but his antagonist made a sudden move which wrenched his head still farther off the line, when he went down on his knees. That settled the contest, for his enemy was upon him before he could recover. He was thrown aside and his flank raked by several ugly upward thrusts of his foe, which left him torn and bruised, all in a heap. As quick as he could get on his feet he limped, crestfallen, away.

The victorious fellow lashed his small tail, tossed his head, and moved in all the pride of his contest up and down through the ranks of his adversary's herd. How exultant he was! We took it to be rank impudence, and though he had exhibited some heroic qualities of strength and daring, it displeased us to see him take on so many airs on account of his victory.

But his conquest of the field was not yet entirely complete. As he strode proudly along his progress was stopped by a loud snort, and, looking aside, he saw a fresh challenge. There, standing out in full view, was another bull, a monster of a fellow belonging to his late enemy's herd. He pawed the earth with great strokes and sent rockets of turf curving high in air, some of which sifted its fine soil down upon the nose of the victor.

As we looked at this new challenger and took in his immense form, we chuckled with the assurance that the haughty fellow would now have some decent humility imposed upon him. The conqueror himself must have been impressed with the formidableness of his new antagonist, for there was a change in his demeanour at once. Of course, according to a well-established buffalo code, he could do nothing but accept the challenge.

Space was cleared as the two monsters went through their gyrations, their tossings of earth, their lashings of tail, their snorts and their low bellows. This appeared to them a more serious contest than the former, if we could judge from the length of the introductory part. They took more time before they settled down to business. We were of the opinion that the delay was caused by the champion, who resorted to small arts to prolong the preliminaries. We watched it all with the most excited interest. It had all the thrilling features of a Spanish bull-fight without the latter's degradation of man. Here was the level of nature. Here the true buffalo instincts with their native temper were exhibiting themselves in the most emphatic and vigorous fashion. It was the buffalo's trial of nerve, strength, and skill.

Numberless as must have been these tournaments, in which the champions of different herds met to decide which was superior, in the long ages during which the buffalo kingdom reigned supreme over the vast western prairies of the United States, yet few had ever been witnessed by man. We were looking upon a spectacle rare to human eyes, and I confess that I was never more excited than when this last trial reached its climax. It was a question now whether the champion should still hold his position. It stimulates one more when he thinks of losing what he has seized than when he thinks of failing to grasp that which he has never possessed. Undoubtedly both of these animals had this same feeling, for as we looked at this latest arrival, we about concluded that he was the real leader, and not the other that limped away vanquished.

While these and other thoughts were passing through our minds, the two mighty contestants squared and made a tremendous plunge for each other. What a shock was that! What a report rolled on the. air! The earth fairly shook with the terrific concussion of buffalo brains, and both burly fellows went down on their knees. Both, too, were on their feet the same instant, and locked horns with the same swiftness and skill, and each bore down on the other with all the power he could summon. The cords stood out like great ropes on their necks; the muscles on thighs and hips rose like huge welts.

We were quite near these fellows and could see the roll of their blood-red fiery eyes. They braced and shoved with perfectly terrible force. The froth began to drip in long strings from their mouths. The erstwhile victor slipped with one hind foot slightly. His antagonist felt it and instantly swung a couple of inches forward, which raised the unfortunate buffalo's back, and we expected every instant that he would go down. But he had a firm hold and he swung his antagonist back to his former position, where they were both held panting, their tongues lolling out.

There was a slight relaxation for breath, then the contest was renewed. Deep into the new sod their hoofs sunk, neither getting the advantage of the other. Like a crack of a tree broken asunder came a report on the air, and one of the legs of the first fighter sank into the earth. The other buffalo thought he saw his chance, and made a furious lunge toward his opponent. The earth trembled beneath us. The monsters there righting began to reel. We beheld an awful rent in the sod. For an instant the ground swayed, then nearly an acre dropped out of sight.

We started back with horror, then becoming reassured, we slowly approached the brink of the new precipice and looked over. This battle of the buffaloes had been fought near the edge of this high bluff. Their great weight—each one was over a ton—and their tremendous struggles had loosened the fibres which kept the upper part of the bluff together, and the foundations having been undermined by the current, all were precipitated far below.

As we gazed downward we detected two moving masses quite a distance apart, and soon the shaggy fronts of these buffaloes were seen. One got into the current of the river and was swept downstream. The other soon was caught by the tides and swept onward toward his foe. Probably they resumed the contest when, after gaining a good footing farther down the banks of the Missouri, they were fully rested.

But more probably, if they were sensible animals, and in some respects buffaloes have good sense, they concluded after such a providential interference in their terrific fight that they should live together in fraternal amity. So, no doubt, on the lower waters of the Missouri two splendid buffaloes have been seen by later hunters paying each other mutual respect, and standing on a perfect equality as chief leaders of a great herd.

Chapter 22

The Black Bear

I have stood several times, when a boy, upon the doorstep of my father's log-cabin and watched the men and dogs in their chase after a bear, only a few hundred yards away. This was, of course, only a few months after the first settlers came into the country, for it was the habit of these bears to leave as soon as they knew the white people had come to stay.

As my knowledge of the bear was obtained by being brought np and living in the portion of the State of Missouri they inhabited, it was natural when I grew up that I became a bear-hunter. I have killed them at all times of the year; when in their caves, shortly after they have come out in the spring, and while in their beds, before going to their caves. I have traced them by their tracks in the snow from their temporary beds to their winter caves.

On account of my own experience, and my association with the best and oldest bear-hunters, I have had good opportunities to learn the nature and habits of black bear. Although I have seen a great many bears of the Rocky Mountains, and have had some little experience with the cinnamon, the brown, and the silver-grey bear, I am not as familiar with their modes of life as I am with those of the black bear that were found in such numbers in the Mississippi Valley when the white people first emigrated to that country. Bears of the Rocky Mountains, and especially grizzly bears, are very much larger than black bears, and, as far as I have been able to learn from those who have hunted them, their meat, as food, does not compare with that of the black bear.

One of my personal experiences in bear hunting occurred about the 15th of December, 1839, in Taney County, Missouri, where I then lived. After a deep snow had fallen, I had provided myself with some bread, a piece of fat bear meat, and a little salt, and some corn for my horse, and unaccompanied, except by my horse and four dogs, I started out to try and kill a bear. On reaching that part of the mountains where I expected to find them, I came across a number of trails, and soon found one which I knew must have been by a very fat bear. Hunters know by the trail whether the bear is fat, for if fat he makes two rows of tracks about a foot apart, while a lean bear makes only one row of tracks, similar to that of a dog. I spent part of one day in tracking this animal, which I was sure would be well worth my pains.

While on this trail I was led to the deserted bed of one of the largest bears I ever saw, for I afterward had ample opportunity of judging of its size and weight. He had lain in his temporary bed during the falling of the snow, after which he had gone in a bee-line to the cave for his intended hibernation. Feeling sure he was such a large animal, I followed the trail four or five miles, going as straight as if I had followed the bearings of a compass. On a very high peak at the mouth of one of those caves, of which there are so many in that country, his trail disappeared. The openings of many of these caves are so small that it is often with great difficulty a large bear effects an entrance.

However, though the openings are so small, the caves are broad and spacious. In these caves bears hibernate. This particular cave had a very small and irregular opening, so that I could not enter it with my gun; but, as is the custom with bear-hunters, I cut a pole ten or twelve feet long, sharpened one end, and to this tied a piece of fat bear meat, set fire to it, and made another attempt to enter the cave. Finding I could not do this, on account of the opening being so irregular, I abandoned the idea of shooting him in his cave, and proceeded to kindle a fire at the mouth, and putting a pole across the opening, hung my saddle-blanket and a green buckskin that I procured the day before, when getting meat for my dogs, upon it.

This covering drove the smoke from the fire into the cave, which soon disturbed the animal, so that he came and put the fire out by striking it with his paws. Instead of coming out of the cave as I supposed he would, after putting out the fire, he went back to his bed. He had gotten such draughts of the suffocating smoke that he made no other attempts to get to the mouth of the cave, where my four dogs were standing, ready, nervous, and trembling, watching for him, and I was standing on one side of the mouth of the cave, prepared to put a whole charge into him if he made his appearance. I waited a few moments after I heard him box the fire for him to return, but as he did not, I took the covering from the mouth of the cave and found the fire was entirely out.

I then rekindled it and replaced the coverings, and it was not long after until I heard him groaning, like some strong-chested old man in pain. I listened eagerly for his meanings to cease, knowing that he must die of suffocation. It was not, however, very long until all was still. I then uncovered the mouth of the cave to let the smoke out. It was some time before I could venture in; before I did so I relit my light, and going in I found my victim not twenty feet from the mouth of the cave, lying on his back, dead; and, as before stated, he was the largest animal of the kind I ever saw or killed. It took me seven or eight hours to slaughter him and carry the meat out of the cave, as I could not carry more than fifty pounds at a time and crawl out and in.

When I opened the chest of this big bear, I found two bullets. These were entirely disconnected with any solid matter. They had been shot into him by some hunter who knew precisely the location of a bear's heart, which is different from what it is in other animals. His heart lies much farther back in his body, being precisely in the centre of the same, while the heart of all other quadrupeds, and I think I have known all those of North America, lies just back of their shoulders; in other words, in the front part of the chest.

These bullets, from the necessity of the case, must have been shot into the animal when he was the very fattest, and when he was ready for hibernation, because they were not lodged in the flesh, but entirely loose in the chest, each one covered with a white film, and tied with a little ligament, about the size of a rye straw, to the sack that contained the heart. When the bear lay down, these bullets could not have been more than half or three-quarters of an inch from each other, for each one was covered separately, and had a separate ligament attaching it to the sack above alluded to; and the two ligaments, where they had grown to the sack, were not more than a quarter of an inch apart.

I cut out the piece containing both the bullets, and taking it in my fingers reminded me of two large cherries with the stems almost touching at the point where they were broken from the limb. What I have just described would indeed have been an interesting study to the medical fraternity, as perhaps there has never been anything like it. It could not have occurred in this particular way, except where the bear had gone through the preparation peculiar to him before

Alexander Majors' first bear hunt

hibernating, and after leaving his temporary bed he could lie dormant and give nature ample opportunity to restore the injury to the system which the bullet had caused. The above facts proved that it was just at the season of the year when the bear was ready to hibernate.

In one of my trips on a steamer of the Upper Missouri, one day while the boat's crew were getting their supply of wood, I took my gun and started along the river-bank in the hope of seeing an elk or deer that I might shoot. I came to a place on the river where the banks were very high, and I observed that a lot of cottonwood saplings from six to eight inches in diameter had been felled and cut into sections. I saw that it had been recently done, and I at first supposed that it had been done by someone with an axe, but when I reached the spot, I saw that it was the work of the beavers and that some of the wood had been dragged away. I followed the trail for a few steps, when I came to the mouth of a tunnel, and discovered that the timber had been dragged through it.

The tunnel had an incline of about thirty-five degrees, and was as straight as if it had been made with an auger. This was in the month of October, at the time when it. was their custom to stow away their food for the winter. They had no dam at this point, as the water was deep, and they were drawing the timbers down through the tunnel and sinking them in the deep water, so that they could have access to it during the period when the river would be frozen over.

The reason for the tunnel, of which I have spoken, was that the river-bank for some distance was high and almost perpendicular, and the beaver, being a very clumsy animal with short legs, his only alternative was to make a tunnel in order to get his winter food. They have a way of sinking the cottonwood and keeping it down in their pond or simply in the deep water when they do not make dams. This family of beavers evidently had their house far under the surface of the ground, for the place was admirably adapted for them to make such a home, the banks being so high above the water.

One could see no trace whatever of the beaver, or have a knowledge of where he was, more than the opening of the tunnel and where the timber had been cut; indeed, one might pass hundreds of times and not be conscious that beavers were living right under one's feet. I picked up one of the chips which the beaver had cut, measuring about seven inches in length, and carried it home with me as a curiosity.

CHAPTER 23

A Boy's Trip Overland

Remembering my own love of adventure as a boy, I cannot refrain from giving here, a chapter contributed by my son, Green Majors, which will be found both instructive and interesting. He says:—

At the inexperienced age of twelve years I was seized with a strong desire to go overland to Montana. For a number of years I had lived at Nebraska City, on the Missouri River, a starting point in those days for west-bound freight and emigrant wagon trains; and having so long seen the stage-coaches go bounding over the hills and rolling prairies, headed for the golden West, it was with a feeling of great satisfaction that on the morning of April 26, 1866, I was seated on top of one of those, same coaches, as a fellow passenger with my father, Alexander Majors, bound for the Rocky Mountains, and Helena, Mont, in particular. To my boyish fancy the never ceasing rocking to and fro of the overland coach of early days was a constant delight.

Denver we reached in six days and nights of incessant travel. Rain nor shine, floods nor deserts, stopped us. If a passenger became too sleepy or exhausted to hold on and sleep at the same time on the outside, he could get inside by submitting to the 'sardining' process. But inside, the clouds of dust and the cramped position necessary to assume made one at times feel like the coach were spinning round like a top in the dark.

At Denver we laid in a big supply of luncheon material, for the next continuous ride, without a town, was for 600 miles, to Salt Lake City. However, before we reached Zion, our troubles were many, one of which was being caught in a violent snowstorm one dark night while bowling along over Laramie Plains. Our driver and his mules both lost the road. He so notified us, and we got out to wade through the innumerable drifts to see if we could feel the hard-beaten trail with our feet. But it was of no use.

So for fear we might wander away from the emigrant road too far, or that he might drive over some precipice or into some hole or other in the blinding storm, we unhitched his four mules and tied each one with its head to a wheel, so there could be no runaway, and then all hands got back into the coach, tucked our wraps about us as best we could, and there we sat, like Patience on a monument, smiling at grief, with the wind whistling in all its many sad cadences through the flapping wings of that desolate coach, until the longest night I ever saw went by. Next morning, we found two and a half feet of 'the beautiful' on the level, and the struggle to gain another station began. We tramped snow and broke trails for that coach to get through the drifts for about ten or fifteen miles, before we got to a lower altitude, out of the path of the storm, for all of which distance we of course paid the stage company 25 cents a mile fare, with no baggage allowance to speak of.

Not a great ways farther on, we struck the famous Bitter Creek country, a section that was the terror of travellers, because of poor grass, water that was foul and bitter, and alkali plains that were terrific on man and beast. At one place along Bitter Creek its water was as red as blood, at another as yellow as an orange; but generally, its colour was a dark muddy drab, and highly impregnated with vegetable and earthy matter.

I suppose Bitter Creek is the only place on earth where highwaymen had the cold-blooded nerve to charge travellers $1.50 for nothing but fat bacon, poorly cooked, and an inferior quality of mustard, as a meal's victuals, but the stage station-keepers had it there. By the time we finished our Bitter Creek experience we were proof against peril, so that subsequent floods in the canons from melting snows in the mountains, sitting bolt upright with three on a seat to sleep over the rough mountain roads at night, and passing over long stretches of country with no water fit to drink, were trivial circumstances.

After a thirty-day siege of this sort of experience, we alighted on the gravelly streets of Helena, Mont., then a town of canvas houses and tents, and log huts. Helena at that time was the liveliest town I have ever seen in my life, either in America or Europe, over the whole of both of which I have since travelled. At that time her business houses were largely propped up on stilts, while underneath the red-shirted placer miner was washing the blue gravel soil for gold-dust.

Her streets, in many places, were bridged over, to allow of the same thing. Sunday was the liveliest day in the week for business. The plainest meal at a restaurant cost $1.50, and bakery pies, with brown paper used for a crust, cost 75 cents each.

Everybody had money, and nobody appeared to want to keep what he had. Gold dust was the money of the country, no greenbacks nor coin being used. A pennyweight of the yellow dust passed for a dollar, but expert cashiers, at the gaming places and stores, were said to know how to weigh the article so deftly that $100 of it in value would only go $50 in distance. However, wages were very high, and so was everything else, so that if a man were robbed pretty badly, he could soon recuperate his lost fortunes. There were no churches in Helena then, if, indeed, there were any in the Territory.

The first Sunday after arriving there, I remember attending divine service in a muslin building, but the blacksmith's hammer next door and the lusty auctioneer's voice in the street made so much noise the congregation could not understand the divine's injunctions, so that church-going there, at that time, was attended with considerable annoyance. Everything was crude and primitive, everybody was cordial, generous, and open-hearted, and anything or anybody justly appealing to those roughly apparelled yeomanry for aid or sympathy invariably opened the floodgates of their plenty and fired the great, deep, warm, heart-throbs of their noble natures.

But they were as prompt in meting out retributive justice to the wrong-doer as in loosing their purse-strings to a worthy applicant, and many were the wayward souls jerked into eternity through the deadly and inexorable noose of the ubiquitous vigilante, whose will was law, and the objects of whose adverse edicts were soon plainly told to recite their last prayers in the body.

Cattle-raising on the rich, nutritious bunch-grass of the broad valleys of the Territory also soon grew to be a very lucrative business, to supply the numerous placer-mining towns of Montana, a number of which were quite important and thrifty camps at that time. Farming was also followed to a limited extent. Inasmuch as potatoes, cabbage, and other vegetables were largely imported from Salt Lake, about five hundred miles, all sorts of soil products yielded handsome returns.

Montana has had her periods of depression as well as of prosperity. For after her then-discovered and easily accessible placer ground became washed out, which took several years, times there grew very dull, but not until something like $200,000,000 worth of gold had

SUNRISE IN CAMP

been washed from her auriferous gulches and hillsides. Quartz mining was rare in those days, because freight and everything else was so high that few had the means to engage in that kind of mining. From a State of such prosperous activity in the sixties, with a large and well-to-do population, in 1874-75 it grew so dull and so many had left the Territory that those remaining wished they could get away too.

In the Centennial year of 1876, however, Montana's true era of prosperity dawned, when rich silver quartz was discovered at the now famous city of Butte, styled 'the greatest mining camp on earth.' The Territory's business in every avenue soon rose from its low ebb to an affluent flood, all kinds and lines almost immediately feeling its vitalizing, stimulating influence. From an isolated mountain fastness, it forthwith again became the theatre of activity and thrift, and the stream of precious metals that it again poured into the world's commercial channels not long after required the capacity of a line of railroad to handle its vast volume.

Chicago, New York, Boston, and other Eastern centres recognised Montana merchants as among their heaviest and best-paying customers, again demonstrating that mining for the precious metals is the great vanguard of a rapid and substantial civilization. The Utah & Northern was the pioneer railroad into her confines, but its business soon grew to such enormous proportions that the Northern Pacific followed in three or four years, and then Jim Hill swooped in with his Great Northern Road. So that that apparently isolated section has three trans-continentals now running east and west through her entire length, with the Chicago, Burlington & Quincy on her eastern border, impatient to share her immense traffic, and the Butte, Boisé & San Francisco soon to give her a direct outlet to San Francisco Bay.

But to return to the early days of Montana, certainly one of the grandest and richest sections of the Union. It is in this State that the muddy Missouri River has its source, although in the mountainous part of its course its water is as clear as crystal. Here, also, the broad and majestic Columbia has its inception, the heads of these two noble streams bubbling up out of her lofty mountains quite close together. And it is a striking coincidence that the same section that sends these two noble streams down through fertile fields to the sea, bearing on their mighty bosoms the wealth and water supply of empires, should also possess the largest and richest deposits of the precious metals that the world has ever known.

But such is the case. Speaking of precious metals recalls some of the 'stampedes' to newly discovered mining camps in early days. A 'stampede' is a panic reversed, usually instigated by the wild and rainbow-coloured statements of over-enthusiastic persons, and often those statements had utterly no foundation in fact. Men would rise from their beds in the middle of the night, if thought necessary, and with insufficient food, clothing, or implements, afoot or horseback, climb dark mountains or canons, swim floods, tramp over alkali plains, or submit to any and all kinds of hardships, all for the sake of being among the first on the ground of newly discovered 'diggins.' 'First come, first served,' was the rule, and each man was determined, as nearly as possible, to be first served.

In the famous Sun River stampede, in the winter of 1866-67, with the mercury *coquetting* with the 30-degree-below-zero point, it was said men actually started out in their shirt sleeves to make a hundred-mile journey through the deep snow to the reputed new camp without food supplies to carry them through. And as it often proved in other cases, there wasn't a particle of truth in the reputed rich fields. Dame Rumour, that ever versatile and fertile-brained jade, had had an inning, and she batted hard, firing her hot balls of deception to all quarters of the field. In those days buffalo were plentiful on the plains of Eastern Montana. I think I have seen from twenty to fifty thousand in a single herd there. They blackened the hills and plains with their shaggy coats, they swarmed the rivers in their peregrinations, and raised clouds of dust like a *simoon* in their journeys across the country.

I have seen hundreds of them in a group mired down in the quicksands along the Upper Missouri River. Hunters walked on their backs and shot the fattest of them as trophies of the chase, and the ever ubiquitous, keen-scented wolves came and gnawed their vitals while they were yet alive, but helpless, in their inextricable positions. At that time bands of stately elk also abounded there. Deer were plentiful, and the fleet-footed antelope bounded over every plain. Mountain sheep, whose tender meat was fat and juicy, climbed the terraced rocky cliffs in great numbers, while ducks, geese, pheasants, fool hens, and many other table fowl were to be had for a little effort on the part of the hunter. A fool hen is a species of bird weighing about two pounds, that is so foolish as to allow the gunner to lay aside his fire-arms and kill the whole flock with sticks and stones, so closely can it be approached without taking flight. Its meat is delicious.

"Many volumes could be written on Montana's early reminiscences, her vast resources, her brilliant past, and her glorious prospective future. But the brief space allotted me precludes the possibility of detailed mention of people, places, or things, and I reluctantly stop sharpening my pencil. Montana has been great in the past, but her future will be much grander and greater still.

CHAPTER 24

The Denver of Early Days

Henry Allen was the first postmaster of Denver, so called, and charged 50 cents for bringing a letter from Fort Laramie. The first Leavenworth and Pike's express coach arrived there on May 17, 1859, having made the trip in nineteen days. This company reduced the postage rates on letters to 25 cents. The first postmaster of this concern was Mr. Fields, who was succeeded by Judge Amos Steck in the fall of 1859.

On June 6, 1866, Horace Greeley, of the New York *Tribune*, arrived in Denver by express coach *en route* to California, and addressed the citizens that same Monday evening. The next day he straddled a mule for the Gregory mines in company with A. D. Richardson, then a Western correspondent of the *Tribune*. On the 11th, they returned from Gilpin County mines, and published under Greeley's signature in a *News* extra his views concerning the extent and richness of the gold diggings which he had just witnessed with his own eyes. The circulation of this extra along the routes to the States soon caused another immense immigration to return there that fall.

On October 3rd the first election for county officers was held under provisional government. B. D. Williams was then elected to represent the new Territory of Jefferson in Congress.

The first marriage took place in Aurora (West Denver) October 16, 1859, Miss Lydia R. Allen to Mr. John B. Atkins, Rev. G. W. Fisher officiating. The first school ever started in Denver was by O. J. Goldrick, October 3, 1859, in a little cabin with a mud roof, minus windows and doors; and the first Sunday-school was organised October 6, 1859, by Messrs. Tappen, Collier, Adrian, Fisher, and Goldrick, in the preacher's cabin on the west bank of Cherry Creek.

The first theatre, called Apollo, was opened in Denver October 3, 1859, by D. R. Thorn's *troupe* from Leavenworth, with Sam D. Hunter for leading man and Miss Rose Wakely for leading lady. Old-timers will remember her well. She was considered the most beautiful lady that had graced Denver City in the first years of its existence.

The first election for territorial officers and legislative, assembly occurred October 24, 1859, when R. W. Steele, a miner, was made first governor. Over 2,000 votes were cast in the twenty-seven precincts of the Territory at that election.

The first legislature assembled in Denver November 7, 1859, comprising eight councilmen and nineteen representatives. On New Year's, 1860, Denver had about 200 houses and Aurora (now West Denver) nearly 400, with a total combined city census of over 1,000 people, representing all classes, creeds, and nationalities; hence its cosmopolitan style from that day to this. Many brick and frame buildings, stores, hotels, shops, and dwellings were put up in both towns during 1860. One was the banking house of Streeter & Hobbs, corner of Eleventh and Laramie streets. The rate of interest charged by them at that time was from 10 to 25 *per cent* per month, according to the collateral security, and from 10 to 25 cents per hundred pounds was the rate from the Missouri River for freight by ox or mule train.

On the 8th of December, the day of the adjournment of the first legislature, an election was held by those in favour of remaining under the Kansas regime, and Capt. Richard Sopris was sent as representative in the Kansas legislature. John C. Moore was elected the first mayor of Denver, December 19, 1859, under a city charter granted by the first provisional legislature. In the fall of '59 there were no particular politics there. The great question of the day was: "Are you a Denver man or an Aurorian?" Rivalry ran high between the two towns until the consolidation of Denver, Aurora, and Highlands, April 3, 1860. The first officers of the Aurora town company were W. A. McFadding, president, and Dr. L. J. Russell, secretary. Those of the Denver town company were E. P. Stout, president, and H. P. A. Smith, secretary. Strange to say, not a single one of these property holders is now living there, or is now the owner of a single lot in this large city.

I must not forget an event that happened in Denver then. A family arrived there from the East, consisting of father, mother, two daughters, and a son. One of the young Denverites took a fancy to one of the young ladies, but parents and son were opposed to the young man;

yet he was not to be got rid of. One evening he took advantage of the absence of the parents and married the girl, and on the return of the parents in the evening the mother and son started to look for them, and threatened to kill the young man if they could find him. They found them at the Platte House, on Blake Street. The mother of the girl went to break in the door, but finally concluded not to do so, and left for her home. The parties are still living in Denver, and are well off and greatly respected.

On November 10, 1859, a lager-beer brewery was established by Solomon, Tascher & Co. It was said that the beer was drinkable. It was as innocent of malt and hops as our early whisky was of wheat or rye.

Thirty-three years ago, next July the patriotic pioneers celebrated the Fourth of July in this city. It took place in a grove near the mouth of Cherry Creek. One Doctor Fox read the Declaration, and James K. Shaffer delivered an oration. There was music by the Council Bluffs band.

July 12, 1860, a series of murders and violence began there by desperadoes who had infested Denver during the summer. They tried to muzzle the mouth of the press, which bravely condemned their dastardly outrages, and as a consequence they raided the *Rocky Mountain News* and tried to kill its proprietor.

The first regular United States mail arrived there on August 10, 1860; P. W. McClure, postmaster. The first Odd Fellows lodge was instituted there on Christmas Eve, 1860.

The close of the year 1860 saw 60,000 people in the Territory, 4,000 of whom were in and around Denver.

At this juncture of time Denver was tolerably well favored with the three great engines of civilization, to-wit, schools, churches, and newspapers. There were three day schools, two or three newspapers, and the following church denominations, each with a place for holding services: Methodist Episcopal, Methodist Episcopal South, Roman Catholic, Presbyterian, and Protestant Episcopal. The latter denomination was well and truly cared for by the Rev. J. H. Kehler, who established St. John's Church in the wilderness, as he then called it. Therefore, to the praise of our pioneers let it be recorded that though then remiss in many of the modern enterprises, their liberality encouraged religion, morality, and popular education. They claimed that Whittier's apostrophe to Massachusetts might and should apply equally to *Colorado in these regards:*

The riches of our commonwealth
Are free, strong minds and hearts of health;
And more to her than gold or grain
The cunning hand and cultured brain.
Nor heeds the sceptic's puny hands,
While near the school the church-spire stands;
Nor fears the blinded bigot's rule,
While near the church-spire stands the school.

The first pioneer's cabin was erected in Denver; the first schoolhouse was built at Boulder; the first church was consecrated at Denver; the first colony located at Greeley, and the first irrigating ditches taken out, all within the Platte Valley. As the valley had been the route of Major Long and other of the early explorers, so, following in the train of the pioneer, came first the pony express, then the stage-coach, then the locomotive and the Pullman car. And it is a fact which I believe has never yet been published, that the last stage-coach of the great overland line was dispatched from the town of Brighton to Denver, thus associating its name with an act, insignificant in itself, but far-reaching in its importance, when it is remembered that that act marked the end of our pioneer period and ushered in the new growth of the railroad era.

We stand today at the distance of three-fourths of a century from the date when the foot of the while man first trod the valley of the Platte. The names of Pike and Long are perpetuated by the two magnificent peaks which raise their summits to the clouds and stand as guardians of the plains below. Fremont lived to see his wildest dreams realised in the progress of the West, but whatever fame he may have achieved as a soldier and a statesman, his name will longest be remembered as the pathfinder of the Rocky Mountains. Wheat-fields now flourish where once stood the trading-posts of Vanquez and St. Vrain. The trails of the early explorers and of the pioneers of 1859 are almost obliterated, and grass is growing upon their once broad and beaten pathways.

A happy, contented, prosperous people possess the land. A great line of railway now rolls the traffic of a continent along the valley where once the stagecoach and ox-trains of Russell, Majors & Waddell wended their slow and weary way. Thriving towns and villages and cities dot the plain, and reflect in the activity of their commercial life the industrial development by which they are surrounded.

CHAPTER 25

Buffalo Bill from Boyhood to Fame

It may not be amiss just here, while writing of this "Land of the Setting Sun," its changes from savagery to civilization, to refer to one who has done so much to aid those who followed the Star of Empire toward the Rocky Mountains.

I refer to Col. W. F. Cody, known in almost every hamlet of the world as Buffalo Bill, one upon whom the seal of manhood has been set as upon few others, who has risen by the force of his own gigantic will, his undaunted courage, ambition, and genius, to be honoured among the rulers of kingdoms, as well as by his own people.

Nearly forty years ago, in Kansas, a handsome, wiry little lad came to me, accompanied by his good mother, and said that he had her permission to take a position under me as a messenger boy.

I gave him the place, though it was one of peril, carrying dispatches between our wagon-trains upon the march across the plains, and little did I then suspect that I was just starting out in life one who was destined to win fame and fortune.

Then it was simply "Little Billy Cody," the messenger, and from his first year in my service he began to make his mark, and lay the foundation of his future greatness.

Next it became "Wild Will," the pony express rider of the overland, and as such he faced many dangers, and overcame many obstacles which would have crushed a less strong nature and brave heart.

Then it became "Bill Cody, the Wagonmaster," then overland stage driver, and from that to guide across the plains, until he drifted into his natural calling as a Government scout.

"Buffalo Bill, the Scout and Indian Fighter," was known from north to south, from east to west, for his skill, energy, and daring as a ranger of mountain and plain.

With the inborn gift of a perfect borderman, Buffalo Bill led armies across trackless mountains and plains, through deserts of death, and to the farthest retreats of the cruel redskins who were making war upon the settlers.

Buffalo Bill has never sought the reputation of being a "man killer."

He has shunned difficulties of a personal nature, yet never backed down in the face of death in the discharge of duty.

Brought face to face with the worst elements of the frontier, he never sought the title of hero at the expense of other lives and suffering.

An Indian fighter, he was yet the friend of the redskin in many ways, and today there is not a man more respected among all the fighting tribes than Buffalo Bill, though he is feared as well.

In his delineation of Wild West life before the vast audiences he has appeared to in this country and Europe, he has been instrumental in educating the Indians to feel that it would be madness for them to continue the struggle against the innumerable whites, and to teach them that peace and happiness could come to them if they would give up the war-path and the barbarism of the past, and seek for themselves homes amid civilized scenes and associations.

Buffalo Bill is therefore a great teacher among his red friends, and he has done more good than any man I know who has lived among them. Courtly by nature, generous to a fault, big-hearted and brainy, full of gratitude to those whom he feels indebted to, he has won his way in the world and stands today as truly one of Nature's noblemen.

One of the strongest characteristics of Buffalo Bill, to my mind, was his love for his mother— a mother most worthy the devotion of such a son. His love and devotion to his sisters has also been marked throughout his lifetime.

When he first came to me he had to sign the pay-roll each month by making the sign of a cross, his mark. He drew a man's pay, and earned every dollar of it.

He always had his mother come to get his pay, and when one day he was told by the paymaster to come and "make his mark and get his money," his face flushed as he saw tears come into his mother's eyes and heard her low uttered words:

"Oh, Willie! if you would only learn to write, how happy I would be."

Educational advantages in those early days were crude in the extreme, and Little Billy's chances to acquire knowledge were few, but from that day, when he saw the tears in his mother's eyes at his inability to write his name, he began to study hard and to learn to write; in fact his acquiring the art of penmanship got him into heaps of trouble, as "Will Cody," "Little Billy," "Billy the Boy Messenger," and "William Frederic Cody" were written with the burnt end of a stick upon tents, wagon-covers, and all tempting places, while he carved upon wagon-body, ox-yoke, and where he could find suitable wood for his pen-knife to cut into, the name he would one day make famous.

With such energy as this on his part, Billy Cody was not very long in learning to write his name upon the pay-roll instead of making his mark, though ever since, I may add, he has made his mark in the pages of history.

All through his life he was ever the devoted son and brother, and true as steel to his friends, for he has not been spoiled by the fame he has won, while today his firmest friends are the officers of the army with whom he has served through dangers and hardships untold, as proof of which he was freely given the indorsements of such men as Sherman, Sheridan, Gen. Nelson A. Miles, Generals Carr, Merritt, Royal, and a host of others.

Buffalo Bill's first situation

Chapter 26

The Graves of Pioneers

Many an Eastern city has more dead people than living. Instead of the West being young, the East is growing old. The antiquities of the Eastern cemetery are often more interesting to the Westerner than the life and energy of the living city. How the old names of Concurrence, Patience, Charity, Eunice, Virtue, Experience, Prudence, Jerusha, Electra, Thankful, Narcissa, Mercy, Wealthy, Joanna, Mehitable, on the tombstones of the old Puritan grandmothers have been supplanted by the new names of these modern times!

And the old-time grandfathers—well, their names suggest a scriptural chapter on genealogy. These old-time names, with quaint and queer epitaphs, on less pretentious monuments than the costly ones now erected, make an interesting study, for the ancient dates and names show that the cemetery has a history from the earliest settlement. The ancestral bones from the Mayflower down to the present have been saved. It is true that the great Western cities now have costly, beautiful, and often magnificent monuments for the dead, for the modern cemetery is becoming aristocratic.

But for the reason it might be considered almost a sacrilege, the model of a typical New England graveyard, with its odd names and quaint epitaphs, would be an interesting historical study at the World's Fair. In fact, it would be as much of a curiosity to millions of people in the West as Buffalo Bill's Wild West Show was in the East.

In all the cities of the West there are more live people than dead ones, which is not always true of the East, where the cemetery population is often larger. With the exception of some of the old Spanish mission cemeteries, those of the West are all new, unless one would wish to explore the ancient homes of the mound-builders and cliff-dwellers. A white man's graveyard is a new thing for the West. There are many thousands among the 17,000,000 people west of the Mississippi River who can tell of the days when Kansas City, Omaha, St. Paul, Minneapolis, Denver, Salt Lake, Galveston, Dallas, Helena, San Francisco, Portland, and Seattle hardly had a cemetery. Even St. Louis and New Orleans have been American cities less than a century.

But during all this time many millions have been added to the silent cities of the dead in the East, and the older the cemetery the more there is to it that is new to a Western tourist. One born in the West, on making his first trip to the East, finds almost as much of interest in a New England burial-ground, and often views it with as little reverence as does the Bostonian in gazing upon the mummies and antiquities of Egypt.

It is interesting to contrast the frontier funeral and burial-ground in the West with that of the East. The cemetery, the necessary but last adjunct to the organisation of a civilized community, follows in the wake of immigration and empire. No monuments mark the last resting-place of those buried in the first five great cemeteries in the far West. They are in the region of nameless and unknown graves.

Those five historic cemeteries, where thousands from the East and South died and fill unknown graves, are the Missouri River, and the Santa Fé, Oregon, California, and Pike's Peak trails. The trans-Alleghany, and later the trans-Mississippi pioneers, followed, in the main, the watercourses. There was no prairie-farming, and hence the term, "backwoodsman." It was a kind of a Yankee trick in the West, in later years, to leave the forests and begin ploughing the prairies, and save the time that had been hitherto used in log-rolling and clearing the river-bottoms for agriculture. The early trappers, hunters, and fur dealers followed up the Missouri River and its tributaries.

Only with great difficulty could a corpse be concealed from wolves and coyotes; the latter animal always having been known as the hyena of the plains country. Hence many an old hunter, when far from the borderland of civilization, has buried his "pard" in the Missouri River! Landsmen and plainsmen with a seaman's burial—a watery grave! The body wrapped in a blanket—when the blanket could be spared—and tied to rocks and boulders, was lowered from the drifting canoe into the "Big Muddy," as that river is commonly known in the West. Many an old hunter and trapper has been buried in the mighty rushing waters of the great Western river, even as the faithful followers of De Soto lowered his remains into the bosom of the Mississippi.

When it was necessary or convenient to bury the dead on land, the greatest precaution was taken to protect the body from wolves and coyotes, which were especially dangerous and ravenous when off of the trail of the buffalo. Rocks and large pieces of timber were placed on the newly made grave, but often these hyenas of the plains could be seen scratching and growling at this debris before the comrades of the dead man were out of sight. With these facts so well known, it is not strange that many in those early days preferred a burial in the rivers to that of the land. It seems almost paradoxical to thus find in the old trapper some of the instincts and traditions of the sailor. Far out on the plains cactus was often put in the grave, just over the corpse, as a protection against the wolves and coyotes.

The earlier expeditions starting from St. Louis went up the Mississippi a few miles, to the mouth of the Missouri River, and then followed the latter stream. For some time, the old Boone's Lick country, now known as Howard County, Mo., and Old Franklin, was the frontier commercial head.

The town of Old Franklin, where was the original terminus of the old Santa Fé trail, when Kit Carson was only an apprentice to a saddler and harness-maker, is now the bottom of the Missouri River, for there a current of seven miles an hour has cut away the old town site.

But the pioneers became bolder. Instead of following the river they began to venture out from St. Louis overland, about the time of the old Boone's Lick settlement. It was considered a brave and hazardous journey to start from St. Louis overland in those days, for it was a village town, and all of the country to the west was a wilderness. It was about the year 1808 that the Workman and Spencer party started from St. Louis, and far out on the plains, before reaching the Rocky Mountains, one of the party sickened and died.

The Indians rendered what assistance they could in bringing herbs and such crude medicines as they used for fevers. The poor fellow died, and they dug for him a grave, which was among the first, if not the first, burial of a white man on the great plains of the West.

It was a novel sight for the Indians to see the hunters and trappers wrap up their dead comrade in a blanket, and put the body into a deep hole they had dug. They piled up brush and what heavy things they could find, and placed on the grave, carved his name in rude letters, and went on their way. But they had hardly resumed their journey before the wolves began to dig at the grave.

Were it not foreign to the purpose of this article, it would be interesting to relate at some length the fate of this expedition. The most of the party were slain in battles with the Indians, and Workman and Spencer are reported to have gone through the grand canons of the Colorado River to California in 1809, but that remarkable feat is discredited by some, leaving honours easier with Major Powell, whose expedition through these *cañons* was in more modern times.

This lonely and desolate grave dug by the Workman and Spencer party is supposed to have been somewhere in what is now Kansas or Nebraska. It was the beginning of making graves on the plains and in the mountains, but time, wind, rain, and sand made them unknown.

Many thousands perished on the old-time trails to Santa Fé, the Rocky Mountains, and the Pacific Coast. Exposure, sickness, thirst, starvation, and massacre were the dangers the immigrants had to face. Many of their graves were marked with slabs, but the inscription was soon effaced. These graves are as unknown in the great ocean of plain, prairie, and mountain as though the pioneer dead had been buried at sea.

The most fatal days was when the cholera raged on the Western trails. Sometimes an entire train would be stricken and the captain would be compelled to corral the wagons until aid could be obtained from other caravans on the desert, then so called, or the teamsters recovered to continue the journey. Women sometimes helped to dig the graves and assisted in burying the dead, and have then taken the dead teamster's place at the wagon, driving the oxen until men could be employed.

With the opening of the Western trails for wagons, a larger number were buried in boxes made from rude pieces of lumber, or sometimes a part of the sideboard of the wagon was utilised for that purpose. The earlier expeditions were on horseback, and hence at that time the best that could be done would be to roll the body in a blanket. Only those in the East who have seen a burial at sea, although they may never have been on the plains, can realize the sadness and desolation of those who left their friends in the nameless graves of the old-time American desert.

Many of the babies lived that were born on the California and Oregon trails, but the saddest of all was when the pioneer mother and babe were added to the thousands of nameless graves. The death-couch was a pile of straw and a few blankets in an old freight wagon. If the angels ever hover over the dying, there never would have been a more appropriate place for their ministrations. Nameless graves! Unknown! Only the drifting sands and the ceaseless flow of the mighty Western rivers know the place of their nameless dead. These are the famous cemeteries of the far West. There are no granite shafts or beautiful emblems carved in marble. Heroic men and women! They died unknown to fame and honour, but they gave their lives that a new civilization and a new empire might be born in the far West.

The brave men, North and South, who fell in battle, have their graves marked "unknown" when they could not be identified, but no one knows where sleep the thousands who died on these trails. Even a slab to the "unknown" could not be placed, for who knows the grave? Farmhouses, fertile fields, cities and towns, and the rushing railway car now mark the spot. The path of civilization and the rapid building of empire in the West is their only living monument.

During the cholera days there was a heavy loss of life on the Western steamboats. On the Missouri River some of the old boats had a burial crew. At night-time, when the passengers were hardly aware of what was going on, the boat would stop near a sand-bar. The bodies of those who had died during the day were taken to the sand-bar, where they were quickly buried. What would have been the use of putting up even a pine board, for the rising waters would soon have washed it away?

But this is not simply Western history. It is a part of the history of the North and the South, for those who came never to return were from those sections. In many an Eastern and Southern home, it is as unknown to them as to the people of the West where sleep their dead on those old trails of the Western empire.

The emigrants and gold-seekers were population in transit. Their burial-places were as fleeting. With the building of new towns and cities were established cemeteries, but there still continued to be the thousands of unknown graves. A father, brother, husband, or son dies away from home. His name may not have been known, or if it was, the pencil-marks on the pine board soon lost their tracing in the weather-beaten changes that time brings. How often in my own experience in the mining-camps I have seen men die far away from the tender and loving care of mother, wife, and sister. How terrible then is the struggle with death! The desire to live and to see the old home-faces again becomes a passion. In their delirium the passion becomes a reality.

In their feverish dreams I have seen the dying miner in his cabin fancy he was home again. He talks to his wife, and with words of endearment tells her that he has found a fortune in the mines. I never knew of a miner who, in the delirium of death, when he was talking of the mines, but what he was rich. He had struck the precious metal. He tells his people at home about it, and many a poor fellow has seemingly died content, founded on the fancy that he had a mine and that his wife and family would always have plenty. Out of many instances. I will relate but one.

A young man from Galena, Ill., eleven years ago, was taken sick and soon the fever was upon him. He grew rapidly worse, but bravely fought the pale' reaper, for he wanted to see home again. But courage was not equal to the task. The poor fellow had to die, and when the fever was at its height, he imagined that he was with his wife and baby. How tenderly he spoke to his young wife. He thought he had a rich mine, and told her where it was located. Then he imagined that his pillow was his baby, and that he was running his fingers through the child's curly hair, and would fondle the child up to his bosom. As I gazed on the bronze and weather-beaten faces of those present in the cabin, I saw tears come into the eyes of some when the dying man was murmuring child-love talk to the baby.

At the time of the great Leadville rush, many came who never returned. Unknown, many of them sleep in their last resting place in the gulches, on the mountain sides, and under the shadows of the pine trees and granite peaks. Exposure and not being prepared to guard against the sudden changes of climate caused many to die of pneumonia and fevers. The writer went through a hard attack of typhoid pneumonia in one of the mining camps. After the worst was over and I was conscious again, one of the boys said to me, "Hello, pard, when you were in the fever you thought you had found enough gold mines to have bought out the Astors and Vanderbilts."

The greatest number of deaths for a while seemed to come from what was known as the "sawdust gang." In the wild excitement of a new mining camp boom, people rush in by the hundreds and thousands. Many have only enough money to get there, and are compelled to sleep on the sawdust floor of the saloons. Thus, they caught cold, which turning into pneumonia often proved fatal. And the cowboys—how often on the long Texas-Montana drives they have dug a hasty grave and with the lassos lowered their dead pard into it.

The sporting and theatrical element always have a swell funeral in the booming mining camps. The musicians from the dance-halls turn out, play dirges, and with due pomp and ceremony the funeral is conducted. The band returns from the new cemetery usually playing some lively air. The deceased has had a fine funeral and a good send-off, and now to business. The dance-halls are crowded again, the music goes on, and men and women gamble, dance, and drink, unmindful of what has occurred.

Those were days of death, hell, and the grave. But what will not men undergo and dare for gold? They have braved anything for it in the past, and will in the future. Friendships and home ties are broken, and in the wild, mad rush for fortune, thousands of gold hunters have lost their lives, and fill nameless and unknown graves in the far West. There is something of romance in the death of a humble prospector searching for wealth on the mountain side. Whether rich or poor the old gold hunter often sees wealth ahead in his last hours. And, perchance, through the fading light on the mountain peaks, may he not see a trail leading to a city where the streets are golden? Who knows?

In 1849 and 1850, all along the trail of the overland freighters' route, were scattered unknown graves, clear into California, my dear father being one of the pioneers who died and filled an unknown grave. In the fall of 1850, on the east bank of the San Joaquin River, he died of cholera, and was buried, and his grave is unknown.

Another instance that I recall was of the death of one of the women of the party. She was buried at the South Pass, and they built a pen of cottonwood poles over the grave, placing her rocking chair to mark the spot, and which had her name carved on it.

Chapter 27
Silver Mining

My son Benjamin and I worked as contractors almost a year in 1868, upon the building of the Union Pacific Railroad, and we were present at the Promontory when the Union and Central Pacific roads met, and saw the gold and silver spikes driven into the California mahogany tie. It was regarded at that time as the greatest feat in railroad enterprise that had ever been accomplished in this or any other country, and it was a day that will be remembered during the lifetime of all that were present to witness this great iron link between the two oceans, Atlantic and Pacific.

My calling as a freighter and overland stager having been deposed by the building of telegraph lines and the completion of a continental railway, I was compelled to look after a new industry, and as the silver mining at that time was just beginning to develop in Utah, I chose that as my next occupation, and my first experience in prospecting for silver mines was in Black Pine District north of Kelton some twenty-five miles, and I believe in the northwest corner of Utah. The district proved to be a failure, but leaving it, I met with Mr. R. C. Chambers, who, upon acquaintance, I found to be a very pleasant gentleman.

I left the camp and went to Salt Lake City, and wrote Mr. Chambers that I thought mines in the mountains were a better show for prospectors than the Black Pine District, and in a few days, he came to Salt Lake City, and we then engaged in prospecting in the American Fork and Cotton wood districts, which lay in the Wasatch Mountains, twenty-five or thirty miles southeast of Salt Lake City.

We had some success, but were not able to find anything in the way of bonanzas. We were connected with each other more or less until 1872, when a gentleman came to me one day in July of that year and told me that he had a bond upon McHenry mine, in Park District, and that the mine was a remarkably rich one. He desired me to telegraph to Mr. George Hearst of San Francisco to come to Salt Lake City and go and see the mine. He said that he wanted me to send the message because he knew Mr. Hearst, with whom I had become acquainted through Mr. Chambers, would come for my telegram, when he would perhaps pay no attention to his. I sent the message, and received a reply forthwith that he would start at once for Salt Lake City. He arrived in due time, and we together went to the McHenry mine.

Upon arrival we found it was not what was represented. We were thoroughly disappointed in our expectations. But while sitting, resting on a large boulder, a man by the name of Harmon Budden (who a day or two before had discovered and located the Ontario mine) approached us and spoke to Mr. Hearst. Mr. H. said he did not remember him, but Mr. Budden said he had previously met him in some mining camp in Nevada, and remarked that he had a prospect that he would like us to look at, only a short distance away. We went with him to the location. His shaft was then only about three feet deep, and when Mr. Hearst jumped down into the hole that he had dug, the surface of the ground was about as high as his waist, and he could jump in and out by putting his hands on the earth.

I saw that he was very much interested in the appearance of the ore, which at that depth and at that time did not show more than a streak of eight or ten inches of mineral. I was at that time what they called a "tenderfoot," and had not been in the mining business long enough to be an expert, and to my inexperienced eye there was nothing unusual in the appearance of the ore, but Mr. Hearst did see something, and he determined then and there to purchase the Ontario prospect, and arranged when we returned to Salt Lake City with Mr. Chambers to keep a watch over its development, and purchase it when he saw an opportunity to do so. Mr. Budden and his associates asked $5,000 for the prospect when we were there, but Mr. Hearst thought it might be bought for less, as it was nothing but a prospect.

But as the development of the mine progressed they raised their price for it $5,000 every time they were asked the terms, until at last it was up to $30,000, when Mr. Chambers purchased it for Mr. Hearst and his associates in San Francisco, Messrs. Tebis and Haggin. Mr. R. C. Chambers was made superintendent of the mine, and has remained its manager from that period until the present, he being one of the stockholders, as well as the superintendent. The mine has grown and developed until it is one of the great mines of the Rocky Mountain region, and under Mr. Chamber's supervision has been extremely successful and profitable to its owners. Its output, up to 1892, has been over $26,000,000, over $12,000,000 of which has been paid in dividends to the stockholders. This showed that Mr. Hearst was an expert, for he was really one of the best judges of minerals I ever met.

Utah has furnished the mining industry with some very remarkably rich silver mines, among them the Eureka, in Tintick District; the Eureka Centennial; the Chrisman Mammoth, a large gold and silver mine, and the Beck and Hornsilver, in the Frisco District; the Crescent; the Daly, in Park City District; and Ontario, as well as a great many smaller mines in the various parts of Utah. In Montana we have one of the greatest copper mines in America, called the Anaconda. It is the leading mine in Butte City, though they have many other remarkable mines in that district.

Then there is the Granite Mountain, the Drumlummen, in Marysville District, also in Montana. But the greatest output from any mine yet discovered was the Comstock, in Virginia City, Nev. It has produced more millions of dollars than any other silver mine in the United States, its output being about one-third gold. The mining industry of the Rocky Mountain States and Territories is only in a fair way for development. The State of Colorado furnishes some very rich mining camps; also New Mexico and Arizona.

In Colorado there is the Central City and Black Hawk, and the adjacent mining district, from which there has been millions of dollars in gold extracted; also, the Leadville, which has produced its millions in silver and lead; the Aspen District, with its Molly Gibson and other immensely rich mines. Then there is the Crede District, with its Amethyst and others, now producing large amounts of silver and some gold; the Silverton, where there are a great many rich mines being opened; the Ouray District and Cripple Creek, a newly discovered gold camp, with various others in that State too numerous to mention.

Nearly all of the entire mining camps of the State produce both gold and silver in greater or less proportions, and with more or less galena or lead contained in the ores with the precious metals, and this great mining industry, when it is allowed to go on as it did before the demonetization of silver, will prove to be among the greatest and best paying industries in the whole Rocky Mountain region.

The Black Hills mining district of South Dakota is a very large mining camp, where millions and millions of dollars in gold and silver have been taken out, and where, no doubt, hundreds of millions more will be produced.

Idaho has also proven to be a very rich State in mineral wealth, both gold and silver, with many places where gold is washed out of the sands and gravel of the valleys.

Silver City, in New Mexico, has produced a great many millions in gold and silver, and at present seems to be a mining camp of great merit.

The mining industry of the mountains has, of course, been the means of influencing the building of numerous railroads through and into some of the most difficult mountain ranges; in fact, wherever there has been a flourishing mining district the railway people have found a way, with capital behind them, to build a road to it, and it has now become apparent that a rich mining camp will have a railway connection sooner or later, no matter how difficult of access it may be. I think the men and the companies who have had the building of roads through and into the Rocky Mountains, and the interests of the country at heart, are deserving of great praise. No doubt, as many camps are discovered, it will be necessary to build many more roads than are now in existence, without which the mining industry could not be conducted with profit.

I may, in concluding this chapter on mining, speak of the great future there is for both Washington and Oregon as mineral States.

CHAPTER 28

The Surgeon Scout

While dwelling upon the scenes and incidents of my life upon the frontier, and speaking of those with whom I came in contact, I wish to refer to one whose meeting with me toward the latter days of overland travel began with a sincere friendship that has lasted until this day, and will continue to the end of our lives.

The person to whom I refer is Dr. D. Frank Powell, an army surgeon in those days, and whose gallant services as an officer and scout, as well as his striking appearance, gained for him the border cognomens of "White Beaver" (by which he is as frequently called today as by his own name) and "The Surgeon Scout," "Mighty Medicine Man," and "Fancy Frank."

Doctor Powell was the firm friend of Buffalo Bill, and his valuable services, rendered as a scout, guide, and Indian-fighter, made him famous as the Surgeon Scout.

His dash and handsome style of dress also gained for him the name of "Fancy Frank," while the other two appellations by which he was known were gained by his skill and service as a surgeon and physician.

When the Indians were stricken with an epidemic of small-pox, although at the time at war with the whites, Surgeon Powell conceived the idea of boldly entering their village and checking the dread disease.

Leaving the fort upon his perilous mission, Surgeon Powell made his way alone to the Indian country, and rode forward at sight of them, making signs of peace.

The astonished red-skins received him with amazement, but, assured that he was in their power, they listened to the bold proposition he had to make them, and which was that he would check the epi-

demic then raging or forfeit his own life.

Struck with the boldness of the man, whom they knew so well as the comrade of Buffalo Bill, and who spoke their language fluently, the chiefs listened to all he had to say and then put him to the test.

Then it was that the strange circumstance occurred of a pale-face foe and medicine man *vaccinating* the Indians, young and old, all except the medicine men of the tribe, who would have nothing to do with him.

The result of Doctor Powell's work was that the dread disease was soon checked, and under his care many desperate cases of sickness were cured, and he became the ideal of his friends, who held a grand *pow-wow*, and presented him with a robe of sixteen white beaver-skins—the white beaver being a sacred animal among them.

Nor was this all, for they made him a mighty medicine man, or chief of their tribe, and bestowed upon him the name of "White Beaver," which he uses today in connection with his own name.

A resident now, (1892), of La Crosse, Wis., Doctor Powell has a large practice there, resides in an elegant home, and is for the fourth time mayor of that beautiful city, and one of the most popular men in the State, socially and politically.

The doctor has been a most extensive traveller, in this country and abroad, and yet each year, for a couple of weeks, entertains as his guests the tribe of Winnebago Indians, of whom he is still the medicine chief, and who make a pilgrimage to see him, consult him as to the affairs of their people, and show him devoted respect during the time they are encamped upon his grounds, where he has a place set apart for them.

A handsome man, of splendid physique, one who has known a strange life of adventure, he is yet as gentle as a woman, and ever generous to those with whom he comes in contact; and this tribute to his worth as a man and skill as physician and surgeon he most justly deserves.

Conclusion

A Summing Up of the Happenings that Occurred or Transpired in Every Decade, Commencing with the Twenties and Ending with Ninety.

There was but little occurred of very great note west of the Mississippi during the twenties. The State of Missouri was admitted into the sisterhood of the States in the beginning of the twenties; after that there was very little of note that transpired during the twenties, with the exception of a few Indian scares on the frontier of Missouri, which, as a rule, were brought about without any real cause, and some trapping expeditions going west to the Rocky Mountains to trap for beaver fur, and also trading expeditions to Santa Fé, in New Mexico. With those exceptions, everything went along as quiet and almost as calm as a summer morning.

In those days the entire community west of the Mississippi River, as well as the States east of it, were self-sustaining, producing all that they consumed in clothing and food, in their own homes, and I might say that this state of things also existed during the term of the thirties. Very little of note occurred outside the regular course of events save the Blackhawk war upon the Upper Mississippi and the appearance of steamboats in the Missouri River, as far west as the west border of the State of Missouri, which commenced in the early thirties, and became a very large source of transportation and passenger travel, and there was also, in the commencement of the thirties, some Mormon elders that came to the county of Jackson, in Missouri, bringing with them the revelations of their prophet Joseph Smith, and claimed that they had been sent to that county by the direction of the Lord to their prophet to establish the Zion of the Lord, or a "New Jerusalem," and, of course, a new church, which has since kept its existence until the

The Retreat on the Colorado of Major John D. Lee, the Mormon

present time, with its headquarters now in Salt Lake City, Utah.

With the arrival of steamboats in the Upper Missouri, farmers commenced to raise hemp and other commodities that they could ship to St. Louis and New Orleans upon the steamers, which was the commencement of the people in that State to market the surplus that they could produce upon their farms; but the advantage of this trade or business only applied to the farmers and producers living in the river counties (I mean the counties located on the river), as it was too costly to haul their products upon wagons and with teams for any great distance; so the steamboat transportation could only be very beneficial to the counties, as above stated, the interior portions of the State having to plod along very much as was the case before steamboats came into use.

There was no finer passenger travel ever inaugurated than the accommodations that travellers enjoyed as passengers upon those floating palaces, and I have lived to see them come and go, so far as their operations upon the Missouri is concerned. The Missouri afforded nearly 3,000 miles of water navigation, measured by the windings of the river. I have travelled on steamboats from its mouth, or St. Louis, to the head of navigation at Fort Benton, in Montana.

Now, commencing with the forties, there was nothing of great moment happened until the great freshet of '44, which was the largest flood that has been known in the Missouri, about the mouth of the Caw, in the last seventy-five years, and I think that there never has been in the history of the country as great a flood in the Missouri at that point. In '46 the Mexican War came up, and produced quite a stir among the business men upon the west border of the Missouri, as at that time there was no Kansas and Nebraska, the whole country being called "the Indian Territory" west of the State of Missouri.

The Santa Fé trade, by this time, had become a regular annual business, and men had learned how to outfit wagons and teams so as to carry large amounts of merchandise and Government stores from the Missouri River to Santa Fé, N. M. and when General Donathan organised his regiment of troops, by the authority of the Governor of the State of Missouri, to march to Santa Fé, H. M., he found no trouble, neither did the government, in securing all the transportation necessary to meet any emergency that might arise, with a plain and well-beaten road the entire route that they had to travel, this road having been opened by the merchant-trains in previous years.

In '47 the Mormon leader, Brigham Young, with a company of his elders and members of the church, left the Missouri River in the early spring and travelled 1,000 miles into the interior of the country, and formed a colony in that year in Salt Lake Valley, and named the city that they found Salt City, which proved to be a half-way house, as we might call it, between the Missouri River and the Pacific Coast, which proved of great advantage to the emigrants who left the Missouri in the spring of '49 to reach the gold-fields of California; for it was in '49, or rather the winter of '48, when the placer-gold in California was discovered, and it was on this account that '49 became one of the most eventful years of the forties, the Mexican War having closed, and peace negotiations established in '48, which gave the United States the entire domain of the Pacific Coast lying north of the line now dividing Old Mexico from the United States.

There were vast numbers of brave and daring citizens from almost every State in the Mississippi Valley who attempted to reach California by the overland route, and at no time, not even during the Mexican War, up to '49, had there ever been any overland travel to compare with that of '49. Tens of thousands of emigrants or gold-hunters left the west border at that time, outfitting themselves, some with ox-teams and some with mules and the best wagons that could be found in the market, loaded to the guards with supplies of food and clothing to make the trip and return, for at that time none of them expected to remain or make their homes in California; if so, it must have been a very small percentage of the number.

Many of them died with cholera on the way; the large majority, however, reached their destination, but many of them through great suffering and privation from one cause or another. One of the misfortunes that attended the majority of them was want of experience in traveling their animals; they started off in too big a hurry, and pressed their teams too much at the outset, the result of which was, many of their animals died from fatigue, caused by over-travelling, long before they reached the Pacific Coast, the result of which was to leave on the road, or rather in the road, often the valuables that they had secured in the outset for their comfort and preservation when they reached the land of gold.

The year '50 was also a very fatal year to emigration, for it did not cease with '49, but the success of the "forty-niners" in gathering gold proved to be a great inducement to the country to continue the movements of '49 in the way of outfitting and emigrating to the Pacific Coast; in fact, it continued in a greater or smaller degree during the entire fifties; but in the year '50, as in '49, there were great numbers died with cholera. It was fatal among the emigrants from their starting point from Missouri till they would reach the Rocky Mountains, after which time the cases of death from cholera were very few compared with what they suffered upon the plains before reaching the mountains. There were but few cases that occurred after they reached the Sacramento Valley in California.

Instead of returning, as the most of the gold-seekers intended to do on leaving their homes, they found California a delightful climate, with rich and fertile valleys, and many, very many of them concluded, after having a year's experience in the country, to become citizens, and a little later in the fifties, there were a great many people in the Western States who sold their homes and started with their families for the golden shores of the Pacific—in other words, for California—in view of adopting that State for their future homes. I was acquainted with numbers who did so, and who I have since met at their homes in California, who were delighted with the change that they made, and it is a very common thing now, after the country has been settled so many years, to find numbers of people there who think that California is the only country fit to live in.

Returning to the fifties, there was nothing of great note happened until the admission of Kansas and Nebraska in 1854, when floods of emigrants, mostly from the Northern States, passed into those Territories. A number, however, were from the Southern States, and held pro-slavery views.

In '56 what is known as the Kansas war occurred, from the invasion of men from Missouri and other States.

In '57 and '58 the Mormon war occurred, when Gen. Albert Sidney Johnston was sent to Utah with an army of 5,000 regulars.

In 1859 the great Comstock mine was developed, and it added to the currency of the world between one and two hundred millions of dollars in gold and silver. Also in '58 began the Pike's Peak excitement, which resulted in the settlement of Denver.

In 1860 the election of Abraham Lincoln was followed, in '61, by the breaking out of the Civil War.

In '62 the initial steps for the establishment of the Union and Central Pacific railroads were taken, and the idea was fulfilled in '69.

Daily stages were put on in 1859 from the Missouri River to Denver and Salt Lake.

It was during the sixties that the telegraph was established across the continent, following in the track of the Pony Express.

Gold was discovered in Montana in the sixties, resulting in the settlement of that Territory.

During the seventies and eighties, the most important happenings in our country were the remarkable growth of the railroad interests.

A Thrilling and Truthful History
of the Pony Express

IN THE ROCKY MOUNTAINS
"Where Nature unto Nature's God her sonorous Aves speaks."

Contents

"The Great American Desert"	211
The Gold Fever	216
Winning the West	220
The Pony Express	227
Off Both Ways	238
Famous Rides and Riders	250
"Pony Bob"—Robert Haslam	259
"Buffalo Bill"—Col. W. F. Cody	265
A Little Pawnee	286
The Telegraph	296
An Incident that Changed a Railroad Terminus	299
"The Iron Trail"	305
General Sheridan's Way	311
The Beginning of the End	318

THE WESTWARD TRAIL

Rising, the sun points westward, by the shadows of the trees.
The shadows of the mountains, and of monuments and men,
And westward is the trending from the continents and seas;
From all the earth, within the scope of mortal sight and ken.

From where the murky waters of the dark Missouri flow,
And blot the blue of Mississippi's clear and placid tide,
Since the dawn of Western Empire, a hundred years ago,
Have ridden bands of hardy men, with Progress for their guide.

Amid the forests and along, where to the tawny stream,
Come branches, lazing eastward, across the desert plain,
They rode, and on, twixt castled buttes, to where the mountains gleam,
'Neath helmets of eternal snow, 'mid Nature's rugged reign.

Among the Sioux and Shoshone, and Cheyenne tribes that roamed,
The region where the riders bold, undaunted took their way;
Along the placid rivers, and where cascades dashed and foamed,
They blazed the way of Empire; lit its wider, brighter day.

Over the mountain ranges, and among the crags and peaks:
Adown the streams that turn toward the great Pacific Sea;
Where Nature unto Nature's God her sonorous aves speaks.
Along the cañons and the dalles, the forests and the lea.

Highways of steel have stretched along the trail the seekers made;
Great mountains have been rent in twain, deep valleys bridged and spanned;
As if by magic, cities rose, and arteries of trade
Have pulsed the blood of enterprise through all this gloryland.

This gloryland where Nature's mood is wild, and free, and strong.
Where awful rise the mountain kings, where sweep the river queens,
In majesty unspeakable, and where the forest's song,
In high hosanna, rolls above its sea of evergreens.

Now hers is high prosperity, and happiness, and health,
With life that throbs in ecstasy amid the golden gifts;

Now the favoured land rejoices in blest, God-given wealth.
And in thanksgiving, ardently, its grateful voice uplifts.

Then Ho! for the land of plenty, under the western sun!
And Ho! for the land of flowers, land of the vine and tree!
Ho! for the land of grit and gold, the land by heroes won!
Ho! for the land of Fortune's home, along the western sea!

And shout for the flag—"Old Glory!" Shout for its waving bars,
Where blaze the crimson tintings of the sunset's lustrous dyes,
And gleams the snow of the mountains that reach toward the stars;
The bravest flag that ever rose to kiss a nation's skies!

'Twas borne by heroes, valiantly, along the Western Trail,
The young republic's light and pride, "Old Glory," Hail! All hail!

W.L.V.

Chapter 1

"The Great American Desert"

The schoolboy of half a century, and more, ago was taught by his geography that a large area west of the Missouri River, and not very far from the banks of that dark stream, was the "Great American Desert."

In somewhat uncertain lines that arid waste was shown on the map of the republic in his atlas, less known than the *sirocco*-swept Sahara. But before this almost unknown territory had been eliminated from his books, he began to learn through the everyday sources of information that this region was being encroached upon by the advance skirmishers of civilization.

The boy did not comprehend it all, but as he stepped along in years it became plainer and plainer, and by the time he had reached manhood and its affairs, his own progress and that of the far West had so broadened and improved that what he had learned of the "Great American Desert" had become a dim reminiscence.

First, the boy had seen a few of the volunteer soldiers of the Mexican War, who had come back to the States, and who had brought with them a mustang pony, curious Mexican jewellery and Indian trappings, a *sombrero*, and a *serape* of bright colours, a buffalo robe, and other things that specially impressed his youthful fancy. He heard the returned Soldier "The Pathfinder" talk to the "old folks" about the West and Southwest—not yet touching the Great American Desert, but getting quite close to it.

This set the boy to looking westward.

Then he heard of the discoveries of gold in California. Sutter's mill-race was his property, in a way, and he was well acquainted with neighbors who went away, far toward the "jumping-off-place," to the "diggings." Then came the song "Joe Bowers," that told the sad tale of

Hon. Thomas Hart Benton
Famous U. S. Senator from Missouri

Gen. John Charles Fremont
"The Pathfinder"

a man who went to "Californy" to win a fortune for his sweetheart, and how she proved false because Joe had gone so far that he never could possibly get back, and she married a redheaded butcher and had a red-headed baby—according; to Joe's wail of woe.

Then, through letters home, from the Argonauts and other adventurers, the boy learned of emigrant trains that crossed the vast plains, and of the Overland Stage coaches, the great, swinging ships of the plains that were nearly like the caravels of Columbus, but following one after another, until there was an undulating line of them stretching from start to finish across the map, in his mind, of billowy prairie, sand-bottomed and treacherous streams, white-faced desert, mountain defiles, snow-crowned peaks, and so on to Sutter's Mill, and thereabout.

And the boy was close to the beginning of the facts.

Much was printed in the newspapers and magazines of the day concerning all this, and the boy devoured it. Now and then a book came within his reach that fairly teemed with the wonderful West and the exploits of men and women, and even some boys, like himself, in the long journey across the continent, and actually over the Great American Desert.

The tales of almost ceaseless fighting with the Indians; the descriptions of the varying way; the pictures of camps on the plains, where the great and curious covered wagons of the emigrant trains and the freighters made a corral, and where some skulls of buffalo, Indian wickiups, Indians themselves, with little else than a head-dress of feathers and a bunch of bows and arrows about them, entered into the striking detail; the riders of the Pony Express who flashed by in a streak of shapeful colour, followed by a long-drawn, quivering whoop; the wealth of hardihood, horse flesh, and brilliant dash that gleamed from these fleet messengers of commerce and romance—all this, and more of its sort, crowded the boy to the very heights of sensational enthusiasm. He revelled in it and wanted it. Sometimes he went after it. When he did, it became his, or he became its. To the boy who only saw it from afar, it was a glorious mental panorama.

To those who were really of it, and in it, and for it, there were manhood, womanhood, bravery, patriotism, trial, pain, fatigue, joy, sorrow, loss, gain, achievement, conquest, success, satisfaction.

To the civilized world, it brought the addition of a vast area of redeemed wilderness.

To the republic it opened an empire of opulent resource and many splendid states.

SUTTER'S MILL-RACE, CALIFORNIA
Where gold was first discovered

To "Old Glory" it was a sprinkling on the blue firmament of another shower of sparkling stars.

To the "Great American Desert" it brought the rains of heaven and the waters of the earth with sane and human climate, undulating meadows, prolific fields, flowering gardens, fruitful orchards, homes, cities, villages, farms, roads, railways, intelligence, wealth, comfort, art, strength, health and happiness; prosperity in all its tints and shades, its elements and degrees.

From the beginning, when man was told to "possess the earth and subdue it," he has thus aspired, and he has thought that he could see afar. According to his individual cosmos, he has looked into the future of the world by aid of reason, science, philosophy and high thought, a great distance, but the *vista* has been shadowy and without detail—merely a long streak of shimmering light. Time, industry, experience, experiment, necessity, ceaseless seeking, have accomplished the world's success, and the same will accomplish far more.

When Greece was the republic of art and science, and Rome had learned from her and advanced to be the mistress of the world, even yet the supply of heat was safeguarded in temple fires, and an emperor was chief priest thereof.

Today, any tramp, or the most indigent beggar, is supplied with matches wherewith he may start a blaze that Caesar might have shivered for the lack of.

When, nearly a century ago, Benton stood in the Senate of this republic, and pointing dramatically toward the west, exclaimed, "There lies the East; there lies India," he saw only a road that led to a point on the Pacific sea from which ships might sail and shorten the way to our trade with the Orient. The mighty empire that arose from the western desert, wilderness, and arid expanse over which he was pointing, was not seen by even so great a mind as his. He simply saw "through a glass, darkly."

Before Benton, a few decades, it was believed that there was more land on the eastern slope of the Allegheny Mountains, and a line running north and south from them, than the people of the United States would ever need, for any purpose, and when Iowa, Missouri, and Arkansas were the western border states, the Great American Desert and the awful Rockies were squat in the middle of an inconceivable area of sand, stone, bleakness, aridity, death, and desolation.

For ages and eons Nature has been building in the space of this desolation the vast heritage that belongs today to the people of the West, and through them to the people of the world.

The hunter, the freighter, the pony express rider, the emigrant, the telegraph, the railroad, irrigation—each in turn—blazed, opened, improved the way; the keys of Energy and Enterprise unlocked the treasure vaults, and Prosperity, before undreamed of, arose as if a special and all-covering benediction from Jehovah. The crops alone from this "desert" are annually more than all the gold money in the world. Days of travel carry the beholder through good growth until the eye becomes weary with it. Millions of prosperous people enjoy it; many, many more millions will be added to these. The waste places have become a glory to the world, under the dancing shadow of the Star-Spangled Banner.

An Emigrant Train

Chapter 2

The Gold Fever

The discovery of gold in California, in the richest and most accessible deposits ever known in the world, of which there is authentic account, had sent a mighty stream of humanity to that region. Its currents had arisen throughout the earth, and converging there, had flooded the region.

The fall of '49 and spring of '50 were the times of the greatest tides of immigration. By sail from the uttermost parts of the earth people had gone along all the ways necessary to reach the land of gold and from the relatively eastern regions of this republic, men, women, and children had taken the "Isthmus Route" and "Round the Horn," long voyages by sea, for the same goal. Countless thousands had also toiled across the plains and mountains, "The Overland Route." To use the mildest terms, it was a strenuous journey. Disease, fatigue, flood, cold, heat, storms, and savages killed thousands. The trail was marked with skeletons and scattered bones of human beings and animals of all kinds. The history of it all groans with pain, privation, and death. The details of adventure that have been written and printed would load a long railway train, and yet the half has not been told.

Notwithstanding the struggle necessary to get there, people in long and lustful lines arrived and immediately sought "the diggings," or fell into other ways of attaining the yellow bait. Commerce in all branches of trade, gambling, robbery, anything to get gold was done. Not all men in all these ways struggled for it, but some men in each. At any rate the magnet drew people in such numbers that California quickly received inhabitants enough to be admitted to the Union as a State, and as the territory belonged to this republic, one of the United States.

Government was rapidly systematised, and business with "the States," was needful, mandatory, strong, and intense. The distance and

"The Central Route"

the perilous and time-consuming means of communication made an ever-pending obstacle to all the ramifications of life between the new state and the older states, commercial, governmental, social. Leading men were constantly calculating ways and means and endeavouring to evolve plans for the bettering of these conditions.

Hon. W. M. Gwin, one of the United States Senators from California, proceeding in the fall of 1854 from San Francisco to Washington City, to take up his legislative duties, rode, horseback, from the Pacific Ocean to the Missouri River, by the way of Sacramento, Salt Lake City, South Pass, and down the Platte to St. Joseph, that way then known as "The Central Route."

One of the standing jokes of that day was that the term of a member of Congress from California might run out while he was on the way to the national capital, if he was much delayed, *en route*.

On a long distance of the journey mentioned, and for many days, Senator Gwin had for a traveling companion Mr. B. F. Ficklin, general superintendent of the pioneer freighting firm, Russell, Majors and Waddell. Between these two earnest, observant, and practical men grew the idea, on this journey, of what afterward culminated in the famous "Pony Express." Both were enthusiastic for closer communication between California and the East, and the Senator became an active and untiring advocate of the freighter's scheme for the unique express service mentioned.

In January following (1855), and almost immediately after Senator Gwin's arrival in Washington, he introduced a bill in Congress looking to the establishment of a weekly mail express between St. Louis

Abraham Lincoln

The News of Lincoln's Election

and San Francisco. The time schedule of this service was to be ten days between the two cities. Five thousand dollars for the round trip was to be the compensation and the Central Route to be the line travelled.

That bill went to the Senate Committee on Military Affairs, and it was relegated to the reserves. At any rate its front never showed again.

"The Irrepressible Conflict" was on for the following five years, until the election of Mr. Lincoln as president precipitated the Civil War, and during all this time Congress and the country east were so entirely absorbed in the impending struggle that nearly all thought of Pacific Coast business was submerged in the intensity of sectional affairs. But the far West, especially California, clamoured more and louder for accelerated mail service. The people of these regions desired to know what was going on and were insistent. The war talk was added to all the other causes of the demand for quicker information. Thus, the West did not cease to agitate the subject.

The South, however, was strongest in Congress. Its interests, pending the struggle, demanded the prevention of legislation favourable to the routes north of "Mason and Dixon's Line" and sought the confining of all government aid in that direction to the southern routes.

In those days there were three trans-continental mail routes, very slow ones, but the great bulk of the mail was sent by the Isthmian Route, *via* Panama, and the time between New York and San Francisco, at its best, was twenty-two days.

The first overland mail route west of the Missouri was a monthly stage line from Independence to Salt Lake, 1,200 miles. Its first trip began July 1, 1850, and its continuance was four years. In 1854, the government paid $80,000 *per annum* for a monthly mail-stage from Missouri, *via* Albuquerque, to Stockton, California. It was one of the failures of the period—during the nine months it ran, its receipts were $1,355. Thus early, as well as later, there were many serious interruptions in the service. The eastern mails for November, 1850, reached California in March, 1851; and the news of the creation of Utah Territory by Congress in September, 1850, arrived at Salt Lake the following January, having gone *via* Panama by steamer to San Francisco, and thence east by private messenger.

Chapter 3

Winning the West

In 1756, it took our great-great-grandfathers three days to "stage it" from New York to Philadelphia; and under Washington's administration, two six-horse coaches carried all the passenger traffic between New York and Boston—six days each way. It was a long step from this to the Overland travel of half a century later, 'the first great transcontinental stage line, and probably the longest "continuous run" ever operated, was the Butterfield "Southern Overland Mail." Its route was 2,759 miles, from St. Louis to San Francisco—being far south, *via* El Paso, Yuma, and Los Angeles, to avoid the snows of the Rockies. or this tremendous distance, its schedule time was at first twenty-five and then twenty-three days; its record run, twenty-one days.

Its first coaches started simultaneously from St. Louis and San Francisco, September 15, 1858; and each was greeted by a mighty ovation at the end. Through fare, $100, gold; letters, ten cents per half ounce. The equipment consisted of more than 100 Concord coaches, 1,000 horses, 500 mules, and 750 men, including 150 drivers. It began as a semi-weekly stage, but was soon promoted to six times a week. The deadly deserts, through which nearly half its route lay, the sand storm, the mirage, the hell of thirst, the dangerous Indian tribes, and its vast length—40 *per cent* greater than that of any other stage line in our history—made it a colossal undertaking; and the name of John Butterfield deserves to be remembered among those Americans who helped to win the West.

This "Southern Overland Mail" was operated till the Civil War utterly precluded mail-carrying so far south, and the Overland had to be transferred to a shorter northern route, where it took its chances with the snows.

The first daily Overland stage on the "Central" line left St. Joe and

Placerville simultaneously July 1, 1861, and each finished its 2,000 mile trip on the 18th.

There have never been compiled even approximate statistics of the overland travel and freighting from 1846 to 1860; nor would it be possible to list the vast throng of emigrants that crossed the Plains. Roughly speaking, 42,000 people did it in 1849 alone. There is no tally of the freighting enterprises that sprang up on the heels of this vast migration, and grew to proportions now-a-days incredible. By the sixties, 500 heavily laden wagons sometimes passed Fort Kearney in a day. In six weeks, in 1865, 6,000 wagons, each with from one to four tons of freight passed that point.

At about this time also, express messenger Frank A. Root—whose book *The Overland Stage to California* deserves to be better known—counted, in one day's ride, 888 westbound wagons, drawn by 10,650 oxen, horses and mules, between Fort Kearney and old Julesburg. A curious connotation as to the relative speed of the Overland stage and the Overland freighting is the fact that Root, starting from Atchison one day, spoke to a bull whacker just "pulling his freight" in the same direction; got to Denver; doubled back, meeting his friend somewhat advanced, and so on; finally bespeaking him as he trundled into Denver. Root had made the single trip five times (3,265 miles) with eighteen days' lay-over, while the freighter was covering the 653mile road once.

The height of this freighting was the period 1850 to 1869; its climax was from 1863 to 1866. The floating population then on the Western Plains was nearly 250,000. In 1865, over 21,000,000 pounds of freight were shipped from Atchison alone, requiring 4,917 wagons and 8,164 mules, 27,685 oxen, and 1,256 men. That is more oxen than there are today in the states of Maine, New Hampshire, and Vermont; and more mules than the census of 1900 gives all New England, New York State, Utah, and the District of Columbia. And this was but a drop in the bucket.

The firms engaged were many; their men an army; their "cattle a host." One firm alone—the greatest, but only one of a multitude—Russell, Majors and Waddell—at top-notch employed 6,250 big wagons and 75,000 oxen. The twelfth census fails to give statistics of working oxen—perhaps this mode of transport has so fallen off in the decade since 1890 (when it was itemized) as no longer to be reckoned important—but probably there are not today so many oxen working in the United States as this one firm used half a century ago.

THE GREAT AMERICAN DESERT OF TODAY

This may give some faint idea of the mighty traffic whose wheels wrinkled the face of the far West, and the smoke of whose dusty torments "ascended up forever" and reddened the prairie sunsets for a generation.

The standard organisation of such a train was twenty-five of the huge, long-geared "prairie schooners" flaring from the bottom upward, and sometimes seventeen feet long, with six feet depth of hold and capacity of from 5,000 to 16,000 pounds each; and each with six to twelve yoke of oxen. The men of the outfit were—a captain or wagon-master, his assistant, a night herder, and the "cavvyard driver" (who had charge of the spare riding horses—a plains corruption of the Spanish *caballada*), and a driver for each wagon. The ox drivers were universally known as "bull whackers," and their beasts as "bull teams." The Jehus, who had long-eared "critters" instead of horned ones, were "mule skinners." "Trailers" did not come in until after 1859.

At high tide, the investment reached a figure beside which the earlier Chihuahua trains seem insignificant. The huge "Conestoga," or "Pittsburgh," or "Pennsylvania" wagons cost $800 to $1,500 each; first-class mules (and no other sort would do), $500 to $1,000 a pair;

harness, $300 to $600 to the ten-mule team—a total of $2,600 to $7,100 per wagon, besides salaries, provisions, and incidentals. In other words, a first-class freighting outfit on the Plains, half a century ago, cost as much as an up-to-date vestibuled passenger train of today.

The largest train ever organised on the Plains was that of General Custer, in his 1868 campaign. He had over 800 six-mule teams—single file four miles long.

The establishment of regular freight caravans from the Missouri River westward greatly reduced the cost of transportation and vastly developed business and immigration. In the days of pack-trains, it was—and still is, where that institution survives in the remoteness of the West—no uncommon thing to pay $1.00 per pound per 100 miles, or $20 per ton per mile. There have been regular tariffs much in excess of this, but this was common. Nowadays it costs a railroad, even on the mountainous grades of the far West, only about seven-eighths of a cent per ton per mile to haul its freights. The tariff of the Overland freighters, between Atchison and Denver (620 miles), averaged as follows:

Flour 9 cents per lb.
Sugar 13½ cents per lb.
Bacon and dry goods 15 cents per lb.
Whisky 18 cents per lb.
Glass 19½ cents per lb
Trunks 25 cents per lb.
Furniture 31 cents per lb.

—and so on. Everything went by the pound. The above trip took twenty one days for wagons drawn by horses or mules; five weeks for ox teams, The quickest time ever made across the continent, before the Pony Express, was twenty-one days by the Butterfield stage line, its schedule for mail from New York to San Francisco being twenty-three days, The Pony Express more than cut this in half. Not only did it never once fail to span the transcontinental desert in ten days; it more than once surpassed any other courier record in history. Buchanan's last message was carried by it from St. Joe to Sacramento, 2,000 miles, in seven days and nineteen hours; and the news of Lincoln's election to Denver (665 miles) in 2 days, twenty-one hours. It whisked Lincoln's inaugural across the 2,000 mile gap in the Nation's continuity in seven days and seventeen hours.

This latter is still the world's record for dispatch by means of men

HORACE GREELEY
Famous Editor who crossed the plains by stage-coach

Governor of Colorado in Gold-Fever days

and horses. There have been times when a railroad train could not reliably cross the continent as swiftly as did the best of the Centaur-Mercuries, organised by that typical frontiersman, Alex Majors, who died about the year 1900, the Kentucky Christian who never drank, never swore, and made his employees sign a contract not to drink, nor gamble, nor swear, under penalty of being "fired" without the pay that was coming.

In his young manhood Majors made the broad-horn record on the Santa Fé Trail—a round-trip with oxen in ninety-two days. Later, he took up government contracts, and in 1858, aside from other activities, was using over 3,500 large wagons merely to transport government supplies into Utah, employing there 4,000 men, 1,000 mules, and more than 40,000 oxen.

Majors was also one of the two stage-line kings. For debt, folly of his partners, or other reasons alien to his choice, in his own despite he became responsible head of more miles, and harder miles, more animals, and less "gentled" ones, more Concord coaches, and more "king whips" than any man before or since, save only Ben Holladay. Between Leavenworth and Denver, Majors had 1,000 mules and fifty coaches. The first of these "hoss-power Pullmans" reached Denver May 17, 1859, six days for the 665-mile journey. Horace Greeley, Henry Villard, and Albert D. Richardson were passengers. The Hockaday and Liggett stage line from St. Joe to Salt Lake had (in 1858) frittered twenty-two days in its semi-monthly trips. Majors cut the 1,200-mile-run to ten days, with a coach each way daily.

The stage from Denver to Salt Lake had a run of over 600 miles without a single town, hamlet, or house on the way. By 1859 there were no less than six mail routes to California (counting the Panama steamer), but Ben Holladay was king. No other one man, anywhere, has owned and managed a transportation system at once so vast and so difficult. He had sixteen first-class passenger steamers plying the Pacific from San Francisco to Oregon, Panama, Japan, and China. At the height of his Overland business he operated nearly 5,000 miles of daily mail stages, with about 500 coaches and express wagons, 500 freight wagons, 5,000 horses and mules, and a host of oxen.

On the main line he used 2,750 horses and mules and 100 Concord coaches. It cost $55,000 for the harness; the feed bill was a million a year. To equip and run this line for the first twelve months cost $2,425,000. The Government paid Holladay a million dollars a year in mail contracts. In 1864, grain was worth 25 cents a pound along the line, and hay up to $125 a ton. In one day, Dave Street contracted, at St. Louis, for seven Missouri River steamers to load with corn for the Overland's army of mules and horses.

Holladay, whose whole career reads like fiction, was the Overland Napoleon for about five years, beginning in December, 1861. The Indian depredations of 1864-66 greatly crippled his stage line, nearly all the stations for one hundred miles being burned, his stock stolen, and his men killed. The loss was upward of half a million. In November, 1866, he sold out the Overland stages to Wells, Fargo & Co., in whose hands the romantic enterprise continued till the railroads drove romance off the plains forever.

STAGE-COACHING ACROSS THE PLAINS

Chapter 4

The Pony Express

The Most Unique and Romantic Mail Service Ever Organised

Despite the consuming interest in the coming war, Senator Gwin kept up his fight for a quick mail route and the reduction of time in sending news to the Pacific Coast and receiving news from that region. Notwithstanding that it was found impossible to obtain any subsidy from Congress, at that time, for the purpose in view, in the winter of 1859-60, Senator Gwin and several capitalists of New York, and Mr. Russell of the Overland transportation firm of Russell, Majors and Waddell, met in Washington City, and the result of that meeting was the real start of one of the most romantic and daring business ventures this country, or any other country, ever knew. That was the Pony Express.

By that the time of transmitting news across the continent was reduced from twenty-one days to ten days. It is about 3,500 miles by our most direct railway route from New York to San Francisco, and it took seven days, three hours, and forty-five minutes actual time to cover the distance on our fastest express trains during the first years of. railroad history. In 1859, there was not a mile of railroad west of the Missouri River. St. Joseph, Missouri, was the western terminus of railway communication, and between that city and the young city of the Golden Gate there intervened but one city, Salt Lake, and 2,000 miles of wild, uninhabited country, infested with warlike Indians. Through this uninviting region led the trails over which it was proposed to ride the flying ponies.

Genghis Khan, the remarkable conqueror of Tartary and China, who flourished in the years between *A. D.* 1203 and 1227, has lately received the credit of having originated the Pony Express. Someone has looked up the fact in the writings of Marco Polo, who says that the ancient Tartar had stations every twenty-five miles over the territory that he wished to send messages, and that his riders made nothing of covering 300 miles a day. However, things have ample time to grow in some centuries, and these rides may have been stretched considerably on the elastic paper used in Polo's time. It is certain, though, that the system has been used in Asia and Europe, even within a century, and may be used there yet in remote regions.

It is also certain that pony express was used in this country about the middle of the first half of the last century. That is to say, two or three decades before the Pony Express across the Great American Desert. David Hale, an enterprising New York newspaper man, used it about 1825 in collecting state news. In 1830, Richard Haughton, editor of the New York *Journal of Commerce,* afterward founder of the Boston Atlas, utilized the system in the collection of election returns. James Watson Webb, of the New York *Courier* and *Enquirer,* established a pony express in 1832 between New York and Washington that wrought dismay among his competitors until railways and telegraphs overlapped him.

These enterprises were, however, as simple and harmless as roller skating compared to the dangers and tests of endurance to which the Pony Express riders of the western plains and mountains were subjected in 1860-61.

Majors, Russell and Waddell established and maintained for a number of years a fourteen-day mail schedule by rail and pony express between New York and San Francisco, making the trip of the running ponies from St. Joseph to Sacramento as exactly upon the schedule time as do our mails today. By using the telegraph to St. Joe and the pony express beyond, news was carried from ocean to ocean in ten days.

Senator Gwin's strongest argument was that if the operating company could carry the mails to the Pacific Coast in quicker time than was then being accomplished, and if it could be shown that the line might be kept open the year round, increased emigration and the building of a railroad by the government would result. The sequel has far exceeded the most extravagant hopes of all who were then concerned.

This able and patriotic statesman who had so deeply interested himself in the project under consideration, not only for the reasons already given, but also in the interest of accelerating communication between the Unionists of the Pacific Coast and the Federal authori-

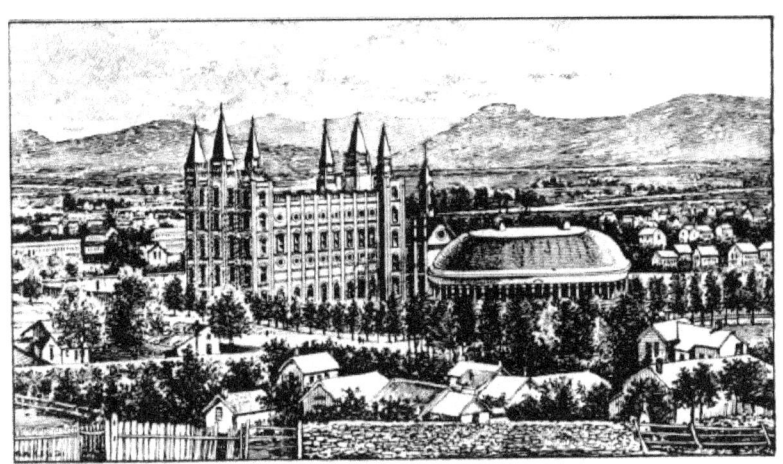

TEMPLE AND TABERNACLE AT SALT LAKE

ties, ended strangely. Stalwart Union senator that he was, he afterward espoused the cause of the Southern Confederacy, when his native state, Mississippi, seceded, and by so doing lost his great prestige, influence, and fortune in California. After the war he drifted into Mexico and the service of the ill-starred Emperor Maximilian, who, in 1866, made him Duke of Sonora in the furtherance of the visionary scheme of western empire. But Gwin shortly afterward died.

Col. Alexander Majors, who long survived his partners, and wrote a highly interesting and instructive book of strictest authenticity, entitled *Seventy Years on the Frontier*, (that appears as first part of this book), gives in substance the following history of the Pony Express, which account necessarily repeats in a few brief instances some of the preceding matter in this chronicle.

Col. Majors says that in the winter of 1859, while the senior member of the firm was in Washington, he became intimately acquainted with Senator Gwin, of California, who, as stated previously, was very anxious that a quicker line for the transmission of letters should be established than that already worked by Butterfield; the latter was outrageously circuitous.

The senator was acquainted with the fact that the firm of Russell, Majors, and Waddell were operating a daily coach from the Missouri River to Salt Lake City, and he urged Mr. Russell to consider seriously the propriety of starting a pony express over the same route, and from Salt Lake City on to Sacramento.

After a lengthy consultation with Senator Gwin, Mr. Russell consented to attempt the thing, provided he could induce his partners to

A MATTER OF MOMENT

take the same view of the proposed enterprise as himself, and he then returned to Leavenworth, the headquarters of the firm, to consult the other members. On learning the proposition suggested by Senator Gwin, both Colonel Majors and Mr. Waddell at once decided that the expense would be much greater than any possible revenue from the undertaking.

Mr. Russell, having, as he thought, partly at least, committed himself to the Senator, was much chagrined at the turn the affair had taken, and he declared that he could not abandon his promise to Mr. Gwin, consequently his partners must stand by him.

That urgent appeal settled the question, and work was commenced to start the Pony Express.

On the Overland Stage Line, operated by the firm, stations had been located every ten or twelve miles, which were at once utilised for the operation of the express; but beyond Salt Lake City new stations must be constructed, as there were no possible stopping places on the proposed new route. In less than two months after the promise of the firm had been pledged to Senator Gwin, the first express was ready to leave San Francisco and St. Joseph, Missouri, simultaneously.

The fastest time ever thus far made on the "Butterfield Route" was twenty-one days between San Francisco and New York. The Pony Express curtailed that time at once by eleven days, which was a marvel of rapid transit at that period.

The plant necessary to meet the heavy demand made on the originators of the fast mail route over the barren plains and through the dangerous mountains was nearly five hundred horses, one hundred and ninety stations, and eighty experienced riders, each of whom was to make an average of thirty-three and one-third miles. To accomplish this, each man used three ponies on his route, but in cases of great emergency much longer distances were made.

As suggested by two members of the firm, when they protested that the business would not begin to meet the expenses, their prophecies proved true; but they were not disappointed, for one of the main objects of the institution of the express was to learn whether the line through which the express was carried could be made a permanent one for travel during all the seasons of the year. This was determined in the affirmative.

In the spring of 1860, Bolivar Roberts, superintendent of the western division of the Pony Express, went to Carson City, Nevada, to engage riders and station agents for the Pony Express route across the

Great Plains. In a few days fifty or sixty riders were engaged—men noted for their lithe, wiry physiques, bravery and coolness in moments of great personal danger, and endurance under the most trying circumstances of fatigue. Particularly were these requirements necessary in those who were to ride over the lonely route. It was no easy duty; horse and human flesh were strained to the limit of physical tension. Day or night, in sunshine or in storm, under the darkest skies, in the pale moonlight, and with only the stars at times to guide him, the brave rider must speed on.

Rain, hail, snow, or sleet, there was no delay; his precious burden of letters demanded his best efforts under the stern necessities of the hazardous service; it brooked no detention; on he must ride. Sometimes his pathway led across level prairies, straight as the flight of an arrow. It was oftener a zigzag trail hugging the brink of awful precipices and dark, narrow canons infested with watchful savages, eager for the scalp of the daring man who had the temerity to enter their mountain fastnesses.

At the stations the rider must be ever ready for emergencies; frequently double duty was assigned him. Perhaps he whom he was to relieve had been murdered by the Indians, or so badly wounded that it was impossible for him to take his tour; then the already tired expressman must take his place and be off like a shot, although he had been in the saddle for hours.

The ponies employed in the service were splendid specimens of speed and endurance; they were fed and housed with the greatest care, for their mettle must never fail the test to which it was put. Ten miles distance at the limit of the animal's pace was exacted from him, and he came dashing into the station flecked with foam, nostrils dilated, and every hair reeking with perspiration, while his flanks thumped at every breath.

Nearly two thousand miles in eight days must be made; there was no idling for man or beast. When the express rode up to the station, both rider and pony were always ready. The only delay was a second or two as the saddle pouch with its precious burden was thrown on and the rider leaped into his place, then away they rushed down the trail, and in a moment, were out of sight.

Two hundred and fifty miles a day was the distance travelled by the Pony Express, and it may be assured the rider carried no surplus weight. Neither he nor his pony were handicapped with anything that was not absolutely necessary. Even his case of precious letters made a bundle no larger than an ordinary writing tablet, but there was $5.00 paid in advance for every letter transported across the continent. Their bulk was not in the least commensurable with their number; there were hundreds of them sometimes, for they were written on the thinnest tissue paper to be procured. There were no silly love missives among them nor frivolous correspondence of any kind; business letters only that demanded the most rapid transit possible and warranted the immense expense attending their journey found their way by the Pony Express.

The mail-bags were two pouches of leather, impervious to rain, sealed, and strapped to the rider's saddle before and behind. The pouches were never to contain over twenty pounds in weight. Inside the pouches, to further protect their contents from the weather, the letters and despatches were wrapped in oil silk, then sealed. The pockets themselves were locked, and were not opened between St. Joseph and Sacramento.

The Pony Express, as a means of communication between the two remote coasts, was largely employed by the government, merchants, and traders, and would eventually have been a paying venture had not the construction of the telegraph across the continent usurped its usefulness.

The arms of the Pony Express rider, in order to keep the weight at a minimum, were, as a rule, limited to revolver and knife.

The first trip from St. Joseph to San Francisco, 1966 in exact miles, was made in ten days; the second, in fourteen; the third, and many succeeding trips, in nine. The riders had a division of from one hundred to one hundred forty miles, with relays of horses at distances varying from twenty to twenty-five miles.

In 1860, the Pony Express made one trip from St. Joseph to Denver, 625 miles, in two days and twenty-one hours.

The Pony Express riders received from $120 to $125 a month. But few men can appreciate the danger and excitement to which those daring and plucky men were subjected; it can never be told in all its constant variety. They were men remarkable for their lightness of weight and energy. Their duty demanded the most consummate vigilance and agility. Many among their number were skilful guides, scouts, and couriers, and had passed eventful lives on the Great Plains and in the Rocky Mountains. They possessed strong wills and a determination that nothing in the ordinary course could balk. Their horses were generally half-breed California mustangs, as quick and full of

BRIGHAM YOUNG

endurance as their riders, and were as sure footed and fleet as a mountain goat; the facility and pace at which they travelled was a marvel. The Pony Express stations were scattered over a wild, desolate stretch of country, 2,000 miles long. The trail was infested with "road agents" and hostile savages who roamed in formidable bands, ready to murder and scalp with as little compunction as they would kill a buffalo.

Some portions of the dangerous route had to be covered at the astounding pace of twenty-five miles an hour, as the distance between stations was determined by the physical character of the region.

For the most part, the employees of the Pony Express were different from the plainsmen of the time, generally. The latter were usually boisterous, profane and intemperate. The organisers of the Pony Express were abstemious, moral and truthful men, and they sought to have their employees observe a high standard of integrity.

When the plans for the Pony Express had been sufficiently matured and all was in readiness to start on the day set, the enterprising firm that had organised the enterprise, and which owned it entirely and without Government subsidy, or other, that is to say the firm of Russell, Majors & Waddell, through Mr. Russell, who was the most enthusiastic and insistent, at first, of the members, caused the following advertisement to be published in the *New York Herald* of March 26, 1860, and the *Missouri Republican* of St. Louis, on the same date:

TO SAN FRANCISCO IN EIGHT DAYS

—)BY(—

THE CENTRAL OVERLAND CALIFORNIA

—)AND(—

PIKE'S PEAK EXPRESS.

The first courier of the Pony Express will leave the Missouri River on Tuesday, April 3d, at 5 o'clock p. m., and will run regularly weekly thereafter, carrying a letter mail only. The point of departure on the Missouri River will be in telegraphic communication with the East and will be announced in due time.

Telegraphic messages from all parts of the United States and Canada, in connection with the point of departure will be received up to 5 o'clock p. m. of the day of leaving, and transmitted over the Placerville and St. Joseph telegraph wire to San Francisco and intermediate points, by the connecting express in eight days.

The letter mail will be delivered in San Francisco in ten days from the departure of the Express. The express passes through Forts Kearney, Laramie, and Bridger, Great Salt Lake City, Camp Floyd, Carson City, the Washoe Silver Mines, Placerville, and Sacramento.

Letters for Oregon, Washington Territory, British Columbia, the Pacific Mexican ports, Russian possessions, Sandwich Islands, China, Japan, and India will be mailed in San Francisco.

Special messengers, bearers of letters to connect with the express of the 3d of April, will receive communications for the courier of that day at No. 481 Tenth Street, Washington City, up to 2.45 p. m. on Friday, March 30, and in New York, at the office of J. B. Simpson, Room No. 8, Continental Bank Building, Nassau Street, up to 6.30 a. m. of March 31st.

Full particulars can be obtained on application at the above place and agents of the Company.

W. H. RUSSELL, President.

Leavenworth City, Kansas, March, 1860.

Office in New York, J. B. Simpson, Vice-President.

Samuel & Allen, Agents, St. Louis.
H. J. Spaulding, Agent, Chicago.

The Civil War began in nine months after the Pony Express was started, and never has news been more anxiously awaited than on the Pacific Coast during the existence of this enterprise. The first tidings of the attack on Fort Sumter was sent by the Pony Express, and its connections, to San Francisco in eight days, fourteen hours. From that time on a bonus was given by California business men and public officials to the Pony Express Company to be distributed among the riders for carrying war news as fast as possible. For bringing the news of the battle of Antietam to Sacramento one day earlier than usual, in 1861, a purse of $300 extra was collected for the riders.

During the last few weeks preceding the termination of the Pony Express, by the opening of the transcontinental telegraph, the express riders brought an average of 700 letters per week from the Pacific coast. In those last few weeks, after the telegraph had been completed to Fort Kearney, the "pony" rates were reduced to $1.00 per half ounce, and each letter was enclosed in a 10-cent government stamped envelope for each half ounce, and this was the only financial interest the government had, at any time, in the Pony Express enterprise, until the remnant of it was transferred by Russell, Majors & Waddell to the Wells-Fargo Company.

In all the trips across the continent, and the 650,000 miles ridden by the Pony Express riders of the Russell, Majors & Waddell Company, the record is that only one mail was lost, and that a comparatively small and unimportant one.

Notwithstanding that the packages of letters were wrapped in oil silk, they were sometimes injured by water when, occasionally, a rider was forced to swim his horse across a swollen stream. Once under such circumstances the horse was drowned, but the rider, with his mail, escaped.

When, on one occasion, the rider was killed by Indians, the pony escaped with the letter pouch which was subsequently recovered, and the letters were promptly forwarded to their destination.

CHAPTER 5

Off Both Ways

The day of the first start, on the 3rd of April, 1860, at noon, says Colonel Majors, Harry Roff, mounted on a spirited half-breed *broncho*, left Sacramento on his perilous ride, covering the first twenty miles, including one change, in fifty-nine minutes. On reaching Folsom he changed again and started for Placerville at the foot of the Sierra Nevada Mountains, fifty-five miles distant. There he connected with "Boston," who took the route to Friday's Station, crossing the eastern summit of the Sierra Nevada. Sam Hamilton next fell into line and pursued his way to Genoa, Carson City, Dayton, Reed's Station, and Fort Churchill, seventy-five miles.

The entire run was made in fifteen hours and twenty minutes, the entire distance being 185 miles, which included the crossing of the western summit of the Sierra Nevada through thirty feet of snow! Here Robert Haslam took the trail from Fort Churchill to Smith's Creek, 120 miles through a hostile Indian country. From that point Jay G. Kelley rode from Smith's Creek to Ruby Valley, Utah, 116 miles. From Ruby Valley to Deep Creek, H. Richardson, 105 miles. From Deep Creek to Rush Valley, old Camp Floyd, 80 miles; from Camp Floyd to Salt Lake City, 50 miles, the end of the western division—in all 130 miles—was ridden by George Thacher.

On the same day, and the same moment, Mr. Russell superintended the start of the Pony Express from its eastern terminus. An arrangement had been made with the railroads between New York and St. Joseph for a fast train which was scheduled to arrive with the mail at the proper time. The Hannibal & St. Joseph Railroad also ran a special engine, and the boat which made the crossing of the Missouri River was detained for the purpose of instantly transferring the letters. Mr. Russell in person adjusted the letter pouch on the pony. Many of the enthusiastic crowd, who had congregated to witness the inauguration of the fast mail, plucked, hairs from the hardy little animal's tail as talismans of good luck. In a few seconds the rider was mounted, the steamboat gave an encouraging whistle, and the pony dashed away on his long journey to the next station.

There has been much discussion among those interested as to who rode the first horse out of St. Joseph at the opening of the Pony Express service, many claiming that the rider was John Frey. Mr. Huston Wyeth, a native of St. Joseph, and one of the most distinguished citizens of Missouri, wrote to his friend, J. H. Keetley, one of the first of the Pony Express riders, now at the head of an extensive mining concern at Salt Lake City, Utah, and Mr. Keetley replied in the following letter, a copy of which Mr. Wyeth gave to the author of this book:

Salt Lake City, Utah,
August 21, 1907

Mr. Huston Wyeth,
St. Joseph, Mo.
Dear Sir:—

Yours of the 17th inst. received, and in reply will say that Alex Carlyle was the first man to ride the Pony Express out of St. Joe. He was a nephew of the superintendent of the stage line to Denver, called the "Pike's Peak Express." The superintendent's name was Ben Fickland. Carlyle, was a consumptive, and could not stand the hardships, and retired after about two months trial, and died within about six months after retiring. John Frye was the second rider, and I was the third, and Gus Cliff was the fourth.

I made the longest ride without a stop, only to change horses. It was said to be 300 miles, and was done a few minutes inside of twenty-four hours. I do not vouch for the distance being correct, as I only have it from the division superintendent, A. E. Lewis, who said that the distance given was taken by his English roadometer which was attached to the front wheel of his buggy which he used to travel over his division with, and which was from St. Joe to Fort Kearney.

The ride was made from Big Sandy to Ellwood, opposite St. Joe, carrying the east-going mail, and returning with the west-bound mail to Seneca without a stop, not taking time to eat, but eating my lunch as I rode. No one else came within sixty miles of equalling this ride, and their time was much slower.

JAMES BUCHANAN
President of the United
States in those days

J. H. KEETLEY
When he was a Pony Express Rider

The Pony Express, if I remember correctly, started at 4 o'clock p. m., April 16, 1860, with Alex Carlyle riding a nice brown mare, and the people came near taking all the hair out of the poor beast's tail for souvenirs. His ride was to Guittard's, 125 miles from St. Joe. He rode this once a week. The mail started as a weekly delivery, and then was increased to semi-weekly inside of two months.

The horses, or relays, were supposed to be placed only ten miles apart, and travelled a little faster than ten miles per hour so as to allow time to change, but this could not always be done, as it was difficult then in the early settlement of the country to find places where one could get feed and shelter for man and beast, and sometimes horses had to go twenty-five to thirty miles, but in such cases there were more horses placed at such stations to do the work, and they did not go as often as the horses on the shorter runs.

At the start the men rode from 100 to 125 miles, but after the semi-weekly started, they rode about 75 or 80 miles. My ride and those of the other boys out of St. Joe was 125 miles, to Guittard's, but later we only rode to Seneca, eighty miles. The first pony started from the one-story brick express office on the east side of Third Street, between Felix and Edmond streets, but the office was afterwards moved to the Patee House. At 7 o'clock a. m. we were ordered from the stables two blocks east of the Patee House by the firing of a cannon in front of the Patee House which was the signal for the ferry boat to come from Ellwood and to lie in waiting at the landing until our arrival.

We rode into the office and put on the mail, which consisted of four small leather sacks six by twelve inches, fastened on to a square macheir which was put over the saddle. The sacks were locked with little brass locks much like one sees today on dog collars, and the sacks were sewed to the macheir, one in front and one behind each leg of the rider.

When the mail was put on, and the rider mounted on his race horse, which was always used out of St. Joe to the Troy Station, nine miles from Ellwood, he bounded out of the office door and down the hill at full speed, when the cannon was fired again to let the boat know that the pony had started, and it was then that all St. Joe, great and small, were on the sidewalks to see the pony go by, and particularly so on the route that they knew the pony was sure to take. We always rode out of town with silver mounted trappings decorating both man and horse and regular uniforms with plated horn, pistol, scabbard, and belt, etc., and gay flower-worked leggings and plated jingling spurs resembling, for all the world, a fantastic circus rider.

This was all changed, however, as soon as we got on to the boat. We had a room in which to change and to leave the trappings in until our return. If we returned in the night, a skiff or yawl was always ready and a man was there to row us across the river, and to put the horse in a little stable on the bank opposite St. Joseph. Each rider had a key to the stable. The next day we would go to the boat, cross the river, bring our regular horse and our trappings across to the St. Joe side. We stayed in St. Joe about three days and in Seneca about the same length of time, but this depended pretty much on the time that we received the mail from the West.

The Pony Express was never started with a view to making it a paying investment. It was a put-up job to change the then Overland mail route which was running through Arizona on the southern route, changed to run by way of Denver and Salt Lake City, where Ben Holladay had a stage line running tri-weekly to Denver and weekly to Salt Lake. The object of the Pony Express was to show the authorities at Washington that by way of Denver and Salt Lake to Sacramento was the shortest route, and the job worked successfully, and Ben Holladay secured the mail contract from the Missouri River to Salt Lake, and the old southern route people took it from Salt Lake City to Sacramento.

As soon as this was accomplished and the contract awarded, the pony was taken off, it having fulfilled its mission. Perhaps the war also had much to do with changing the route at that time. I hope the data I have given you will be satisfactory and of value to you. I have been asked for it many times, but have always refused. You will please excuse me for not sending my photo or allowing my people at home to furnish the old daguerreotype there that was taken when I made the ride as I am much opposed to publicity and newspaper notoriety or any other puffs, but it is impossible to always keep clear of reporters and to keep them from saying something.

I will add that the letters were all wrapped in oil silk, in case the pony had to swim, to keep the mail dry, and the regular charge was $5.00 a half ounce.

Yours truly,

J. H. Keetley.

The route of the riders from St. Joseph, after crossing the Missouri River, lay a little southwest until it struck the old military road forty-four miles out, at Kennekuk, then it turned a little north-westerly across the Kickapoo Indian Reservation, by the way of Grenada, Log-chain, Seneca, Ash Point, Guittard's, Marysville, Hollenburg, up Little Blue Valley to Rock Creek, Big Sandy, Liberty Farm, over prairies to Thirty-two-mile Creek, across the divide, over sand hills and prairies to Platte River, and due west up that valley to Kearney. This was the trail taken by the Mormons in 1847, and afterward by the gold seekers to California in 1848-9, and by General Albert Sidney Johnston and his army of 5,000 men, who marched from Fort Leavenworth to Salt Lake City in 1857-8.

From Fort Kearney the train led westward 200 miles along the Platte to old Julesburg, then across the South Fork of the Platte north-westerly to Fort Laramie, then over the foothills at the base of the Rockies to South Pass, by Fort Bridger to Salt Lake. Thence by the route of the riders from the Sacramento end, as given heretofore, to the steamer at Sacramento for San Francisco.

J. H. KEETLEY.
As he is to-day, a prosperous Salt Lake business man.

A Pressing Situation

Of the riders from the St. Joseph start, after those mentioned by J. H. Keetley in his letter to Mr. Wyeth, printed earlier in this chapter, Alex Carlyle, John Frye, Keetley himself, and Gus Cliff; the first named died of consumption shortly after the service was inaugurated. Frye joined the Union Army as a member of Gen. Blunt's scouts, and was killed in Arkansas in 1863 in a hand-to-hand fight with a company of "Arkansas rangers" in which battle he killed with his own hand, before being overcome, no less than five of his antagonists. Gus Cliff died in Los Angeles, California, in 1865, of bronchitis, while serving with a government freighting outfit.

Melville Baughn was another of the riders who alternated with Carlyle, Frye, Keetley, and Cliff from St. Joseph to Seneca, but was afterward transferred to the Fort Kearney and Thirty-Two-Mile Creek. Once on this run his pony was stolen. Baughn followed the thief to Loup Creek, secured his pony, and rode back to Kearney where he found the mail pouch and finished his trip, a little behind schedule time. The record is that Baughn, a few years afterward, lost his life at the hands of the law, at Seneca, upon a charge of murder.

Jim Beatley, whose name "in the States" was Foote, rode from Seneca to Big Sandy, fifty miles, and doubled his route twice a week. He was a native of Richmond, Va., and was killed in a quarrel at Farrell's ranch in Southern Nebraska in 1862, by an Overland employee named Milt Motter.

Will Boulton, who rode opposite to Beatley, was living in Minnesota at last accounts. Once while Boulton was within five miles of his station, Guittard's, his pony becoming disabled, he was forced to abandon the animal and "foot it" with his pouch and accoutrements to the station, where he received another mount and completed his trip.

Don C. Rising for a time rode from Big Sandy to Fort Kearney. He was not seventeen, but it is reported that he made two runs, on special orders, when he averaged twenty miles an hour. He was from Steuben County, N.Y., and now resides at Wetmore, Neb.

"Little Yank" rode between Cottonwood Springs and Julesburg, and often covered 100 miles at a trip. He weighed not over one hundred pounds, and was twenty-five years old.

Hogan was the name of the rider from Julesburg to Mud Springs, near historical Chimney Rock, about eighty miles. He lives somewhere in Nebraska.

Theodore Rand's run was 110 miles, from Box Elder to Julesburg. He covered the entire distance always at night. He was a Pony Express rider from the time the system was inaugurated until it was withdrawn. While the schedule time was ten miles an hour, he generally averaged twelve miles an hour. When he first went on the line he rode each animal twenty-five miles, but later he was given a fresh horse every fifteen miles. Rand is now a railroad man living at Atchison, Kansas. James Moore, whose most remarkable rides and adventures are mentioned elsewhere in these chronicles, was one of the riders between St. Joseph and Salt Lake, as was W. F. Cody, who is also spoken of at length in a separate chapter.

Bill Cates was one of the riders along the Platte who had many exciting adventures with Indians.

James W, Brink was one of the early mail-carriers on the plains, and was one of the first Pony Express riders on the eastern half. He was known as "Dock" among the early stage drivers, and was with Hickok—Wild Bill—in the fight at Rock Creek Station when five of the McCandless band of outlaws were killed.

Upon the day of this writing the author talked with Charles Cliff—brother of Gus Cliff— at St. Joseph, Mo., where he is engaged in merchandizing. Charles was only seventeen when he was a Pony

COL. W. F. CODY
As he was in Union Pacific Building Days.

Express rider, and he was one of the most daring. He rode on alternate days from St. Joseph to Seneca, and generally covered his eighty miles in eight hours. Three years after the closing of the Pony Express enterprise he was freighting on the plains and one day became engaged in a battle with Indians. In this fight he received three bullets in his body and twenty-seven more in his clothes. His party, composed of the men necessary to the piloting of nine wagons, was besieged three days by a war band of 100 Sioux, which was held at bay until the arrival of a large train with men enough to put the Indians to flight.

Will D. Jenkins, now a distinguished citizen of Washington State residing at Olympia, the capital, and who has frequently held high office in that commonwealth, was at times employed as a Pony Express rider, his home being at Big Sandy, Nebraska, in those days. Writing of the Pony Express he says:

> Although only a substitute, I shall always retain a certain degree of pride in the fact that I rode stations on the old Pony Express, and that at a time and place when it was far safer to be at home. I remember also Bob Emery's wild stage drive from 'The Narrows.' I was an eye witness of that exciting event. During my boyhood days on the plains I witnessed many exciting chases, but none that would compare with that wild drive. One Sioux warrior mounted on a fleeter pony than the other Indians would make a complete circle of the stage, and at each circle would send in a volley of arrows. But Bob succeeded in landing his passengers at the station, none of them injured.

Captain Levi Hensel has been for many years an honoured citizen of Pueblo, Colorado, and is well known to this writer. He says in a letter:

> I had the contract to shoe the Overland stage and Pony Express horses that ran from "Kennekuk to Big Sandy up to the time that I threw down my hammer and went into the army. I missed the best three years to make money by doing so, but don't regret that I helped to save the Union. Sometimes they ran ponies in from Fort Kearney and beyond to be shod. The animals that John Frye and Jim Beatley used to ride were the worst imps of Satan in the business. The only way that I could master them was to throw them and get a rope around each foot, stake them out, and have a man on the head and another on the body, while I trimmed the hoofs and nailed on the

shoes. They would squeal and bite all the time I was working with them. It generally took half a day to shoe one of them. But travel! They seemed never to get tired.

I knew John Frye to ride one of them fifty miles without change. He was about as tough as the ponies, and Jim Beatley was another off the same piece. Jim was murdered in some sort of a cowboy row up the road, and poor Johnnie Frye was killed on the Canadian River by bushwhackers. I saw him within a few minutes after he was killed. He was one of General Blunt's sharpshooters, along with W. S. Tough, John Sinclair, and other of the pony riders who had turned soldier. We were returning from chasing Stan Watie and gang through the Indian Nation, almost to Bogy Depot, Texas. The scouts ran into a band of Indian bushwhackers at Canadian Crossing. Frye was one of the most noted of all the Pony Express riders, and had many hairbreadth escapes from Indians on the plains. He never knew what fear was, and several times made runs through hostile bands when others weakened.

The large newspapers of both New York and the Pacific Coast were ready patronisers of the Express. The issues of their papers were printed on tissue manufactured purposely for this novel way of transmitting the news. On the arrival of the pony from the West, the news brought from the Pacific and along the route of the trail was telegraphed from St. Joseph to the East the moment the animal arrived with his important budget.

To form some idea of the enthusiasm created by the inauguration of the Pony Express, the *St. Joseph Free Democra*t said in relation to this novel method of carrying the news across the continent:

> Take down your map and trace the footprints of our quadrupedantic animal: From St. Joseph, on the Missouri, to San Francisco, on the Golden Horn—two thousand miles—more than half the distance across our boundless continent; through Kansas, through Nebraska, by Fort Kearney, along the Platte, by Fort Laramie, past the Buttes, over the Rocky Mountains, through the narrow passes and along the steep defiles, Utah, Fort Bridger, Salt Lake City, he witches Brigham with his swift pony-ship—through the valleys, along the grassy slopes, into the snow, into sand, faster than Thor's Thialfi, away they go, rider and horse—did you see them?

"They are in California, leaping over its golden sands, treading its busy, streets. The courser has unrolled to us the great American panorama, allowed us to glance at the home of one million people, and has put a girdle around the earth in forty minutes. Verily the riding is like the riding of Jehu, the son of Nimshi, for he rideth furiously. Take but your watch. We are eight days from New York, eighteen from London. The race is to the swift.

The expenses of the Pony Express during the part of two years that it was operated were, approximately, as follows:

Equipping the line	$100,000
Maintenance, $30,000 per month	480,000
Nevada Indian war	75,000
Miscellaneous	45,000
	$700,000

While it is true that the receipts did not reach as high as $1,000 per trip, in all they did not exceed $500,000, leaving a net loss of $200,000.

CHAPTER 6

Famous Rides and Riders

Of the brave deeds, stirring incidents, and romantic adventures of the gallant riders of the West, and especially of the Pony Express riders and other employees of that unique organisation, volumes have been written, and much must forever remain unwritten, as it cannot ever be known. Nearly all of the participants in the memorable enterprise have "gone over the Divide," and the bullet of Indian or border ruffian "blue pencilled" many a story that would have been startling, ere the man who knew it best could turn it in.

Perhaps the greatest physical achievement of all the performances of the horsemen of the West, as a matter of endurance, was the ride of F. X. Aubrey from the *plaza* of Santa Fé, N.M., to the public square at Independence, Mo., a distance of nearly 800 miles, through a country inhabited by warlike Indians, a large part of which was then a sandy desert. It was about the year 1851 that Aubrey gave his wonderful test of human endurance, before which all other attempts of the kind pale into insignificance.

He was a short, heavy set man, thirty-eight years of age, in the prime of manhood and strength. His business for ten years as a Santa Fé trader had made him perfectly familiar with the trail and all the stopping places. He was a perfect horseman, and although there were great riders in those days, none of them cared to dispute the palm with Aubrey. On a wager of $1,000, he undertook to ride alone from Santa Fé to Independence inside of six days. It was fifty-five years ago that he undertook the terrible feat. It was to be the supreme effort of his life, and he sent half a dozen of the swiftest horses ahead to be stationed at the different points for use in the ride.

He left Santa Fé in a sweeping gallop, and that was the pace kept up during every hour of the time until he fell fainting from his foam-

A FLANK MOVEMENT

covered horse in the square at Independence. No man could keep up with the rider, and he would have killed every horse in the line rather than to have failed in the undertaking. It took him just five days and nineteen hours to perform the feat, and it cost the lives of several of his best horses. After being carried into a room at the old hotel at Independence, Aubrey lay for forty-eight hours in a dead stupor. He would never have recovered from the shock had it not been for his wonderful constitution. The feat was unanimously regarded by western men as the greatest exhibition of strength and endurance ever known on the plains.

The ride of Jim Moore, a noted frontiersman of the pioneer days, was another remarkable performance. Moore was a man of almost perfect physique; in fact, by military standards he was a model. He weighed 160 pounds, stood five feet ten inches, straight as an arrow, with good neck well set on his shoulders, small waist, but good loins, and had the limbs of a thoroughbred. No finer looking man physically ever rode a *broncho* than Jim Moore. He could run like an Indian, was as active as a panther, the best natured man in the world, but as courageous as a lion. He was one of the first Pony Express riders.

His route was from Midway Station, half way between Fort Kearney and Cottonwood Springs, to Julesburg, a distance of 140 miles. Moore rode the round-trip of 280 miles once a week. The stations were from ten to fourteen miles apart, and a fresh horse, Spanish blood, was obtained at each station. There was little delay in these changes of horses, as the rider gave the "coyote yell" half a mile away, and, day or night, the station men had the pony ready, so that the rider had only to dismount from one horse, saddle and mount the other, and with a dig of his spurs, he was on a run again.

On each route there were two express riders, one going each way. As easy as it may seem to some for a man to bestride horse after horse for 140 miles, there were few men able to endure it. Upon the occasion of which I speak, Moore's route partner had been ailing and Moore was anticipating and dreading that he might have to double the route. In this anticipation he realised that there is a time limit to endurance, and therefore he gave the *"bronchos"* a little more of the steel than usual and made the trip to Julesburg in eleven hours. Arriving at Julesburg, he had his fears confirmed. His partner was in bed. He had hoped that he might have a few hours for rest, but before he had time to dismount and stretch his cramped and tired muscles, the "coyote yell" of the east-going rider was heard. He drank some cold coffee, filled his pocket with cold meat, and was in the saddle again for another 140-mile ride.

In order to be able to live the route out, he sent his ponies for all there was in them, with the result that he arrived at Midway after having ridden 280 miles in twenty-two hours from the time he had left there. Ben Holladay gave him a gold watch and a certificate of this remarkable performance. Many of the old frontiersmen now living knew Moore, knew of his 280-mile ride in twenty-two hours, and have seen the watch and certificate.

J. G. Kelley, one of the veteran riders, now living in Denver, tells his story of those eventful days, when he rode over the lonely trail carrying despatches for Russell, Majors and Waddell.

> Yes, I was a Pony Express rider in 1860, and went out with Bolivar Roberts, and I tell you it was no picnic. No amount of money could tempt me to repeat my experience of those days. To begin with, we had to build willow roads, corduroy fashion, across many places along the Carson River, carrying bundles of willows two and three hundred yards in our arms, while the mosquitoes were so thick that it was difficult to tell whether the man was white or black, so thickly were they piled on his neck, face, and arms.
>
> Arriving at the Sink of the Carson River, we began the erection of a fort to protect us from the Indians. As there were no rocks or logs in that vicinity, it was built of *adobes*, made from the mud on the shores of the lake. To mix this and get it to the proper consistency to mould into *adobes*, we tramped all day in our bare feet. This we did for a week or more, and the mud being strongly impregnated with alkali carbonate of soda, you can imagine the condition of our feet. They were much swollen and resembled hams. We next built a fort at Sand Springs, twenty miles from Carson Lake, and another at Cold Springs, thirty-seven miles east of Sand Springs. At the latter station I was assigned to duty as assistant station-keeper, under Jim McNaughton.
>
> The war against the Pi-Ute Indians was then at its height, and as we were in the middle of their country, it became necessary for us to keep a standing guard night and day. The Indians were often skulking around, but none of them ever came near enough for us to get a shot at him, till one dark night when I

was on guard, I noticed one of our horses prick up his ears and stare. I looked in the direction indicated and saw an Indian's head projecting above the wall. My instructions were to shoot if I saw an Indian within rifle range, as that would wake the boys quicker than anything else; so I fired and missed my man. Later on, we saw the Indian campfires on the mountain and in the morning many tracks. They evidently intended to stampede our horses, and if necessary kill us. The next day one of our riders, a Mexican, rode into camp with a bullet hole through him from the left to the right side, having been shot by Indians while coming down Edwards Creek, in the Quaking Aspen Bottom. He was tenderly cared for, but died before surgical aid could reach him.

As I was the lightest man at the station, I was ordered to take the Mexican's place on the route. My weight was then one hundred pounds, while I now weigh one hundred and thirty. Two days after taking the route, on my return trip, I had to ride through the forest of quaking aspen where the Mexican had been shot. A trail had been cut through these little trees, just wide enough to allow horse and rider to pass. As the road was crooked and the branches came together from either side, just above my head when mounted, it was impossible for me to see ahead for more than ten or fifteen yards, and it was two miles through the forest. I expected to have trouble, and prepared for it by dropping my bridle-reins on the neck of the horse, putting my Sharp's rifle at full cock, and keeping both my spurs into the pony's flanks, and he went through that forest 'like a streak of greased lightning.'

At the top of the hill I dismounted to rest my horse, and looking back saw the bushes moving in several places. As there were no cattle or game in that vicinity, I knew the movements to be caused by Indians, and was more positive of it, when, after firing several shots at the spot where I saw the bushes in motion, all agitation ceased. Several days after that two United States soldiers, who were on their way to their command, were shot and killed from the ambush of those bushes, and stripped of their clothing by the red devils.

One of my rides was the longest on the route. I refer to the road between Cold Springs and Sand Springs, thirty-seven miles, and not a drop of water. It was on this ride that I made a trip which possibly gave to our company the contract for carrying the mail by stage coach across the Plains, a contract that was largely subsidised by Congress.

One day I trotted into Sand Springs covered with dust and perspiration. Before I reached the station, I saw a number of men running toward me, all carrying rifles, and one of them with a wave of his hand said, 'All right, you pooty good boy; you go.' I did not need a second order, and as quickly as possible rode out of their presence, looking back, however, as long as they were in sight, and keeping my rifle handy.

As I look back on those times I often wonder that we were not all killed. A short time before, Major Ormsby of Carson City, in command of seventy-five or eighty men, went to Pyramid Lake to give battle to the Pi-Utes, who had been killing emigrants and prospectors by the wholesale. Nearly all of the command were killed. Another regiment of about seven hundred men, under the command of Colonel Daniel E. Hungerford and Jack Hayes, the noted Texas ranger, was raised. Hungerford was the beau-ideal of a soldier, as he was already the hero of three wars, and one of the best tacticians of his time.

This command drove the Indians pell-mell for three miles to Mud Lake, killing and wounding them at every jump. Colonel Hungerford and Jack Hayes received, and were entitled to, great praise, for at the close of the war terms were made which have kept the Indians peaceable ever since. Jack Hayes died several years ago in Alameda, California. Colonel Hungerford, at the ripe age of seventy years, is hale and hearty, enjoying life and resting on his laurels in Italy, where he resides with his granddaughter, the Princess Colonna.

As previously stated, it is marvellous that the pony boys were not all killed. There were only four men at each station, and the Indians, who were then hostile, roamed over the country in bands of from thirty to a hundred.

What I consider my most narrow escape from death was being shot at by a lot of fool emigrants, who, when I took them to task about it on my return trip, excused themselves by saying 'We thought you was an Indian.'

Stories of the pony express riders, their adventures with Indians and outlaws, and "hairbreadth 'scapes by field and flood" could be told at sufficient length to fill a hundred volumes as large as this, but many of them were so much alike that they would appear in the narration to be simply repetition, yet one required as much dash and nerve as another. The service created the greatest enthusiasm, not only among the riders, but among all others of the employees and all along the route, and to aid a "pony" in trouble was jumped at as a high privilege. For instance, on the first trip the west-bound rider, between Folsom's and Sacramento, was thrown and his leg broken.

A stage of the Wells-Fargo Company found him in this plight, and the special agent of the stage company volunteered to finish the ride, which he succeeded in doing so well as to arrive at Sacramento only one hour and thirty minutes late. This agent was J. G. McCall who was for many years afterward the Pacific Coast agent of the Erie Railroad. McCall often afterward told of the great reception that he got at Sacramento, and how the whole town turned out to enthusiastically welcome him.

The service also created much interest among Eastern newspapers, the more prominent of which kept representatives at St. Joe to collect news from this source. Henry Villard, afterward president of the Northern Pacific, was at the time under consideration the representative of the *New York Tribune*.

Beside "Buffalo Bill" and "Pony Bob," written of at length later in these chronicles, those of the pony riders who have been heard of within the last few years are these:

Jay G. Kelley was captain of Co. C, First Nevada Infantry, during the Civil War, after which he resumed the business of mining and was engaged at that at last accounts. Sam and Jim Gilson long ago became millionaires at mining in Utah. Mike Kelley became a successful miner at Austin, Nevada. Jim Bucklin, "Black Sam," Jim and Bill McNaughton died many years ago. Bill Can was hanged at Carson, Nevada, for the murder of Bernard Cherry, his being the first legal execution in that territory. H. J. Faust became a prominent physician in Utah. Of "Irish Tom" and Jose Zongoltz, nothing has been learned since the service ended.

Among other noted Pony Express riders, not specially mentioned elsewhere in these pages, were Jim Clark, George Spurr, Henry Wallace, George Towne, Jim McDonald, Win. James, John Burnett, Jim Bucklin, Wm. Carr, Wm. Carrigan, Major Egan, J. K. Ellis, H. J. Faust, John Fisher Jim Gentry, Jim Gilson, Sam Gilson, Lee Huntington, James William, Bob Martin, J. G. McCall, Jim McNaughton, Josh Perkins, Johnson Richardson, Bart Riles, George Thacher, Henry Wallace, Dan Wescott, and as many more whose names and gallant deeds are lost from the records as have been the names and deeds of thousands of other heroes who helped to make the great West the rich heritage of pioneer valour, endurance, and enterprise.

Among the humorous incidents associated with the Pony Express was one associated with "Artemus Ward"—Charles Farrar Browne—that has come to be a joke classic.

ARTEMUS WARD

Artemus was at the zenith of his fame as a humorous writer and lecturer at the time of the starting of the Pony Express. Thomas Maguire, the most prominent promoter of amusements in San Francisco at that time, desired to employ Ward for a series of entertainments in California. He sent one of the expensive dispatches from San Francisco to New York asking Ward:

"What will you take for a hundred nights?"

Ward promptly responded, by the same means:

"Brandy and water."

Artemus made the trip to California, going by steamer *via* Panama, and returning overland. The engagement was profitable and hilarious to Artemus and Maguire, and gave much joy to the genial humourist's audiences everywhere, *en route*.

Chapter 7

"Pony Bob"—Robert Haslam

As nervy and daring as possible for a man to be, and the most famous of the Pony Express riders, except Col. W. F. Cody, "Buffalo Bill," was Robert Haslam, known throughout the West as "Pony Bob," and yet so-called by his intimates. He was the hero of many fights with Indians and "road agents," and the principal actor in such a number of hair-breadth escapes and all manner of peril incident to the westward trail that they alone would make a great volume of intense and strenuous adventure.

In his own modest way Mr. Haslam tells here of some of these and others are briefly told by persons acquainted with the facts as participants in the history-making of those times.

> About eight months after the Pony Express was established, the Pi-Ute War commenced in Nevada. Virginia City, then the principal point of interest, and hourly expecting an attack from the hostile Indians, was only in its infancy. A stone hotel on C Street was in course of construction and had reached an elevation of two storeys. This was hastily transformed into a fort for the protection of the women and children. From the city the signal fires of the Indians could be seen on every mountain peak, and all available men and horses were pressed into service to repel the impending assault of the savages.
> When I reached Reed's Station, on the Carson River, I found no change of horses, as all those at the station had been seized by the whites to take part in the approaching battle. I fed the animal that I rode, and started for the next station, called Bucklands, afterward known as Fort Churchill, fifteen miles farther down the river. It was to have been the termination of my

journey, as I had changed my old route to this one, in which I had had many narrow escapes, and been twice wounded by the Indians.

I had already ridden seventy-five miles; but, to my great astonishment, the other rider refused to go on. The superintendent, W. C. Marley, was at the station, but all his persuasion could not prevail on the rider, Johnson Richardson, to take the road. Turning then to me, Marley said:

'Bob, I will give you $50 if you make this ride.'

I replied, 'I will go at once.'

Within ten minutes, when I had adjusted my Spencer rifle, which was a seven-shooter and my Colt's revolver, with two cylinders ready for use in case of emergency, I started. From the station onward, it was a lonely and dangerous ride of thirty-five miles, without a change, to the Sink of the Carson. I arrived there all right, however, and pushed on to Sand Springs, through an alkali bottom and sand hills, thirty miles farther, without a drop of water all along the route. At Sand Springs I changed horses and continued on to Cold Springs, a distance of thirty-seven miles. Another change and a ride of thirty more miles brought me to Smiths Creek. Here I was relieved by J. G. Kelley. I had ridden 190 miles, stopping only to eat and change horses.

"PONY BOB"—from a painting by H. H. Cross

The rider is pictured as carrying the news of Lincoln's election as President, riding 120 miles, in 8 hours, 10 minutes using 13 relays of horses. He was ambushed by Indians, shot with flint-head arrows through the lower jaw, fracturing it on both sides and knocking out 5 teeth.

This run is on record as the fastest of the entire route of 2,000 miles.

Continuing, Bob says:

After remaining at Smith's Creek about nine hours, I started to retrace my journey with the return express. When I arrived at Cold Springs to my horror I found that the station had been attacked by Indians, the keeper killed, and all the horses taken away. I decided in a moment what course to pursue—I would go on. I watered my horse, having ridden him thirty miles on time, he was pretty tired, and started for Sand Springs. Thirty-seven miles away. It was growing dark, and my road lay through heavy sage brush, high enough in some places to conceal a horse. I kept a bright lookout, and closely watched every motion of my poor pony's ears, which is a signal for danger in an Indian country. I was prepared for a fight, but the stillness of the night and the howling of the wolves and coyotes made cold chills run through me at times; but I reached Sand Springs in safety and reported what had happened.

Before leaving, I advised the station keeper to come with me to the Sink of the Carson, for I was sure the Indians would be upon him the next day. He took my advice, and so probably saved his life, for the following morning Smith's Creek was attacked. The whites, however, were well protected in the shelter of a stone house, from which they fought the savages for four days. At the end of that time they were relieved by the appearance of about fifty volunteers from Cold Springs. These men reported that they had buried John Williams, the brave keeper of that station, but not before he had been nearly devoured by the wolves.

When I arrived at the Sink of the Carson, I found the station men badly frightened, for they had seen some fifty warriors decked out in their war-paint and reconnoitring. There were fifteen white men here, well-armed and ready for a fight. The station was built of *adobe*, and was large enough for the men and ten or fifteen horses, with a fine spring of water within a few feet of it. I rested here an hour, and after dark started for Buckland's, where I arrived without a mishap and only three and a half hours behind schedule time. I found Mr. Marley at Buckland's, and when I related to him the story of the Cold

PONY BOB AS HE IS TO-DAY

Springs tragedy and my success, he raised his previous offer of $50 for my ride to $100.

I was rather tired, but the excitement of the trip had braced me up to withstand the fatigue of the journey. After a rest of one and a half hours, I proceeded over my own route from Bucklands to Fridays Station, crossing the Sierra Nevada. I had travelled 380 miles within a few hours of schedule time, and was surrounded by perils on every hand.

After the Pony Express was discontinued, Pony Bob was employed by Wells, Fargo & Company as an express rider in the prosecution of their transportation business. His route was between Virginia City, Nevada, and Friday Station and return, about one hundred miles, every twenty-four hours; schedule time, ten hours. This engagement continued for more than a year; but as the Pacific Railway gradually extended its line and operations, the Pony Express business as gradually diminished. Finally, the track was completed to Reno, Nevada, twenty-three miles from Virginia City, and over this route Pony Bob rode for more than six months, making the run every day, with fifteen horses, inside of one hour.

When the telegraph line was completed, the Pony Express over this route was withdrawn, and Pony Bob was sent to Idaho, to ride the company's express route of 100 miles, with one horse, from Queen's River to the Owyhee River. He was at the former station when Major McDermott was killed at the breaking out of the Modoc War.

On one of his rides he passed the remains of ninety Chinamen who had been killed by the Indians, only one escaping to tell the tale. Their bodies lay bleaching in the sun for a distance of more than ten miles from the mouth of Ives Cañon to Crooked Creek. This was Pony Bob's last experience as Pony Express rider. His successor, Sye Macaulas, was killed by the Indians on his first trip.

Bob bought a Flathead Indian pony at Boise, Idaho, and rode to Salt Lake City, 400 miles away. Joshua Hosmer, his brother-in-law, was United States marshal for Utah, and Haslam was appointed deputy marshal, but that business not being to his liking, he became again an employee of the Wells-Fargo Company, as first messenger from Salt Lake City to Denver, 720 miles by stage, and filled that position for several years.

At this writing, the Autumn of 1907, Mr. Haslam, who is still called "Pony Bob" by his intimates, is a hale, happy, and prosperous citizen of Chicago, attending industriously every day to his business, which is associated with the management of the vast Congress Hotel organisation that includes the Auditorium Hotel and its magnificent annexes.

To see Mr. Haslam as he is in the conventional garb and. quiet calling that are now of his life, one would find a test of credulity when informed that the bland, mild mannered, and affable gentleman indicated had ever experienced the dangers, privations, and hazardous adventures that have marked the career of "Pony Bob" in blazing the western way.

Chapter 8
"Buffalo Bill"—Col. W. F. Cody

On "Cody Day" at the Trans-Mississippi Exposition in Omaha, in the summer of 1898, this writer had the good fortune to be among the guests at a banquet given by distinguished citizens to Col. W. F. Cody, famed throughout the world as "Buffalo Bill." On this occasion Col. Alexander Majors, frequently mentioned in these chronicles, told in a speech at the table of how Will Cody, a fatherless western lad, whose sire had been slain by Indians, came to him for employment, and how he had engaged the boy to ride as a messenger between the freight trains of great wagons that the firm of Russell, Majors and Waddell were at that time sending to and fro in long caravans across the western plains.

Col. Majors spoke in high laudation and deep affection of Cody, both as man and boy, and told much concerning this famous plainsman's career as messenger, Pony Express rider, guide, hunter, and Indian fighter. Among other things he told of how Will Cody, when he received his first month's pay, which was a considerable sum for a boy in his "teens" to earn, took the coin to his mother, and in his exhilaration spread it out over the table and said: "Ain't it splendid, mother, that I can get all this money for you and my sisters?"

Someone in the party exclaimed, much to the amusement of the banqueters: "Yes, and he has been spreading it ever since."

Col. Majors dwelt with the eloquence of truth, high character, earnestness, and affection upon the faithfulness and intrepidity of Cody, and mentioned that part of the line over which Cody rode in the express service as being particularly hazardous. This route lay between Red Buttes and Three Crossings, so called because the trail ran through a canon where the Sweetwater reached from wall to wall, and had to be crossed three times in a short distance. It was a most dangerous, long, and lonely trail, including the perilous crossing of the North Platte River, which at that place was half a mile wide, and, though generally shallow, in some places reached a depth of twelve feet, a stream often much swollen and very turbulent. An average of fifteen miles an hour had to be made, including change of horses, detours for safety, and time for meals.

He passed through many a gauntlet of death in his flight from station to station, bearing express matter that was of the greatest value.

Colonel Cody, in telling the story of his own experiences with the Pony Express, says:

> The enterprise was just being started. The line was stocked with horses and put into good running order. At Julesburg I met Mr. George Chrisman, the leading wagon-master of Russell, Majors and Waddell, who had always been a good friend to me. He had bought out 'Old Jules,' and was then the owner of Julesburg Ranch, and the agent of the Pony Express line. He hired me at once as a Pony Express rider, but as I was so young he thought I was not able to stand the fierce riding which was required of the messengers.
>
> He knew, however, that I had been raised in the saddle, that I felt more at home there than in any other place, and as he saw that I was confident that I could stand the racket, and could ride as far and endure it as well as some of the old riders, he gave me a short route of forty-five miles, with the stations fifteen miles apart, and three changes of horses. I was fortunate in getting well-broken animals, and being so light I easily made my forty-five miles on my first trip out, and ever afterward.
>
> As the warm days of summer approached, I longed for the cool air of the mountains; and to the mountains I determined to go. When I returned to Leavenworth I met my old wagon-master and friend, Lewis Simpson, who was fitting out a train at Atchison and loading it with supplies for the Overland Stage Company, of which Mr. Russell, my old employer, was one of the proprietors. Simpson was going with this train to Fort Laramie and points farther west.
>
> 'Come along with me, Billy,' said he. 'I'll give you a good lay-out. I want you with me.'
>
> 'I don't know that I would like to go as far west as that again,' I replied. 'But I do want to ride the Pony Express once more;

SITTING BULL AND COL. CODY

SITTING BULL
Chief of Dakota Sioux-Uncapapas

there's some life in that.'

'Yes, that's so; but it will soon shake the life out of you,' said he. 'However, if that's what you've got your mind set on, you had better come to Atchison with me and see Mr. Russell, who, I'm pretty certain, will give you a situation.'

I met Mr. Russell there and asked him for employment as a Pony Express rider; he gave me a letter to Mr. Slade, who was then the stage-agent for the division extending from Julesburg to Rocky Ridge. Slade had his headquarters at Horseshoe Station, thirty-six miles west of Fort Laramie, and I made the trip thither in company with Simpson and his train.

Almost the first person I saw after dismounting from my horse was Slade. I walked up to him and presented Mr. Russell's letter, which he hastily opened and read. With a sweeping glance of his eye he took my measure from head to foot, and then said:

'My boy, you are too young for a Pony Express rider. It takes men for that business.'

'I rode two months last year on Bill Trotter's division, sir, and filled the bill then; and I think I am better able to ride now,' said I.

'What! Are you the boy that was riding there, and was called the youngest rider on the road?'

'I am the same boy,' I replied, confident that everything was now all right for me.

'I have heard of you before. You are a year or so older now, and I think you can stand it. I'll give you a trial, anyhow, and if you weaken you can come back to Horseshoe Station and tend stock."

Thus, ended our interview. The next day he assigned me to duty on the road from Red Buttes on the North Platte to the Three Crossings of the Sweetwater—a distance of seventy-six miles—and I began riding at once. It was a long piece of road, but I was equal to the undertaking, and soon afterward had an opportunity to exhibit my power of endurance as a Pony Express rider.

For some time, matters progressed very smoothly, though I had no idea that things would always continue so. I was well aware that the portion of the trail to which I had been assigned was not only the most desolate and lonely, but it was more eagerly watched by the savages than elsewhere on the long route.

Slade, the boss, whenever I arrived safely at the station, and before I started out again, was always very earnest in his suggestions to look out for my scalp.

'You know, Billy,' he would say, 'I am satisfied yours will not always be the peaceful route it has been with you so far. Every time you come in I expect to hear that you have met with some startling adventure that does not always fall to the average express rider.'

I replied that I was always cautious, made detours whenever I noticed anything suspicious. 'You bet I look out for number one.' The change soon came.

One day, when I galloped into Three Crossings, my home station, I found that the rider who was expected to take the trip out on my arrival, had gotten into a drunken row the night before and had been killed. This left that division without a rider. As it was very difficult to engage men for the service in that uninhabited region, the superintendent requested me to make the trip until another rider could be secured.

The distance to the next station, Rocky Ridge, was eighty-five miles and through a very bad and dangerous country, but the emergency was great and I concluded to try it. I, therefore started promptly from Three Crossings without more than a moment's rest: I pushed on with the usual rapidity, entering every relay station on time, and accomplished the round trip of 322 miles back to Red Buttes without a single mishap and on time. This stands on the records as being the longest Pony Express journey ever made.

A week after making this trip, and while passing over the route again, I was jumped on by a band of Sioux Indians who dashed out from a sand ravine nine miles west of Horse Creek. They were armed with pistols, and gave me a close call with several bullets, but it fortunately happened that I was mounted on the fleetest horse belonging to the express company and one that was possessed of remarkable endurance. Being cut off from retreat back to Horseshoe, I put spurs to my horse, and lying flat on his back, kept straight for Sweetwater, the next station, which I reached without accident, having distanced my pursuers.

Upon reaching that place, however, I found a sorry condition of affairs, as the Indians had made a raid on the station the

GEN. GEORGE CROOK

JOHN NELSON
Typical Frontiersman

morning of my adventure with them, and after killing the stock tender had driven off all the horses, so that I was unable to get a remount. I, therefore, continued on to Ploutz Station, twelve miles farther, thus making twenty-four miles straight run with one horse. I told the people at Ploutz what had happened at Sweetwater Bridge, and went on and finished the trip without any further adventure.

About the middle of September, the Indians became very troublesome on the line of the stage road along the Sweetwater. Between Split Rock and Three Crossings they robbed a stage, killed the driver and two passengers, and badly wounded Lieutenant Flowers, the assistant division agent. The red-skinned thieves also drove off the stock from the different stations, and were continually lying in wait for the passing stages and Pony Express riders, so that we had to take many desperate chances in running the gauntlet.

The Indians had now become so bad and had stolen so much stock that it was decided to stop the Pony Express for at least six weeks, and to run the stages only occasionally during that period; in fact, it would have been impossible to continue the enterprise much longer without restocking the line.

While we were thus all lying idle, a party was organised to go out and search for stolen stock. This party was composed of stage drivers, express riders, stock tenders, and ranchmen—forty of them altogether—and they were well armed and well mounted. They were mostly men who had undergone all kinds of hardships and braved every danger, and they were ready and anxious to 'tackle' any number of Indians. Wild Bill, who had been driving stage on the road and had recently come down to our division, was elected captain of the company. It was supposed that the stolen stock had been taken to the head of the Powder River and vicinity, and the party, of which I was a member, started out for that section in high hopes of success.

Twenty miles out from Sweetwater Bridge, at the head of Horse Creek, we found an Indian trail running north toward Powder River, and we could see by the tracks that most of the horses had been recently shod and were undoubtedly our stolen stage stock. Pushing rapidly forward, we followed this trail to Powder River; thence down this stream to within about forty miles of the spot where old Fort Reno now stands. Here the trail took

Maj. Gen. Eugene A. Carr
Wounded in 1854 with Indian Arrow

Gen. N. A. M. Dudley
Noted Indian-fighter

a more westerly course along the foot of the mountains, leading eventually to Crazy Woman's Fork—a tributary of Powder River. At this point we discovered that the party whom we were trailing had been joined by another band of Indians, and judging from the fresh appearance of the trail, the united body could not have left this spot more than twenty-four hours before.

Being aware that we were now in the heart of the hostile country and might at any moment find more Indians than we had lost, we advanced with more caution than usual and kept a sharp lookout. As we were approaching Clear Creek, another tributary of Powder River, we discovered Indians on the opposite side of the creek, some three miles distant; at least we saw horses grazing, which was a sure sign that there were Indians there.

The Indians, thinking themselves in comparative safety, never before having been followed so far into their own country by white men, had neglected to put out any scouts. They had no idea that there were any white men in that part of the country. We got the lay of their camp, and then held a council to consider and mature a plan for capturing it. We knew full well that the Indians would outnumber us at least three to one, and perhaps more. Upon the advice and suggestion of Wild Bill, it was finally decided that we should wait until it was nearly dark, and then after creeping as close to them as possible, make a dash through their camp, open a general fire on them, and then stampede the horses,

This plan, at the proper time, was very successfully executed. The dash upon the enemy was a complete surprise to them. They were so overcome with astonishment that they did not know what to make of it. We could not have astounded them anymore had we dropped down into their camp from the clouds. They did not recover from the surprise of this sudden charge until after we had ridden pell-mell through their camp and got away with our own horses as well as theirs. We at once circled the horses around toward the south, and after getting them on the south side of Clear Creek, some twenty of our men, just as the darkness was coming on, rode back and gave the Indians a few parting shots.

We then took up our line of march for Sweetwater Bridge, where we arrived four days afterward with all our own horses and about one hundred captured Indian ponies.

The expedition had proved a grand success, and the event was celebrated in the usual manner—by a grand spree. The only store at Sweetwater Bridge did a rushing business for several days. The returned stock hunters drank and gambled and fought. The Indian ponies, which had been distributed among the captors, passed from hand to hand at almost every deal of cards. There seemed to be no limit to the rioting and carousing; revelry reigned supreme. On the third day of the orgy, Slade, who had heard the news, came up to the bridge and took a hand in the 'fun,' as it was called. To add some variation and excitement to the occasion, Slade got into a quarrel with a stage driver and shot him, killing him almost instantly.

The boys became so elated as well as 'elevated' over their success against the Indians, that most of them were in favour of going back and cleaning out the whole Indian race. One old driver especially, Dan Smith, was eager to open a war on all the hostile nations, and had the drinking been continued another week he certainly would have undertaken the job, single handed and alone. The spree finally came to an end; the men sobered down and abandoned the idea of again invading the hostile country. The recovered horses were replaced on the road, and the stages and Pony Express again began running on time.

Slade, having taken a great fancy to me, said, 'Billy, I want you to come down to my headquarters, and I'll make you a sort of supernumerary rider, and send you out only when it is necessary.' I accepted the offer and went with him down to Horseshoe, where I had a comparatively easy time of it. I had always been fond of hunting, and I now had a good opportunity to gratify my ambition in that direction, as I had plenty of spare time on my hands. In this connection I will relate one of my bear hunting adventures. One day, when I had nothing else to do, I saddled up an extra Pony Express horse, struck out for the foothills of Laramie Peak for a bear hunt.

Riding carelessly along, and breathing the cool and bracing mountain air which came down from the slopes, I felt as only a man can feel who is roaming over the prairies of the far West, well-armed and mounted on a fleet and gallant steed. The perfect freedom which he enjoys is in itself a refreshing stimulant to the mind as well as the body. Such indeed were my feelings on this beautiful day as I rode up the valley of the Horseshoe. Occasionally I scared up a flock of sage hens or a jack rabbit. Antelopes and deer were almost always in sight in any direction, but, as they were not the kind of game I was after on that day, I passed them by and kept on toward the mountains. The farther I rode the rougher and wilder became the country, and I knew that I was approaching the haunts of the bear. I did not discover any, however, although I saw plenty of tracks in the snow.

About two o'clock in the afternoon, my horse having become tired, and myself being rather weary, I shot a sage hen, and, dismounting, I unsaddled my horse and tied him to a small tree, where he could easily feed on the mountain grass. I then built a little fire, and broiling the chicken and seasoning it, with salt and pepper which I had obtained from my saddlebags, I soon sat down to a 'genuine square meal,' which I greatly relished.

After resting for a couple of hours, I remounted and resumed my upward trip to the mountain, having made up my mind to camp out that night rather than go back without a bear, which my friends knew I had gone out for. As the days were growing short, night soon came on, and I looked around for a suitable camping place. While thus engaged, I scared up a flock of sage hens, two of which I shot, intending to have one for supper and the other for breakfast.

By this time, it was becoming quite dark, and I rode down to one of the little mountain streams, where I found an open place in the timber suitable for a camp. I dismounted, and after unsaddling my horse and hitching him to a tree, I prepared to start a fire. Just then I was startled by hearing a horse whinnying farther up the stream. It was quite a surprise to me, and I immediately ran to my animal to keep him from answering as horses usually do in such cases. I thought that the strange horse might belong to some roaming band of Indians, as I knew of no white men being in that portion of the country at that time. I was certain that the owner of the strange horse could not be far distant, and I was very anxious to find out who my neighbour was, before letting him know that I was in his vicinity.

I, therefore, resaddled my horse, and leaving him tied so that I could easily reach him, I took my gun and started out on a scouting expedition up the stream, I had gone about four hundred yards when, in a bend of the stream, I discovered ten or fifteen horses grazing. On the opposite side of the creek a light was shining high up the mountain bank. Approaching the mysterious spot as cautiously as possible, and when within a few yards of the light, which I discovered came from a dugout in the mountain side, I heard voices, and soon I was able to distinguish the words, as they proved to be in my own language. Then I knew that the occupants of the dugout were white men.

Thinking that they might be a party of trappers, I boldly walked up to the door and knocked for admission. The voices instantly ceased, and for a moment a deathlike silence reigned inside. Then there seemed to follow a kind of hurried whispering—a sort of consultation—and then someone called out:

'Who's there?'

'A friend and a white man,' I replied.

The door opened, and a big ugly-looking fellow stepped forth and said;

'Come in.'

I accepted the invitation with some degree of fear and hesitation, which I endeavoured to conceal, as I thought it was too late to back out, and that it would never do to weaken at that point, whether they were friends or foes. Upon entering the dugout my eyes fell upon eight as rough and villainous looking men as I ever saw in my life. Two of them I instantly recognised as teamsters who had been driving in Lew Simpson's train, a few months before, and had been discharged.

They were charged with the murdering and robbing of a ranch-

Newspaper cut of a Pony Express
Rider published in 1860

man; and, having stolen his horses, it was supposed that they had left the country. I gave them no signs of recognition, however, deeming it advisable to let them remain in ignorance as to who I was. It was a hard crowd, and I concluded the sooner I could get away from them the better it would be for me. I felt confident that they were a band of horse thieves.

'Where are you going, young man, and who's with you?' asked one of the men, who appeared to be the leader of the gang.

'I am entirely alone. I left Horseshoe Station this morning for a bear hunt, and not finding any bears I had determined to camp out for the night and wait till morning,' said I; 'and just as I was going into camp a few hundred yards down the creek, I heard one of your horses whinnying, and then I came to your camp.' I thus was explicit in my statement, in order, if possible, to satisfy the cut-throats that I was not spying upon them, but that my intrusion was entirely accidental.

'Where's your horse?' demanded the boss thief.

'I left him down at the creek,' I answered.

They proposed going after the horse, but I thought that would never do, as it would leave me without any means of escape, and I accordingly said, in hopes to throw them off the track, 'Captain, I'll leave my gun here and go down and get my horse, and come back and stay all night.'

I said this in as cheerful and as careless a manner as possible, so as not to arouse their suspicions in any way or lead them to think that I was aware of their true character. I hated to part with my gun. but my suggestion of leaving it was a part of the plan of escape which I had arranged. If they have the gun, thought I, they will surely believe that I intend to come back. But this little game did not work at all, as one of the *desperadoes* spoke up and said:

'Jim and I will go down with you after your horse, and you can leave your gun here all the same, as you'll not need it.'

'All right,' I replied, for I could certainly have done nothing else. It became evident to me that it would be better to trust myself with two men than with the whole party. It was apparent from this time on I would have to be on the alert for some good opportunity to give them the slip.

'Come along,' said one of them, and together we went down the creek, and soon came to the spot where my horse was tied.

One of the men unhitched the animal, and said, 'I'll lead the horse.'

'Very well,' said I; 'I've got a couple of sage hens here. Lead on.' I picked up the sage hens which I had killed a few hours before, and followed the man who was leading the horse, while his companion brought up the rear. The nearer we approached the dugout, the more I dreaded the idea of going back among the villainous cut-throats. My first plan of escape having failed, I now determined upon another. I had both of my revolvers with me, the thieves not having thought it necessary to search me. It was now quite dark, and I purposely dropped one of the sage hens, and asked the man behind me to pick it up.

While he was hunting for it on the ground, I quickly pulled out one of my Colt's revolvers and struck him a tremendous blow on the back of the head, knocking him senseless to the ground. I then instantly wheeled around and saw that the man ahead, who was only a few feet distant, had heard the blow and had turned to see what was the matter, his hand upon his revolver We faced each other at about the same instant, but before he could fire, as he tried to do, I shot him dead in his tracks. Then jumping on my horse, I rode down the creek as fast as possible, through the darkness and over the rough ground and rocks.

The other outlaws in the dugout, having heard the shot which I had fired, knew there was trouble, and they all came rushing down the creek. I suppose by the time they reached the man whom I had knocked down, that he had recovered and hurriedly told them of what had happened. They did not stay with the man whom I had shot, but came on in hot pursuit of me. They were not mounted, and were making better time down the rough mountain than I was on horseback. From time to time I heard them gradually gaining on me.

At last they came so near that I saw that I must abandon my horse. So, I jumped to the ground, and gave him a hard slap with the butt of one of my revolvers, which started him on down the valley, while I scrambled up the mountain side. I had not ascended more than forty feet when I heard my pursuers coming closer and closer; I quickly hid behind a large pine tree, and in a few moments, they all rushed by me, being led on by the rattling footsteps of my horse, which they heard ahead of them. Soon they began firing in the direction of the horse, as they no doubt supposed I was still seated on his back.

As soon as they had passed me I climbed further up the steep mountain, and knowing that I had given them the slip, and feeling certain I could keep out of their way, I at once struck out for Horseshoe Station, which was twenty-five miles distant. I had very hard traveling at first, but upon reaching lower and better ground I made good headway, walking all night and getting into the station just before daylight—footsore, weary, and generally played out.

I immediately waked up the men of the station and told them of my adventure. Slade himself happened to be there, and he at once organised a party to go out in pursuit of the horse thieves. Shortly after daylight twenty well-armed stage drivers, stock tenders, and ranchmen were galloping in the direction of the dugout.

Of course, I went along with the party, notwithstanding that I was very tired and had had hardly time for any rest at all. We had a brisk ride, and arrived in the immediate vicinity of the thieves' rendezvous at about ten o'clock in the morning. We approached the dugout cautiously, but upon getting in close proximity to it we could discover no horses in sight. We could see the door of the dugout standing wide open, and we marched up to the place. No one was inside, and the general appearance of everything indicated that the place had been deserted—that the birds had flown. Such, indeed, proved to be the case.

We found a new-made grave, where they had evidently buried the man whom I had shot. We made a thorough search of the whole vicinity, and finally found their trail going southeast in the direction of Denver. As it would have been useless to follow them, we rode back to the station, and thus ended my eventful bear-hunt. We had no trouble for some time after that."

A friend, who was once a station agent, tells two more adventures of Cody's:

It had become known in some mysterious manner, past finding out, that there was to be a large sum of money sent through by Pony Express, and that was what the road agents were after. After killing the other rider, and failing to get the treasure, Cody very naturally thought that they would make another effort to secure it; so, when he reached the next relay station, he walked about a while longer than was his wont.

This was to perfect a little plan he had decided upon, which was to take a second pair of saddle pouches and put something in them and leave them in sight, while those that held the valuable express packages he folded up in his saddle blanket in such a way that they could not be seen unless a search was made for them. The truth was Cody knew that he carried the valuable package, and it was his duty to protect it with his life.

So, with the clever scheme to outwit the road agents, if held up, he started once more upon his flying trip. He carried his revolver ready for instant use and flew along the trail with every nerve strung to meet any danger which might confront him. He had an idea where he would be halted, if halted at all, and it was a lonesome spot in a valley, the very place for a deed of crime.

As he drew near the spot he was on the alert, and yet when two men suddenly stepped out from among the shrubs and confronted him, it gave him a start in spite of his nerve. They had him covered with rifles and brought him to a halt with the words: 'Hold! Hands up, Pony Express Bill, for we knew yer, my boy, and what yer carried.'

'I carry the express; and it's hanging for you two if you interfere with me,' was the plucky response.

'Ah, we don't want you, Billy, unless you force us to call in your checks; but it's what you carry we want.'

'It won't do you any good to get the pouch, for there isn't anything valuable in it,'

'We are to be the judges of that, so throw us the valuable or catch a bullet. Which shall it be, Billy?'

The two men stood directly in front of the pony rider, each one covering him. with a rifle, and to resist was certain death. So, Cody began to unfasten his pouches slowly, while he said, 'Mark my words, men, you'll hang for this.'

'We'll take chances on that, Bill.'

The pouches being unfastened now, Cody raised them with one hand, while he said in an angry tone, 'If you will have them, take them.' With this he hurled the pouches at the head of one of them, who quickly dodged and turned to pick them up, just as Cody fired upon the other with his revolver in his left hand. The bullet shattered the man's arm, while, driving the spurs into the flanks of his mare, Cody rode directly over the man who was stooping to pick up the pouches, his back turned to the pony rider.

The horse struck him a hard blow that knocked him down, while he half fell on top of him, but was recovered by a touch of the spurs and bounded on, while the daring pony rider gave a wild triumphant yell as he sped on like the wind.

The fallen man, though hurt scrambled to his feet as soon as he could, picked up his rifle, and fired after the retreating youth, but without effect, and young Cody rode on, arriving at the station on time, and reported what had happened.

He had, however, no time to rest, for he was compelled to start back with his express pouches. He thus made the remarkable ride of 324 miles without sleep, and stopping only to eat his meals, and resting then but a few moments. For saving the express pouches he was highly complimented by all, and years afterward he had the satisfaction of seeing his prophecy regarding the two road agents verified, for they were both captured and hanged by vigilantes for their many crimes.

'There's Injun signs about, so keep your eyes open.' So said the station boss of the Pony Express, addressing young Cody, who had dashed up to the cabin, his horse panting like a hound, and the rider ready for the 15-mile flight to the next relay. 'I'll be on the watch, boss, you bet,' said the pony rider, and with a yell to his fresh pony he was off like an arrow from a bow.

Down the trail ran the fleet pony like the wind, leaving the station quickly out of sight, and dashing at once into the solitude and dangers of the vast wilderness. Mountains were upon either side, towering cliffs here and there overhung the trail, and the wind sighed through the forest of pines like the mourning of departed spirits. Gazing ahead, the piercing eyes of the young rider saw every tree, bush, and rock, for he knew but too well that a deadly foe, lurking in ambush, might send an arrow or a bullet to his heart at any moment. Gradually far down the valley, his quick glance fell upon a dark object above the bowlder directly in his trail.

He saw the object move and disappear from sight down behind the rock. Without appearing to notice it, or checking his speed in the slightest, he held steadily upon his way. But he took in the situation at a glance, and saw that on one side was a fringe of heavy timber, upon the other a precipice, at the base of which were massive rocks.

'There is an Indian behind that rock, for I saw his head,' muttered the young rider, as his horse flew on. Did he intend to take his chances and dash along the trail directly by his ambushed foe? It would seem so, for he still stuck to the trail.

A moment more and he would be within range of a bullet, when suddenly dashing his spurs into the pony's side, Billy Cody wheeled to the right, and in an oblique course headed for the cliff. This proved to the foe in ambush that he was suspected, if not known, and at once there came the crack of a rifle, the puff of smoke rising above the rock where he was concealed. At the same moment a yell went up from a score of throats, and out of the timber on the other side of the valley darted a number of Indians, and these rode to head off the rider. Did he turn back and seek safety in a retreat to the station? No! he was made of sterner stuff and would run the gauntlet.

Out from behind the bowlder, where they had been lying in ambush, sprang two braves in all the glory of their war paint. Their horses were in the timber with their comrades, and, having failed to get a close shot at the pony rider, they sought to bring him down at long range with their rifles. The bullets pattered under the hoofs of the flying pony, but he was unhurt, and his rider pressed him to his full speed.

With set teeth, flashing eyes, and determined to do or die, Will Cody rode on in the race for life, the Indians on foot running swiftly toward him, and the mounted braves sweeping down the valley at full speed.

The shots of the dismounted Indians failing to bring down the flying pony or their human game, the mounted redskins saw that their only chance was to overtake their prey by their speed. One of the number, whose war bonnet showed that he was a chief, rode a horse that was much faster than the others, and he drew quickly ahead. Below, the valley narrowed to a pass not a hundred yards in width, and if the pony rider could get to this wall ahead of his pursuers, he would be able to hold his own along the trail in the 10-mile run to the next relay station.

But, though he saw that there was no more to fear from the two dismounted redskins, and that he would come out well

SHORT BULL, KICKING BEAR,
War Chief Medicine man
Ogallala Sioux, leaders of Ghost Dance War
and Messiah Craze

BRIG. GEN. JACK HAYES

in advance of the band on horseback, there was one who was most dangerous. That one was the chief, whose fleet horse was bringing him on at a terrible pace, and threatening to reach there at the same time with the pony rider.

Nearer and nearer the two drew toward the path, the horse of Cody slightly ahead, and the young rider knew that a death struggle was at hand. He did not check his horse, but kept his eyes alternately upon the pass and the chief. The other Indians he did not then take into consideration. At length that happened for which he had been looking.

When the chief saw that he would come out of the race some thirty yards behind his foe, he seized his bow and quick as a flash had fitted an arrow for its deadly flight. But in that instant Cody had also acted, and a revolver had sprung from his belt and a report followed the touching of the trigger. A wild yell burst from the lips of the chief, and he clutched madly at the air, reeled, and fell from his saddle, rolling over like a ball as he struck the ground.

The death cry of the chief was echoed by the braves coming on down the valley, and a shower of arrows was sent after the fugitive pony rider. An arrow slightly wounded his horse, but the others did no damage, and in another second Cody had dashed into the pass well ahead of his foes. It was a hot chase from then on until the pony rider came within sight of the next station, when the Indians drew off and Cody dashed in on time, and in another minute, was away on his next run.

On one of Cody's rides he was halted in the *cañon* one day by an outlaw named ——, who said to him:

"You are a mighty little feller to be takin' such chances as this."
"I'm as big as any other feller," said Cody.
"How do you make that out?" the highwayman asked.
"Well, you see Colonel Colt has done it," the youngster replied, presenting at the same time a man's size revolver of the pattern that was so prevalent and useful among the men of the frontier. "And I can shoot as hard as if I was Gin'ral Jackson," he added.
"I spect you kin an' I reckon you would," was the laconic response of the lone highwayman as with a chuckle he turned up a small *cañon* toward the north. Cody flew on as if he were going for the doctor. The man escaped the law, reformed, and

became a respectable citizen-farmer in Kansas, and in 1871 told this writer, in St. Joseph, Missouri, of the incident as here related. (Therefore, his name is omitted.)

Of all the Pony Express riders Cody has become the best known. His rank as colonel belongs to him by commission. Indeed, he has been commissioned as brigadier-general. He has also been a justice of the peace in Nebraska, and was Once a member of the Legislature, which entitles him to the "Hon." that is sometimes attached to his name. But he only cares to be a colonel on the principle, perhaps, of the Kentuckian who, being addressed as "General," refused the title on the ground that there is no rank in Kentucky higher than colonel. But of all his titles Cody prefers that of "Buffalo Bill," by which he is known throughout the world, and which he obtained while filling a contract on the plains in furnishing buffalo meat to feed the workmen of General Jack Casement and brother, contractors in the building of the Union Pacific Railroad.

Chapter 9

A Little Pawnee

Among the many romantic stories connected with the Pony Express service is the following concerning old "Whipsaw" and "Little Cayuse."

"Whipsaw," if he ever had any other name than this rather sudden one, never informed his associates of it, and it was seldom in those days that anyone cared to learn another's "story of his life" or what his name was "in the States." However, "Whipsaw" had been for many years a trapper until he became a station agent of the Pony Express on the Platte.

One day while "Whipsaw" was in his lonely camp attending to his work of packing his pelts, mending his traps, and the like, a Sioux Indian brought to him a captive Pawnee child about two years old. The little savage was stark naked and almost frozen. The Sioux, who was vividly marked by a long, repulsive scar across his face, desired to dispose of the child to the trapper, and the latter, as was every one of that class—now vanished forever—full of pity and kind hearted to a fault, did not hesitate a moment, but traded a knife for the helpless baby—all the savage asked for the little burden of humanity.

The old trapper took care of the young Pawnee, clothed him in his rough way, encased the little feet in *moccasins*, and with a soft doe-skin jacket the little fellow throve admirably under the gentle care of his rough nurse.

When the young Pawnee had reached the age of four years, the old trapper was induced to take charge of one of the overland stations on the line of the Pony Express. The old agent began to love the young savage with an affection that was akin to that of a mother; and in turn the Pawnee baby loved his white father and preserver. As the little fellow grew in stature, he evinced a most intense hatred for all members of his own dark-skinned race. He never let an opportunity go by when he could do them an injury, however slight.

Of course, at times, many of the so-called friendly Indians would visit the station and beg tobacco from the old trapper, but on every occasion the young Pawnee would try to do them some injury. Once, when he was only four years old, and a party of friendly Indians as usual had ridden up to the station, the young savage quietly crept to where their horses were picketed, cut their lariats, and stampeded all of them. At another time he made an attempt to kill an Indian who had stopped for a moment at the station, but he was too little to raise properly the rifle with which he intended to shoot him.

As it is the inherent attribute of all savages to be far in advance of the whites in the alertness and acuteness of two or three of the senses, the baby Pawnee was wonderfully so. He could hear the footsteps of a bear or the scratching of a panther, or even the tramp of a horse's hoof on the soft sod long before the old trapper could make out the slightest sound. He could always tell when the Pony Express rider was approaching, miles before he was in sight, if in the daytime, and at night many minutes before the old trapper's ears, which were very acute also, could distinguish the slightest sound.

The boy was christened "Little Cayuse," because his ears could catch the sound of an approaching horse's foot long before anyone else.

In the middle of the night, while his white father was sound asleep on his pallet of robes, the little Pawnee would wake him hurriedly, saying "Cayuse, cayuse," whenever the Pony Express was due. The rider, who was to take the place of the one nearing the station, would rise, quickly put the saddle on his *broncho*, and be all ready, when the pony arrived, to snatch the saddle bags from him whom he was to relieve, and in another moment dash down the trail mountain ward.

It was never too cold or too warm for the handsome little savage to get up on these occasions and give a sort of rude welcome to the tired rider, who, although nearly worn out by his arduous duty, would take up the baby boy and pet him a moment before he threw himself down on his bed of robes.

The young Pawnee had a very strange love for horses. He would always hug the animals as they came off their long trip, pat their noses, and softly murmur, "*Cayuse, cayuse.*" "*Cayuse*" means horse in some Indian dialects.

The precocious little savage was known to every rider on the trail

RED CLOUD
Chief of Ogallala Sioux

RED CLOUD
Big Ogallala Sioux Chief from another view

from St. Joe to Sacramento. Of course, the Indians were always on the alert to steal the horses that belonged to the stations, but where Little Cayuse was living they never made a success of it, owing to his vigilance. Often, he saved the animals by giving the soundly sleeping men warning of the approach of the savages who were stealthily creeping up to stampede the animals.

The boy was better than an electric battery, for he never failed to notify the men of the approach of anything that walked. So famous did he become that his wonderful powers were at last known at the headquarters of the great company, and the president sent Little Cayuse a beautiful rifle just fitted to his stature, and before he had reached the age of six he killed with it a great grey wolf that came prowling around the station one evening.

One cold night, after 12 o'clock, Whipsaw happened to get out of bed, and he found the little Pawnee sitting upright in his bed, apparently listening intently to some sound which was perfectly undistinguishable to other ears.

The station boss whispered to him, "Horses?"

"No," replied the little Pawnee, but continued looking up into his father's face with an unmistakable air of seriousness.

"Better go to sleep," said Whipsaw.

Little Cayuse only shook his head in the negative. The station boss then turned to the other men and said, "Wake up, all of you, something is going wrong."

"What is the matter?" inquired one of the riders as he rose.

"I don't exactly know," replied the boss. "But Cayuse keeps listening with them wonderful ears of his, and when I told him to go to sleep he only shook his head, and that boy never makes a mistake."

A candle was lighted; it was long after the express was due from the east.

The little Pawnee looked at the men and said. "Long time, no *cayuse*—no *cayuse*."

They then realised what the Pawnee meant: it was nearly two o'clock, and the rider from the East was more than two hours behind time. The little Pawnee knew it better than any clock could have told him, and both of the men sat up uneasy, fidgeting, for they felt that something had gone wrong, as it was beyond the possibility for any rider, if alive, to be so much behind the schedule time. They anxiously waited by the dim light of their candle for the sound of horses' feet, but their ears were not rewarded by the welcome sound.

BRULE SIOUX CHIEF LONG DOG

OGALLALA SIOUX CHIEF AMERICAN HORSE

Cayuse, who was still in his bed watching the countenances of the white men, suddenly sprang from his bed, and, creeping cautiously out of the door, carefully placed his ear to the ground, the men meanwhile watching him. He then came back as cautiously as he had gone out, and merely said, "Heap *cayuses*."

It was not the sound of the rider's horse whom they had so long been expecting, but a band of predatory Sioux bent on some errand of mischief; of that they were certain, now that the Pawnee had given them the warning. Little Cayuse took his rifle from its peg over his bed, and, walking to the door, peered out into the darkness. Then he crept along the trail, his ears ever alert. The men seized their rifles at the same moment, and followed the little savage to guard him from being taken by surprise.

All around the rude cabin which constituted the station, the boss had taken the precaution, when he first took charge, to dig a trench deep enough to hide a man, to be used as a rifle pit in case the occasion ever offered.

It was to one of these ditches that Little Cayuse betook himself, and the men followed the child's example, and took up a position on either side of him. Lying there without speaking a word, even in a whisper, the determined men and the brave Little Cayuse waited for developments.

Soon the band of savage horse thieves arrived at a kind of little hollow in the trail, about an eighth of a mile from the door of the station. They got off their animals and, Indian fashion, commenced to crawl toward the corral.

On they came, little expecting that they had been long since discovered, and that preparation was already made for their reception. One of them came so near the men hidden in the pit that the boss declared he could have touched him with his rifle. The old trapper was very much disturbed for fear that Little Cayuse would in his childish indiscretion open fire before the proper time arrived, which would be when the savages had entered the cabin. The child, however, was as discreet as his elders, and although it was his initial fight with the wily nomads of the desert, he acted as if he had thirty or forty years of experience to back him.

The band numbered six, as brave and determined a set of cutthroats as the great Sioux Nation ever sent out. The clouds had broken apart a little, and the defenders of the station could count their forms as they appeared between the diffused light of the horizon and the

RAIN-IN-THE-FACE
The Ogallala Sioux who killed Gen. Custer

GEN. CUSTER

roof of the cabin.

On reaching the door the Indians stopped a moment, and with their customary caution listened for some sound to apprise them that the inmates were sleeping. Suspecting this to be the case, they pushed the door carefully open and entered the cabin, one after another.

Now had come the supreme moment which the boss had so patiently hoped for! Whipsaw rose to his feet, and without saying a word to them, his comrades, including Little Cayuse, followed him. He intended to charge upon the savages in the cabin, although there were six to three, for it would hardly do to count the little Pawnee in as a man. The rider who had been waiting for the arrival of the other then placed his rifle on the ground, and each taking their revolvers, two apiece in their hands, ready cocked, advanced to the door.

They knew that the fight would be short and hot, so with the Pawnee between them they arrived at the entrance. Now, the Sioux evidently heard them, and came rushing out, but it was too late! The Pony Express men opened fire, and two of the savages bit the dust. They returned the salute, but with such careless aim that their shots were perfectly harmless; but as the white men fired again, two more of the savages fell, and only two were left. The rider got a shot in the shoulder, but he kept on with his revolver despite his pain, while the boss, who had fired all his shots, was compelled to throw the empty weapon into the persistent savage's face, while Little Cayuse kept peppering the other with small shot from his rifle.

Then the Indian at whom the boss had thrown his revolver came at him with his knife, and was getting the best of it, when Little Cayuse, watching his chance, got up close to the savage who was about to finish his father, and let drive into the brute's side a charge of shot that made a hole as big as a water-bucket, and the red devil fell without knowing what had hit him.

Both of the men were weak from loss of blood, and when they had recovered a little, not far away in the hollow they found the horses the savages had ridden and that of the express rider, all together. About a mile farther down the trail they found the dead body of the rider, shot through the head. His pony still had on the saddle and the mail pouch, which the Indians had not disturbed. In the morning the men carried the remains of the unfortunate rider to the cabin and buried it near the station, and it may be truthfully said that if it had not been for the plucky little Pawnee, there would have been no mourners at the funeral.

GHOST DANCERS

That afternoon the men dug a trench into which they threw the dead Indians to get them out of the way, but while they were employed in the thankless work, Little Cayuse was discovered most unmercifully kicking and clubbing one of the dead warriors; then he took his little rifle and cocking it emptied its contents into the prostrate body.

The boss then took the weapon away from him, but the boy cried out to him, "See! See!"

Looking down closely into the face of the object of the boy's wrath, he discovered by that hideous scar the fiend who had captured Little Cayuse when a mere baby, the scar-faced Sioux from whom Whipsaw had purchased the boy. (Cy Warman vouches for this incident in his *Frontier Stories*.)

CHAPTER 10

The Telegraph

Mr. Edward Creighton—of blessed memory—had, during many years of his life, been engaged in constructing telegraph lines throughout the United States. He had long contemplated the construction of such a line from the Missouri River to the Pacific Coast. In 1860, after many consultations with the Western Union Telegraph Company, a preliminary survey for the line was agreed upon. Notwithstanding that the trip across the plains and mountains was a trying one at best, beset as it was in dangers from attacks by Indians and highwaymen, added to the chances of storm and flood, Mr. Creighton made the journey by Overland stagecoach in the winter of the year mentioned. He halted at Salt Lake City, and there enlisted the very valuable interest and support of President Brigham Young, the great head of the Mormon church.

Desirous of also engaging the association of the California Telegraph Company in the enterprise, Mr. Creighton pressed, by saddle and horse, from Salt Lake to Sacramento, across the alkali desert and the Sierra Nevada range, in mid-winter, an appalling trip for even a hardy plainsman, inured to such journeyings, which Creighton was not. But he had a stout heart and a strong intent, added to a vigorous constitution, thus he accomplished the trip and his mission, and returned to Omaha in the spring of 1861, prepared to proceed with the work of construction.

The government granted a subsidy of $40,000 *per annum* which was to go to the first company that should establish a telegraph line across that part of the continent, and this stimulated a mighty rivalry between the Creighton forces and those of the California company, the first building westwardly and the second eastwardly, each endeavoring to reach Salt Lake before the other.

Eleven hundred miles was the distance that the Creighton company had to build, while the California company's line for construction was only 450 miles, the obstacles, so far as nature was concerned, being about equal, mile for mile. The Creighton forces reached Salt Lake City with the completed line on the 17th of October, the California company connecting a week later. A telegram from ocean to ocean was sent October 24th, the line having been completed within little more than half a year from the time that construction began.

Mr. Creighton's financial interest in the line was eventually more than a million dollars. His original stock was worth $100,000 at 18 cents per share. This, stock was afterward increased to $300,000, which rose to 85 cents per share, and Creighton sold an interest for $850,000, retaining $200,000 worth of stock.

Edward Creighton died in 1874, of paralysis, but there are many monuments to his memory not the least of which is Creighton College in Omaha, and the kindliest remembrance of the man by all who were acquainted with him in life.

The telegraph across the continent instantly, by the flashing of its first message, obviated the necessity for the Pony Express; the unique, highly romantic, and yet intensely practical and distinctly successful enterprise became a brilliant tradition.

Aside from the immediate purpose that it served so well, accelerating communication between the East and West at a particularly critical period, it demonstrated the feasibility of telegraph and railway lines across the continent at the latitude over which its course was laid, and was, in short, the *avant-courier* of the mighty and progress-diffusing Union and Central Pacific Railway systems that have been, and are, the immeasurable agencies for the upbuilding of the vast and resourceful empire, the glorious West that was the "Great American Desert."

On what a slender thread oft hang the weightiest things.

EDWARD CREIGHTON

SENATOR CHARLES SUMNER
Who changed a city's destiny

CHAPTER 11

An Incident that Changed a Railroad Terminus

National Flag on Turner Hall in 1861 Turner Hall, in St. Joseph, Missouri, was located on Charles Street, between Sixth and Seventh streets.

It was a 2-storey stone and brick structure, say 30 x 50 feet, shingle roof, gable fronting north on street, flag staff about three feet south of street line, at summit of roof.

The St. Joseph Turn Verein Society was composed of "unqualified Union men." Their hall was the meeting place of men holding like views. The United States flag was kept flying over said building in token of their loyalty to the United States Government.

The City Council of St. Joseph, Missouri, early in April, 1861, passed an ordinance prohibiting the hoisting of flags, either United States or secession. The Turn Verein Society paid no attention to said proposition, but kept the national flag flying with the approval of Union men.

In 1860, the Hannibal & St. Joseph Railroad was the only line west of the Mississippi River and east of the Sierra Nevada range, in all of the then "far West," except a short line from St. Louis to Jefferson City, the capital of Missouri. The western terminus of the Hannibal & St. Joseph road was at St. Joseph, on the Missouri River and the starting point for the route westward of a transcontinental railway seemed, naturally, to be from St. Joseph, not only because it was the terminus of the only road so far west, but for topographical reasons, involving grades and other *desiderata*.

St. Joseph was at that time easily the most important city on the Missouri River. Kansas City was little known other than as "Westport

GEN. GRANVILLE M. DODGE
Civil Engineer who surveyed the line
of the Union Pacific

GEN. NELSON A. MILES

Landing," a straggling village under the bluffs, most important as the steamboat landing for Westport, a small town a few miles inland, in Missouri, the outfitting depot for much overland traffic. Now, however, Kansas City is, as is well known, a mighty metropolis for a vast tributary region.

Omaha was then little more than a trading-post opposite Council Bluffs, Iowa. But there another great city has grown.

The designation of the termini of the transcontinental railway was an official prerogative of the President of the United States, and it is said that Hon. Charles Sumner, who was a highly influential United States Senator, from Massachusetts, and afterward Secretary of State in President Lincoln's cabinet, was an ardent partisan of St. Joseph as the starting point for the great road which was to be opulently subsidized by the Government.

After the election of Mr. Lincoln in 1860, and his inauguration in 1861, as President, which precipitated the secession of the southern states, Jeff Thompson, a prominent citizen of St. Joseph committed an act that, though an apparently trifling affair, comparatively, resulted in many wondrous changes.

Thompson became an intense secessionist and was afterward an officer of high rank in the Confederate army.

The tradition is that he, with some other young men, tore down the United States flag from the St. Joseph post office and replaced it with the flag of the Southern Confederacy. The story, which seems to be of strong foundation in truth and vouched for by many persons of the time and place, further relates that Mr. Sumner, when informed of the St. Joseph incident, became as strenuously opposed to that city, in the premises, as he had been in its favour theretofore, and that he had much to do with influencing Mr. Lincoln to name Omaha as the beginning of the "Iron Trail" westward.

Hon, John L. Bittinger, who was lately U. S. Consul General at Montreal, many years a leading journalist of St. Joseph, Mo., and now a highly esteemed citizen there, was post-master at St. Joseph at the time of this incident. He apprehended Thompson in the act of destroying the flag that he had pulled down and recovered the fragments at the muzzle of Bittinger's revolver.

Major Bittinger was one of the first three post-office appointees of President Lincoln's administration that began March 4, 1861. This writer conversed with Major Bittinger on the subject of the flag incident, in October, 1907—since the foregoing statement was written—and he confirmed the story as here given. At the same time Mr. Purd B. Wright, Librarian of the St. Joseph Public Library, gave to this writer the following affidavit, made by Robert C. Bradshaw, which is self-explanatory:

> On or about May 23, 1861, I, Robert C. Bradshaw, was going south on Second Street in the city of St. Joseph, Missouri. When opposite the post office I saw men rushing east on Francis Street. I followed the crowd, arriving at "alley" between Second and Third streets. On looking north where the crowd was going, I saw M. Jeff Thompson and others tearing into shreds the United States flag which had just been torn from the flag-staff of the post office building. The mob continued to increase, and in a few minutes fully five hundred men had assembled, when the cry was raised "Now for the dirty rag on Turner Hall."
>
> Hearing this I hastened to Turner Hall seven blocks away. On arriving there I found only a boy in charge of the building, whom I sent to notify members of the society that a "secession mob" was approaching the building with threats of destroying the same; therefore, for them to come immediately to my assistance. I then locked the back or side door and took my stand in front of Main or Charles Street entrance. A few moments later the "mob" headed by M. Jeff Thompson appeared coming towards the building. They crossed Sixth Street, and when forty feet from the hall they were halted by M. Jeff Thompson.
>
> Then Alonzo W. Slayback and Thomas Thourghman (both well known to me) came forward, and in the name of peace and the welfare of the city, they asked me to take the flag down, saying that "Jeff" Thompson was drunk, and no one could tell what a "mob" under a drunken leader would do. I declined to comply with their request, and the parley was continued, when a Mr. Miller, a justice of the peace, came forward and demanded in the name of the "mayor and city council" that the flag be taken down immediately, or he would have me (Bradshaw) arrested, as I claimed to be in charge of the building, for violating the city ordinances.
>
> I then asked Mr. Slayback if he would take charge of the door and not allow anyone to enter during my absence. He said he would. I then told the parties I would take the flag down, but

before doing so I claimed the right to salute it. Leaving Mr. Slayback in charge of the door, I went upstairs, then out on the roof. When half way from exit in roof to the flagstaff, the "mob" raised the cry to "Shoot him!" I stopped and told them I would take the flag down agreeable to the demands of the mayor and the city council, but no mob could compel me to do it, that I would salute the flag before lowering it, well knowing that ere long it would float in triumph over every seceding state.

Again, the cry "Shoot him! Shoot him!" Revolvers in great numbers were drawn and pointed at me; I could hear the click as they were being cocked. Therefore, I drew my revolvers (two, before concealed on my person), cocked one, then advanced to the flag staff, seizing the halyard; I gave three cheers for the national flag, and raising my revolver, I fired six shots over the flag in token of salute, then lowering it, I took the flag and returned to the second story where it was deposited in safety.

Going downstairs I found Mr. Slayback at his post, whom I thanked for his manner in keeping the promise. I also told him, while on the roof, I could see and face the mob, but I could not see him (Slayback) at the door; but when the "mob" yelled "Shoot him," I heard him tell them "that he would kill the first man that shot at Bradshaw."

The foregoing is a succinct but true report of the "Turners Hall" flag episode.

    (Signed)   Robert C. Bradshaw.

ss:

State of Kansas
County of Shawnee

Subscribed and sworn to before me this 28th day of November, 1905: I further certify that I am in no wise interested in the claim nor concerned in its prosecution, and that said affiant is personally known to me, and he is a credible person.

    (Signed)   H. I. Monroe,
Deputy County Clerk,
Topeka, Kansas.

Original on file in office of Librarian, Public Library, St. Joseph, Mo.

                 Purd B. Wright, Librarian.

At any rate Omaha became the starting point of the Union Pacific railroad, which has been immeasurably potent in the upbuilding of the mighty West, and in a few years afterward Kansas City was the starting point of another great line of the system, the Kansas Pacific Railroad, that, crossing Kansas and Colorado, joins other branches at Denver that ramify the Rocky Mountains, one line connecting at Cheyenne with the Union Pacific that connects at Ogden, Utah, with the Central Pacific, which two made the first of the lines that reached across the continent.

If it is true that Thompson's act in hauling down "Old Glory" from its staff in St. Joseph caused the change in the starting point for the transcontinental road, that act also did much for the initiatory of two splendid cities on the Missouri River as well as for that of many other thriving cities further west.

Saving for a short distance west of St. Joseph, the Union Pacific and Central Pacific original lines follow practically the route taken by the Pony Express, and thus did those gallant Centaur-Mercurys with the caduceus of courage, fidelity, and endurance pave the way to an empire of prosperity now, that, great as it is, glows only as a sign of what it will be to coming millions.

Chapter 12

"The Iron Trail"

In all the stories of romance, or reality, colossal performance and accomplishment under difficulties, energy, enterprise, push, and get-there, the building of the Union Pacific and Central Pacific Railroad—the first transcontinental line—stands out in history as the greatest of all the achievements of its kind, in any age, when the conditions and facilities for the work are understood.

However, it is all a matter of record and the story compiled, in all its phases, would make a vast volume. It is a history that lives in the reports of congressional proceedings in which the legislation necessary to the government's official part in the work is set forth; in the reports of surveyors and civil engineers and of the work of contractors; in the details of the proceedings of the syndicates of capitalists who financed the scheme; in the narration of incidents of bloodshed and wild and startling adventure, Indian fighting, affrays with outlaws and desperadoes, the trying service of soldiers, the hardships and exposure associated with weather, rugged nature and thousands of other difficulties that can better be imagined than described when what has been told is considered.

Hundreds of books have been written and printed that, in varying ways, give disunited details, but the whole story of the great work in all its ramifications, atmosphere, and environment has not been written into one great volume and probably never will be. Certainly, it will not be undertaken here, not only because it would require a thousand times the space contemplated in this book, but because only a casual glance at the great enterprise has been intended, and that merely as a result leading up from the success of the Pony Express.

Explorations and surveys, desultory, fitful, deviating, at first, by private parties and corporations, with spasmodic ambitions to build a road across the continent, began as early as 1853, and continued with increasing design and purpose until 1861, when Congress passed the bill favouring a Pacific railway, that was known as the s Law of 1862. As a result of that bill, the Union Pacific Company was organised at Chicago, September a, 1862. The effort to engage capital in the scheme was a failure. The war being under way, the government had its hands full and could only aid slightly in the enterprise.

The road, however, was deemed by the administration a military necessity, and in 1864 a bill was passed by Congress that by subsidy and countenance so strengthened the situation that under it the Union and Central Pacific railroads, constituting one continuous line, from the Missouri River to the Pacific Coast, were built. Ground was broken at Omaha for the Union Pacific on the fifth day of November, 1865, and the last spike was driven at Promontory Point, Utah, where the Union Pacific met the Central Pacific, on the tenth day of May, 1869.

On the occasion of the ceremony of "breaking ground" at Omaha, George Francis Train, an enthusiastic speaker, declared that the road would be completed in five years. He was laughed at as a dreamer. The road was completed in three years, six months, and ten days, about a year and a half less time than had been estimated by Mr. Train.

At the beginning of the work of building the Union Pacific, the nearest railroad to Omaha was 150 miles eastward. Over this distance all the material for construction was hauled by wagon. This included rails, spikes and other iron, necessary machinery, that had been purchased in eastern cities. The laborers, the tools with which they were to work, and the supplies necessary for their sustenance were transported the same way.

West of Omaha for 500 miles the route of the railroad lay over a region bare of timber except for the few cottonwoods that grew along the banks of the streams, and they were useless for railroad building purposes. The ties that were used in the construction of the road were cut in Michigan, Pennsylvania, and New York, and were delivered at Omaha at $2 50 per tie.

In January, 1866, forty miles of the Union Pacific Railroad had been constructed. During the remainder of that year 265 miles further were completed, and in 1867 there were added 285 miles, a total of 550 miles. During the next fifteen months, the remaining distance, 534 miles, was completed, that being at the rate of about one and one-fifth miles per day.

General Jack Casement, who went into the Civil War as colonel of an Ohio regiment, and who rose to the rank of brigadier-general, and a command in the 23rd Army Corps, was on the construction of the Union Pacific. Hundreds of his soldiers, and even soldiers of the Confederate Army, went with General Casement from war to work. Thus, during this period of railway construction, his track train had with it, at any moment, a thousand men who at a word could be transformed into an army of veterans inured to war, and with men who had ranked from general to private, being thus entirely able to whip three times their number of undisciplined men.

It was distinctly needful that this condition should exist, there and then, for occasions were frequent when the men in small or great detachments found it necessary to change a working line into a battle front on account of the attacks of Indians, generally in numbers five, or more, to one of the railroad hands.

The exigencies of the previous war and its diversified experiences were potent in the construction of this transcontinental road. The war had actually made the undertaking possible, physically and financially. Physically it produced the men, and financially public consent.

Notwithstanding that the government was already loaded monstrously with an almost inconceivable war debt, it floated for the enterprise fifty millions of a subsidy, and by this step created for the undertaking a credit that enabled the constructing organisation to bond an equal amount, and this combination of capital, in the hands and at the disposal of the strong and courageous men in charge, who also ventured their personal fortunes and services in the work, triumphantly accomplished the scheme in a manner far beyond the most sanguine expectations of all concerned.

The proposition before the war to construct a railway across the continent 2,000 miles, and through an uninhabited wilderness, except for warlike savages, and for the most part over barren plains, shifting streams, and chaotic mountains, without a dollar of way traffic in sight, would have appalled the nation, had it been asked to give its credit, or even countenance, to such an apparently crazy scheme. In short, the people and their authorities would have promptly estopped even talk of an undertaking so utterly absurd, preposterous, and extravagant as this would have seemed to be.

The mighty achievements of the republic in carrying on a war so prodigious and stupendous in magnitude, and so far reaching in all its physical and financial ramifications, as well as in its social and com-

BUILDING THE UNION PACIFIC RAILROAD UNDER FIRE

mercial effects, widened and enlarged the public mind in many ways, and especially in the direction of structural possibilities in domestic utilities and internal improvements. Thus, the public became far more tolerant as to great undertakings by Government, particularly because the possibilities of finance on a huge scale were made more apparent and the viewpoint was generally widened. In short, ours had become a nation with a big "N."

Touching the matter of railroad construction, distinguished civil engineers declared that necessity brought out during the war bold structures that in their rough were models of economy in material and strength and brought about the adoption of principles in superstructure that are used today in the highest and boldest work of the builders. The simple principles thus evolved out of necessity were applied whenever demanded in the construction of this great work, the transcontinental road, and though they had been reported against at the outset, during the war, by experienced and reliable engineers, were found to be most effectual in this work that tested all the forces in that line because of the difficulties to be overcome.

The enterprising and venturesome men, who with brain, brawn, and capital persisted in forwarding this undertaking, that has since worked inconceivable benefit to the region of its locale, to the nation, and the world, were, notwithstanding the progressive bent of the time, deemed by many persons of importance to be "fools and fanatics" in this particular. But other and greater spirits applauded and encouraged them, and this was particularly true of the great military geniuses of the time and country.

Oakes Ames, who was of the very soul of the enterprise, once remarked in this connection, speaking to an army officer of distinction, "What makes me hang on is the faith of you soldiers," and he was referring to such men of the army as Grant, Sheridan, Sherman. Dodge, Pope, Thomas, Augur, Crook, and many others who were in touch with the building of the road, in the field or otherwise officially. That part of the army which was brought into juxtaposition with the work was enthusiastic in aid of it, and there was nothing that the builders could ask, that the army could give, which was not at all times forthcoming, even in instances where the regulations did not authorise it, and where it took a violent stretch of authority to meet it. The commissary department was nearly always under requisition to the working force and was incalculably valuable. The troops guarded the line, and it was surveyed, located, and constructed within the army's picket posts.

A distinguished man, who has been a potent factor in the country's material advancement, and who had special advantages for observation of the things concerning which he was speaking, once said:

> But for the railroads the great central region of this continent would be indeed a howling wilderness.

Nothing has ever been plainer to those who have had the opportunity and the satisfaction of seeing it all—as have many thousands who are yet strong men and women—than the wondrous changes that have been wrought upon the region that they traverse by the transcontinental roads, of which the Union Pacific and Central Pacific were the pioneers and pace-makers. With the progress of civilization that followed, the turning of the soil and the planting of trees, associated with other attendant influences, the climate changed, the rain-belt advanced, agriculture took possession of the desert and all the adjuncts, accessories, benefits and beatitudes that adorn and embellish enlightened life, came along to stay and increase. In the history of the world there has been no event that did more to directly upbuild a mighty empire of resource and blessed reciprocity.

All in all, the Great Iron Trail has been the working arm of Civilization that has built for herself a palace and planted a garden in the desert, to the glory of the Republic and the benefit of the world.

For all this the fleet, nervy, and gallant riders of the Pony Express were advance couriers who definitely marked the Westward Way.

THE AMES MONUMENT

CHAPTER 13

General Sheridan's Way

American history, especially since the latter fifties, has been made so rapidly that it eclipses the revels of romantic dreamers and embarrasses the writer with its abundance of thrilling episodes, scenes, incidents, and occurrences in the region whose first regularly transacted business affair was the Pony Express. So prolific are they that volumes could be filled, and consequently the latitude of this publication is confined to what was practically the last chapter of Indian warfare so far as it deals with that subject; as growing out of the great things that followed the Pony Express.

Every inch of ground on the historic Overland trail has been made sacred by events, adventures, and experiences that will fill libraries in the future when the local legends are compiled, and the time will come when the legendary lore of Europe, from the time of the Crusaders to historic Waterloo, will be eclipsed by the deeds of daring and hair-breadth escapes, trials, sufferings, and hardships of the early explorers, pioneers, scouts, and army folks that opened the way from the days of Lewis and Clark to the time of the fur traders, trappers from Fort St. Louis, led by the Choteaus and others; during the expeditions of Pathfinder Fremont, guided by Kit Carson, carving the way from the Missouri to the new acquisitions in California, on down to the time when it became necessary to grapple with the obstructing savage for final decision as inaugurated by General Sheridan with the superbly equipped army he found under his command at the finish of the Civil War.

Prolific as was and is the story of a most strenuous, sanguinary invasion of the lands west of the Alleghany Mountains, the crossing of the Ohio and reaching the Mississippi, the occupation of the great central plains, from the Missouri to the Rockies, and from the Red River

Gen. Phil. Sheridan

Kit Carson
Famous scout who guided Fremont's
Exploring Expedition

in the North to the Rio Grande in the South, surpassed it in bloody story and rapidity of action, and there is no doubt that in no epoch of history were there so many startling incidents as resulted from the vigorous contest and settlement of the "Great American Desert."

The marvellous progress and prosperity succeeding the establishment of the Union Pacific Railroad has partaken almost of the miraculous, and the evolution from savage conditions to the height of civilization has wiped out apparently the scars so deeply made as to cause them to be almost forgotten. In fact, the transition has taken place during the lives—the adult active lives, of many of the participants, both red and white, still living. It is here but just, to refer to the nation's debt of gratitude to the army men and their associate scouts and guides that were the 'wedge' that ploughed the way in achieving the results.

In this arena was fought, the reader must remember, the last battles of the struggle that had lasted nearly three hundred years with a gallant foe stubborn to almost the extent of suicide, as were the primitive protestors against the march of civilization. The fate of the American Indian is an example of the survival of the fittest. These people were once the sole owners of the trackless forests, the mighty rivers, the great mountains, woodlands, and plains of the then unknown and even unheard-of country that we now call America. They were in the full sense of the term "monarchs of all they surveyed."

As far as eye could reach or limbs could bear them, whatsoever the sole of their foot rested upon, was theirs. They had a religion, a history, traditions, a nation all their own, a Utopia. The poet Longfellow has done much to bring before the mind's eye a true picture of the primitive life:

With the odours of the forest
With the dew and damp of meadows
With the curling smoke of wigwams,
With the rushing of great rivers.

From the Great Lakes of the Northland,
From the land of the Ojibways,
From the land of the Dacotahs
From the mountains, moor, and fernlands
Where the heron, the Shuh-shuh-hag,
Feeds among the reeds and rushes.

The centuries of deadly combat between the white man and the

CHIEF GALL
A Brilliant Ogallala Leader

CURLEY
A great Warrior of the Brule Sioux

red was the result of the then existing belief on the one hand that the right of discovery gave the right of conquest and acquisition; and on the other that possession is nine points of the law, and that equity and honour demanded the defence of his home. The Indian knew nothing of the much-vaunted beauties of civilization or the fruit of the so-called progress, having only an innate sense of what was justice and equity.

The army and the scout were the ones who fell heir to precedence and consequent prominence on the firing line in this "irrepressible conflict," whose merit must be decided by the results of the greatest good to the greatest numbers. The pages of the world's history held nothing to equal it in sanguinary character and bitterness of feeling, no warfare required such strategic skill, personal qualities and resourcefulness.

In certain characteristics the Indian excelled, and this necessitated the acquisition of similar qualities by his white opponent ere success could be attained.

After the results, none respected each other more and none became more sympathetic than did the old white and red campaigners.

The red man of the western mountains and plains was brave, reckless, and wily; his white enemy had to keep every faculty on the alert to escape the results or counteract his cunning. The result was that American officers trained in that school acquired qualities that made them preeminent among military men when opportunity occurred in civilized warfare.

It is fitting here to remark and call attention of the reader to the difference between Indian warfare and civilized warfare. One was a fight to the death, with torture preceding it if captured, while the other was governed by certain amenities if captured. Capture generally meant good treatment. It was in this school of savage warfare where every faculty was developed that graduated the great chieftains of the Civil War on both sides. The Lees, Van Dorns, Wheelers, of the South, and the Shermans, Sheridans, Merritts, Crooks Emorys, Frenches, Royals, Hayses, and Carrs, of the North, became distinguished leaders in the great civil strife.

At the finish of this struggle General Sheridan found himself possessed of an army of veterans recruited from both sides, when he took command of the Division of the West. While the whites were occupied with their own conflict of opinion and arms, the Indian had revelled almost unmolested on the plains, and in winter was perfectly immune on account of the climatic conditions, and lived in his isolated camp in luxurious ease and domestic comfort. In fact, up to that time the Indian and the white man, if possible, generally avoided each other, but Sheridan conceived the idea of inaugurating new methods. He introduced the new system of Indian fighting, which was to "trail, hunt for, follow, find, and kill under any conditions at the time, season, or climate," believing this would strike a telling blow to the red marauder in winter when he dwelt in fancied security and was not prepared to make long forced marches as in the summer, when nature supplied his commissary with game and his horses and cattle with an abundance of grass. This, of course, meant the white man confronting the difficulties of campaigning in the deep snow, the death-dealing blizzards and the difficulties of climate, at times 40 below zero.

We quote his own description of the conditions from his autobiography: published in 1888, concerning the first winter campaign against Indians on the then uninhabited and bleak plains, in the winter of 1868; he says:

> The difficulties and hardships to be encountered had led several experienced officers of the army and some frontiersmen like old Jim Bridger, the famous scout and guide of earlier days, to discourage the project. Bridger even went so far as to come out from St. Louis to discourage the attempt. I decided to go in person, bent on showing the Indians that they were not secure from punishment because of inclement weather, an ally on which they had hitherto relied with much assurance. We started, and the very first night a blizzard struck us and carried away our tents. The gale was so violent that they could not be put up again; the rain and snow drenched us to the skin.
>
> Shivering from wet and cold, I took refuge under a wagon, and there spent such a miserable night that, when morning came, the gloomy predictions of old man Bridger and others rose up before me with greatly increased force. The difficulties were now fully realised, the blinding snow mixed with sleet, the piercing wind, thermometer below zero—with green bushes only for fuel—occasioned intense suffering. Our numbers, and companionship alone prevented us from being lost or perishing, a fate that stared in the face of the frontiersmen, guides, and scouts on their solitary missions.
>
> During these times occurred innumerable contests of various de-

grees and importance, such as the Battle of The Wichita, under the dashing Custer; Summit Springs, under that wily commander in Indian warfare, the gallant Eugene A. Carr; and the fight on the Canadian between Gen. Sandy Forsythe and Roman Nose, in which Lieut. Beecher was killed; and numerous similar sanguinary contests, each worthy of extended attention from the pen of the historian and the pencil of the painter.

These covered the period of the days of the Pony Express, succeeded by the stage coach and the telegraph wire, and the railroad was thus enabled to be built under the protection thus afforded. It was in these times that Red Cloud, then Red Emperor of the American plains, became a terror, his very name creating confusion when his proximity was heard of, and who made such audacious forays as to attack, capture, and massacre the soldiers at Fort Kearney.

Then came the period when, with the aid of the telegraph and the railroad, rapidity of information and facility of transportation enabled the troops to beat back the savage hordes and drive them northward, culminating in the campaign of '76, giving the bloody chapter of Custer's annihilation with his entire command, but resulting in a very perceptible breaking up of the red man's power. With some desultory forays this continued to fill the atmosphere with danger to the encroaching settlements until 1890 when it was destined to be fought out in the expiring effort of the despairing foe, "The Ghost Dance War."

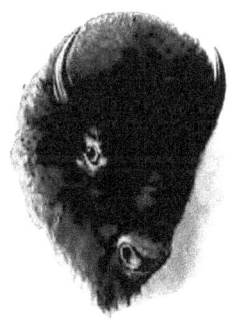

CHAPTER 14

The Beginning of the End

We deem it of importance and interest to refer to this Ghost-Dance War and its causes, as its results have been so stupendous in accomplishing the absolute eradication of anything approaching Indian war again; it cleared the atmosphere so effectively that it is worthy of mention in detail as being the finish at the foothills of the Rocky Mountains of the contest waged from the shores of New England across a vast continent and settling forever the fate, of the red man, which is assimilation into the political body and social conditions of its conqueror.

At this time the Sioux nation was the most powerful, possessing about twenty-five thousand members, distributed between the various tribes, from the Sitting Bull's Uncapapas of the North or Sitting Bull tribe and the Brule and the Ogallalas, or Red Cloud contingent in the south of Dakota. These Indians retained pretty much the "blanket Indian" condition and were somewhat morose in character, deprecating the loss of the Black Hills, and quietly resenting continued encroachments of the settlers, with thousands of the old warriors still living who regaled the young with stories of the glories of the times just alluded to when they roamed at will, gathered the trophies of war and the honours of the chase.

There were about three hundred thousand Indians on the different reservations from the British possessions to the Rio Grande. These Indians had become friendly with each other instead of as in old, being enemies; and the discontented rode from band to band on visits, until there became a community of sentiment and feeling among them as regards the wrongs that they felt they had suffered. This was quietly cultivated to an extent known to but few in the government service, but the Argus eye of the army discovered that something was be-

GEN. CROOK GOV. FOSTER SENATOR WARNER
The Sioux Commission

ing done. In the summer of 1889, Government commissioners came among the Indians and persuaded them to sign away several million acres of land on promises that were not promptly kept; this was owing to the delay of Congress in appropriating the money.

Gen. Crook, who had conducted the negotiations, it was said, was so much affected by the delay and the breach of faith as it appeared to the Indians, which he regarded as a personal dishonour, that many believed it to have hastened his sudden death.

Add to this the influence of the Sioux Chief, Sitting Bull, the red man's Oliver Cromwell—from their view a patriot and a leader of rare ability—ever ready and eager to retrieve his people's birth-right, and it is easy to see that the material for general conflagration was at hand and the conditions for it were timely. This condition was created when the Utes through some machination of an inspector or some of their own fanatical medicine men claimed to have had a visit from the Messiah. The Messiah was the red man's Manitou or God, and the teaching of the missionaries had fully instructed the Sioux, and the Indians in general, in the story of our Saviour's coming on earth, his persecution and crucifixion, and they were taught by the white man that he was to return to earth again.

This doctrine fitted well into the argument of the class of Indians that always desired to fight and played into the hands of the discontented and spread with amazing rapidity all through the Sioux nation, and eventually to every tribe, even inoculating the civilized ones, from the Red River in the North down to the Yaqui Indians of Mexico. In fact, it was like all religious crazes among our coloured races, and even among the whites. It played upon the emotions and worked its victims up to a fanatical frenzy that made them invite death or torture if they could have the satisfaction of fighting or killing their enemies. Some of the teachings were, of course, of the glorious future in the happy hunting grounds that could be achieved by death in battle, accepted with as strong a faith as ever those of Christian martyrs.

To explain the attention, they had paid to the arguments that our Saviour was coming on earth again, but to them only, this story, which the writer knows to be true from the lips of Short Bull, the Messiah high-priest of the Ogallala, will assist. When asked why he advocated the doctrine of the return at this time of our Saviour to the Indians and with the intention of annihilating the white man from the earth, he replied, through an interpreter, as follows:

MAJOR JOHN M. BURKE
Assisted with Gen. J. M. Lee in peace negotiations

GEN. JESSE LEE
Burke's confrère in peace negotiations

You white people here have three religious sects at the agency, three different churches; each one preaches to the Indian what you call Christianity. (He alluded to the Methodist, Episcopal, and Catholic churches that were at the agency.) Now all these three medicine men of these churches differ in every respect and preach different things to us, but mainly impress us, each one, that the other two are very wrong. In fact, out of about fifty white people at the agency, they are the only people who do not speak as they pass by, but they all agree and all preach these four or five facts, agreeing on the same.

They teach that the Messiah once came on earth for the good of the white man. They teach he is the Son of God and the wisest man that ever came on earth. They teach he had miraculous power. They teach that the white man tortured, crucified, and killed him, and they teach that he will return to earth again. These are about all the things they agree on, and we have a right to expect that they are nearer truth than anything they say. Now, if the Messiah came on earth, and was the wisest man, and if the white man tortured and killed him, and he is going to come on earth again, would he not be a heap fool to come back to the white man? That is the reason we believe he is coming again, and if he is all powerful, as they say, he must be coming to avenge himself by helping the red man and with his miraculous power annihilate the white man. How?

This reply simply shows the thoughtfulness given and the argumentativeness created by delving into a subject so mysterious that it creates food for thought among the white men. The Indian, one can see from this, is a thinker, and really not so much of a fool as he looks. He is, for instance, a naturally gifted orator, when occasion requires, but he seems to know generally that silence is golden. Those who have met such men as "Sitting Bull," "John Grass," "Running Antelope," "Red Cloud," American Horse," "Short Bull," and others with an intelligent interpreter found them in argument, foemen worthy of the most astute statesman's consideration.

On the occasion of the Congressional Committee visiting the northern Sioux at Fort Yates (Standing Rock Agency) for a consultation in regard to selling the land, Sitting Bull was as usual doggedly opposed to the scheme. This red statesman was always anxious to show his people his contempt for the white men and his aptness for repartee. The distinguished committee, individually, all referred to the fact that the red men and white men were brothers, and the same God of the white man was the Manitou of the Indian. After an exhaustive session, Sitting Bull arose after the last had concluded and alluded to the fact that each had reiterated and emphasised the fact of the universal God. Pointing his finger at them, he said:

> You say red and white have the same God, who created all mankind and everything in the world; that his all-seeing eye pervades the universe, and that he knows everything even to the fall of the bird (the sparrow). If such is the case, he must have known what he was doing when he created me. He made me a free man and not an agency Indian and by the Eternal (only a little more plainly) I will never consent to be one.

Rising, the old warrior walked out with impressive dignity, and the council would have ended but for the action of Indian agent, Major McLaughlin, who arrested Sitting Bull, and compelled him to permit the negotiations to proceed.

When one considers the Indians, numbering 300,000, North and South, could practically have recruited 50,000 able warriors, armed and mounted, one may conceive what might have occurred had the fanatical conspiracy broken out at the opening of summer, when nature's commissary was available for them, and the rich settlements, with myriad hordes of cattle and provisions of all kind, would have given a grand feast to these nomadic people such as has never been enjoyed by murdering marauders.

The craze as to the imminent return of the Messiah, man of supreme ability, who was to give back America to its original owners, wiping out the whites and their sties, and bringing with him great store of game with which to re-stock the purified plains and prairies, was started first among the Utes. That the Indians should have thereupon originated the Messiah dance should not be considered extraordinary. They have a special dance to suit every occasion. The was dance is the style of gyration most familiar to the white intelligence, and naturally when it was rumoured that the Indians were dancing, the neighbouring settlers took alarm. If it seems a ridiculous thing to invoke the Saviour by a series of frenzied jumpings and howlings, we have only to consider the peculiarities of many existing sects of our people, and it will be clear that we are not so far ahead of them in this respect. The dance, at first, was a form of prayer, engaged in by the young braves after a sort of Turkish bath, and accompanied by the singing of hymns after their own savage fashion.

Some of the Pine Ridge Sioux went up on a visit to the Utes in July of 1890, and found this lively business going on. They were much interested, and took back a report to their own tribes, who held that if the Messiah were really coming, it would not do to let him fall short of a welcome on their part. Their medicine men, accompanied by Short Bull, of the Ogallalas, saw that they must either lead the dancing or get left, so, like medicine men in all times, and all nations, they took it cordially in hand, provided the music, and arranged the figures.

By the usual train of logic in such religious movements, they arrived at a further conclusion: If the Messiah were going to stamp out the whites, should his children sit idly by and let him do all the hard work unaided? Just as Peter the Hermit reasoned that as Heaven desired to drive the Turks out of Palestine, it was clearly the duty of the Crusaders to take a hand and go and knock the said Turks over the head with battle axes, so the Sioux, incited by Sitting Bull, The Right Reverend Short Bull now become "High Priest"—and Kicking Bear, got out their guns and prepared to help divine Providence to the best of their ability whenever the Messiah should appear. It doesn't seem to have struck them as at all ridiculous that Wankantanka, the Great Spirit, being omnipotent, should require the help of the Sioux, Brules, or others, in working out his designs.

Let us not sneer at the half-starved Indians. The extent to which the armies of Europe have sought to assist the Almighty to crush out the opposition, even in recent times, may be read in the sermons of archbishops and the thanksgivings of emperors. In this respect the ancient Jews set them a pious example.

At this supreme psychic moment, when the dancing at Pine Ridge was waxing fast and furious, and the fanatical creatures were falling into swoons, seeing visions under the influence of some sort of hypnotism when prophecies of earthquakes and drought were being strangely fulfilled, a superior genius of Washington stepped into the thick of the trouble and brought about a crisis. The agent in charge of the Pine Ridge reservation was ordered, with fourteen Indian police, up to the camp of a gentleman named White Bird to "stop the dancing" of five or six hundred crazy warriors. He was confronted by a score of braves, armed with Winchester rifles, and made to turn back to the agency.

This, of course, was an act of rebellion. The report spread, the epi-

JAMES B. HICKOK
Known as "Wild Bill." In one fight, single-handed and alone, he killed ten desperadoes

GEN. "TONY" FORSYTH

sode was magnified into a successful battle, and every pious Indian in America commenced dancing the Ghost Dance to the best of his ability. The settlers near the reservations packed up their traps and fled to the cities, and Kicking Bear, with Short Bull and a considerable following of enthusiastic braves, under the venerable Two Strike, High Pipe, and High Hawk, put on full uniforms of war paint, and made for what is known as the Bad Lands, in the central fastness of which is a natural fortress, approachable only by one path, twenty feet wide.

Here they pitched their camp, and breathed defiance to sixty millions of Americans. The plateau was 150 feet above the surrounding country. They requisitioned all the cattle and everything movable for miles around, and while the young braves were out thieving, the High Priest made them highly decorative shirts, which he assured them were bullet-proof. The "medicine" in these shirts was so potent that they would turn a bullet or the edge of a sharp knife. But it was understood that any brave who attempted to cut them by way of experiment would be suddenly paralyzed by divine interposition. These were the famous "Ghost Shirts."

This condition of affairs created intense excitement through the West, and the whole country being inflamed with incendiary reports, Washington became agitated, and the military was ordered to the points of danger. It might here be remarked that Gen. Nelson A. Miles, commanding the West, had been thoroughly informed, and was equal to the emergency. As usual, a great many divergent opinions contended for supremacy at Washington as to what should be done, and as usual "too many cooks spoiled the broth." In the course of a short time a conflict was precipitated that resulted in the death of Sitting Bull and a further inflaming of the excited red men of the North. But Gen. Miles had his troops quickly placed in position to prevent a general conflagration by preventing communication over an extensive area.

Many bands deserted the Standing Rock Agency of the North and started to make junction with the Ogallalas, Brules, and other discontented tribes of the South that had already thrown down the gauntlet and become hostile in quite formidable numbers and began to wage war upon the whites and also the neutral and conservative members of their own tribes who refused to join in the forays. These neutral and conservative Indians, hundreds of whom had travelled extensively with Col. Cody, became a great factor for peace in the stirring conditions. Some even enlisted as scouts and guides and assisted

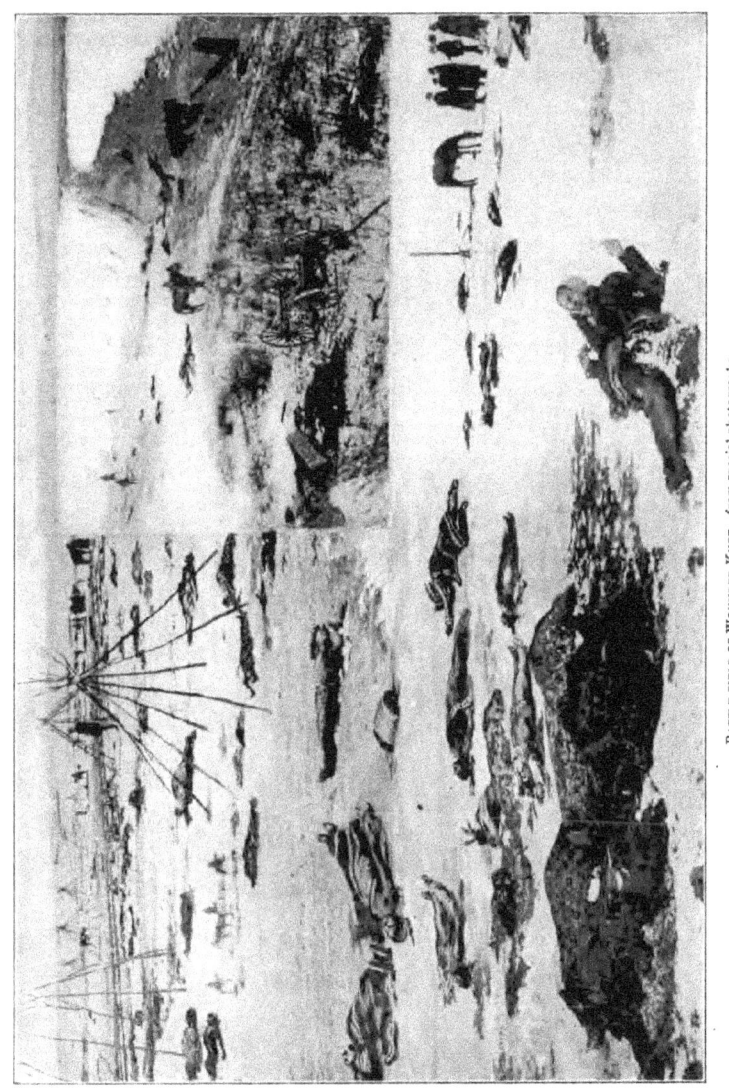

BATTLE-FIELD OF WOUNDED KNEE—from special photographs

In the foreground is the pile of dead Indians under which two Indian baby girls were found on Wednesday who had been there since Monday, a blizzard raging all the time. These lives were saved.

very materially.

As the principal outbreak culminated in December, the reader can imagine what the climatic conditions were for a campaign amidst snow and blizzard and how trying it was on the white soldiers, to an extent only appreciated by those who have endured such privations. One of the first moves of the Indians had been to capture provisions, taking Government herds wherever possible, and supplies of all kind where available. Marches and counter marches, scalpings and skirmishes innumerable resulted in the efforts to corral the recalcitrants, at the same time prevent communications. This was fairly well accomplished, and eventually the Brules and Ogallalas were segregated and prevented from escaping southward and precipitating a guerrilla warfare on the settlements. The national troops were assisted by the Nebraska militia under Gen. Colby of the Nebraska National Guard, on whose staff was Brigadier Gen. W. F. Cody ("Buffalo Bill"), and was so placed as to be of great assistance, Buffalo Bill joining Gen. Miles as volunteer advisory scout with Frank Gruard as headquarters' scout.

The formidable bands under Chiefs Big Foot and Hump from the Northern Sioux escaped southward with the purpose of joining Kicking Bear and Short Bull in the Bad Lands. Miles had sent Capt. Baldwin (now major-general) and Capt. Maus (now colonel) under a flag of truce to talk with Hump and Big Foot for the purpose of

CHIEF GOOD HORSE AND WIFE
Prominent man of present-day Dakota Sioux

getting them to come in, assuring them of proper treatment. He had previously defeated both of these chiefs, and Hump paid attention to the invitation and came in with a powerful band of warriors. All the Indians liked "Beaver Coat," as they called Gen. Miles. Big Foot's band refused to come in, but Hump and his warriors came.. It was' lucky they did. Had they been with the other band that attacked the white men at Wounded Knee or at Pine Ridge, it would have been a repetition of the Custer massacre. However, Gen. Miles, with his characteristic diplomacy, arranged places on his staff with rank and showy uniforms for Hump and seven of his leading warriors as scouts, taking them with him to Pine Ridge, and leaving the warriors in charge of military in Black Hill camp.

But Big Foot was not to be pacified so easily. He and his fighters passed Gen. Sumner and all the other outposts, succeeded in getting almost within hailing distance of Kicking Bear, and were discovered by Major Whiteside of the seventh cavalry, who was reinforced by General "Tony" Forsythe, who commanded in the battle. Little Bit, Lew Changrau, White, and "No Neck," and "Tanklin Charlie," Indian scouts, tried to induce the Indians to surrender. The terms were partly agreed upon. Capt. Wallace was with Phillip Wells in the village to superintend the surrender of Big Foot, when the medicine man, who believed in the bullet deflecting qualities of the ghost-dance shirt, gave a signal that precipitated the Battle of Wounded Knee.

There were about two hundred and forty-five Indians when the battle began. When it was over, 225 of them were dead and the rest wounded; three of the wounded escaped to the hostiles, and an immediate attack the same day was made on the Agency at Pine Ridge. The agency was garrisoned with 450 men under Gen. Brooks; the attack of the Indians came near being a surprise, but with the troops, the Indian police, and Indian scouts the attack was repulsed, and the agency was saved. The fight at Wounded Knee was about one of the first to demonstrate the destructiveness of the modern rifle, as nearly twenty years had elapsed since either Europe or America had tried perfected fire-arms.

The fact that 60 *per cent* of the combatants, white and red, were killed or wounded, in the space of about half an hour, testified that a new epoch in war was at hand, which has since been demonstrated in Manchuria. The accuracy of the aim of Uncle Sam's boys was attested, and the dogged stubbornness of the Indian was proven. Seventy-eight of the soldiers were disabled and some of the Indian allies.

THE PRESS CONTINGENT AT WOUNDED KNEE

Reading from left to right the persons standing are: Buckskin Jack; Kelly, Lincoln Journal; Crissy, Omaha Bee; Charles Seymour, Chicago Herald; Bracket, Chicago Inter-Ocean; Smith, Omaha Herald; Clark, Chicago Tribune; Charles Allen, N. Y. Herald; O'Brien, Associated Press; Clark, Scout. Sitting are John M. Burke, McDonough, N. Y. World; Indian Commissioner Cooper.

One peculiarity of the Indian in war is that he reaches a state of ecstasy of excitement when he wants blood and plenty of it, and in that condition, regards the prospect of death as a pleasure. That feeling gives him an advantage over the white warrior, who, of course, does not desire to die uselessly. It makes the Indian reckless, daring, and aggressive.

In this instance, inspired additionally by the confidence in the "Ghost Shirts," they stood up bravely until struck down to the last man.

The battle of Wounded Knee was a surprise as it was understood that Big Foot had agreed to surrender, and Capt. Wallace and some others—among them Scout Wells—were in the camp about to receive their firearms, when Big Foot's medicine man threw a handful of earth up and shouted out a cue that meant to fire and fight. Brave Capt. Wallace was killed, and afterwards his body was found surrounded by five dead warriors with five chambers of his revolver empty. His skull had been smashed and he was shot through the stomach. Philip Wells, interpreter, had his nose almost severed from his face, so close was their contact. His nose was only hanging by a shred when Surgeon Ewing, right there amid the flying bullets, sewed back the olfactory arrangement, plastered it over with strips, and with a handkerchief bound round it, Wells picked up his rifle and continued the fight. The temperature was so far below zero that the mended nose healed, and today, with *pince-nez* spectacles on it, no one can notice the scar.

Capt. Capron (whose son, Capt. Capron, was killed in the Battle of Santiago with Roosevelt's Rough Riders, while the father was commander of the artillery in the same battle) received a close call, the bullet penetrating overcoat, belt, and underclothes, and making a warm trail around his left side. Lieutenant Garlington (of Arctic fame) was desperately wounded, and Lieutenant Hawthorne (now colonel) was struck by a bullet that hit his watch, driving the works into his body, making a fearfully dangerous wound, but from which he recovered to become famous in the Philippines. Lieutenant Mann of Wallace and Garlington's company was so seriously wounded he died on reaching Fort Riley.

In this fight, young Corporal Heimer, after all his officers and the sergeant had been disabled, handled the gun single-handed, and with one shot, it is reported, killed seven Indians. He was honourably mentioned and received a congressional medal.

One little Indian boy, after the battle, was found behind a bush clapping, his hands in childish glee in imitation of rifle fire, seemingly pleased with the racket the melee created. He is now a successful young ranchman on the reservation known as Johnny Burke No Neck, after his red and white adopters on the day of the fight.

That night there came up a terrible blizzard during which Forsythe succeeded in returning to the agency with his dead and wounded. It might here be remarked that three days afterward, under the pile of dead, was found two little Indian female *papooses*, one frozen so it died that night, and the other survived. The other is now a young lady in the family of Gen. Colby of Nebraska.

The next day there was a very heavy skirmish around the agency on what is called The Mission, in which the Indians showed considerable strategy and came near making another surprise. The arrival at an opportune moment of Gen. "Fighting" Guy Henry's cavalry, after covering 125 miles in twenty-four hours, turned the tide of events, and the Indians soon found themselves surrounded in a cordon of sixteen miles by about 3500 soldiers with Gatling guns accompanying them, under the command of the flower of the old Indian fighters of experience, and the Indians, though outnumbering the whites, became amenable to suggestions from their friends under the circumstances.

Many of the conservative and neutral Indians, like Man-Afraid-Of-His-Horses, Rocky Bear, American Horse, Major MacGillicudy (one of their former celebrated agents), Charley Allen, Father Juet, and Major John M. Burke had spent weeks of hardship and toil in efforts to pacify and bring to reason the excited red skins. Major Burke had come from Alsace-Lorraine (Europe) with Col. Cody and seventy-five travelled Indians for the purpose of helping to stem the tide in a condition of affairs that threatened to give excuse for the eventual annihilation of the recalcitrant Sioux.

Red Cloud, He Dog, and others had been "rushed" out to the hostile camp by the war party during the attack on the agency, and Rocky Bear and a band of pacificators gained access to the leaders through a night march with instructions to give them an ultimatum. It was, that Gen. Miles prayed for, hoped for, and desired to lead them to an honoured peace as their friend, but failing in which their chastisement would be such as to leave few of them to weep at the ensuing obsequies.

After repeated exchanges between the negotiators, a flag of truce party informed the general that hostilities would be stopped until they could meet some white friends "that would talk straight and not with

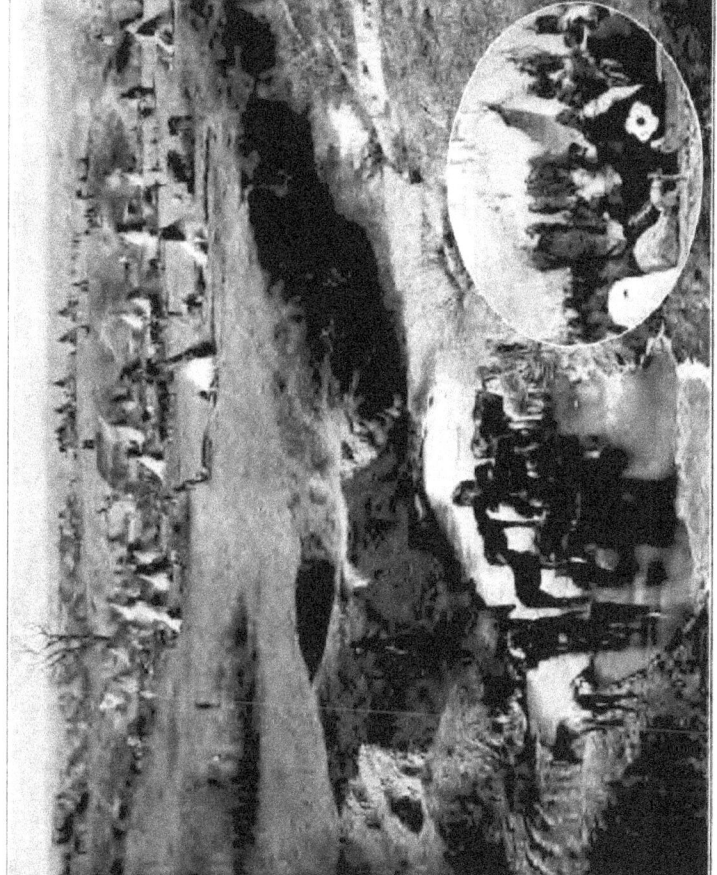

HOSTILE CAMP

Peace meeting of Gen. Lee, Major Burke, and Indian Leaders

forked tongues."

An armistice was arranged, the Indians in the cordon anxiously waiting and the troops on hill and dale standing guard day and night—both at a tension liable at any moment to be broken by the most trivial incident or injudicious move of the lined-up guard or guarded.

Many names were parleyed over, and at last the general commanding was informed that the Brules Sioux would listen to and believe in the Great Father's "First Good Man" that had been sent to them as agent after the War of 1876, Capt. Jesse M. Lee. (Capt. Lee afterwards attained distinction in the Spanish-American War, in the Philippines, and was wounded at Tien Tsin in China, and lately retired as major-general.)

Capt. Lee was in California, and this necessitated a further delay of seven days before his possible arrival—seven days and nights of the most intense anxiety on the part of Gen. Miles and the white peace party as well as the red pacificators, as the younger warriors on both sides had had just enough "baptismal fire" to inspire them for further war.

An incident occurred that only the distance of the outpost, the lateness in the evening, the suppression at the moment of the fact, and the coolness of the old veteran commanders, prevented this tension from snapping and precipitating a sanguinary combat that would have eclipsed anything ever known in Indian warfare—a slaughter from the Gatling gun advantage of the whites that would have been simply appalling. At the same time, it would have been unexplainable to the many well-meaning busybodies who presume to intrude their philanthropies on occasions of impracticability—who know the better side of the red man in repose, but cannot imagine the fanatical zeal, the terrible implacability with which when aroused he wages war to the death, torture to the limit, on the expiring victim, so that an engagement is necessarily a fight to the finish.

This incident was the killing of the brave and excellent young officer, Lieut. Casey, who, as chief of a band of Cheyenne scouts, had made a record for daring and ability that promised him a great future as a military man of rare initiative.

This time the pitcher went once too often to the well, for in trying to locate the topographical conditions of the hostile camp, in case of action, and while spying into its secrets, he was detected and killed by a young Sioux named "Plenty Horses."

SPOTTED TAIL.
Chief of the Brule Sioux assassinated by Crow Dog

Plenty Horses was afterwards acquitted in a civil trial for murder on the testimony of army officers that "it was war" and excusable, and that similar action would have been justifiable on the part of an army outpost guard.

Fortunately, the armistice lasted until Capt. Lee's arrival, as had it not, no doubt, an action might have permitted numerous bands to escape, bands sufficiently strong to have swept down through the settlements carrying death and devastation so disastrously as to check for years the growth of the great Northwest.

With little delay the two accredited peace commissioners, accompanied by Man-Afraid, legitimate hereditary leader of all the Sioux, Rocky Bear, in veracity the George Washington of red men, American Horse, famed as an orator, and other Indian allies, started for the rendezvous of Wolf Creek.

As the cavalcade moved out of sight over the Pine Ridge Hills, many a group of officers and men discussed the fate of former commissioners, and allusions were whisperingly made to the death of Gen. Canby and the massacre of Meeker. When, at sundown, the commissioners returned accompanied by cheering hostiles to within eye sight of their waiting, anxious friends at headquarters, cheers that presaged the success of their pacific efforts, thus assuring the prevention of the sacrifice of many gallant lives—the *peons* were taken up—the news ran around the cordon and mountain, plain and dale resounded with hosannahs of joy as the result was the promise of "peace."

The time will come when the picturesque scene of the racial conference on Wolf Creek will inspire some artist's pencil to adorn the capitol's walls with the reproduction of the "Red Man's Last Stand," as in a natural amphitheatre of hills rising from the valley, ten thousand blanket Indians (hostiles, friendlies, and neutrals having all assembled) gathered to listen to assurances to "come in and all will be forgiven." Hearkening to the voices of two men—Capt. Lee and Major Burke—whom they knew, respected, and could believe—men whose familiar faces dispelled the uncertainty and suspicion that such a generous clean-slate offer was not a deception—the next day a flag-of-truce party concluded with Gen. Miles the terms of surrender, liberal in every way, only stipulating that twenty-seven of the most active hostiles of Kicking Bear and Short Bull's followers should accompany him to (Fort Sheridan) Chicago as hostages.

Next came the surrender, followed by reviews of each other on opposite sides of the stream of both white and red warriors; reviews that inspired additional respect for each other, the red man's review challenging the admiration of veterans, some of whose experiences dated from the fifties in border warfare, such as Generals Carr, Wheating, Whiteside, Hayes, Henry, and others; from the sixties, Generals Miles, Brooks, Corbin, Shafter, Lawton, Chaffee, Young, Baldwin, Sumner, and King; Colonels Egbert and Worth, who figured in connection with the Spanish-American War, and the then young, now leading lights of improved war tactics, such as Generals Franklin Bell, Barry, Humphries, Hall—graduates of the prairies, Indian, Spanish, and Chinese campaigns.

Thus, ended in the Ghost Dance War an epoch in American history that dates the finish of a racial strife—in "Wounded Knee," a battle more noted in its absolute finality of a question than Waterloo and Sedan, the Boyne Water, Magenta, Solferino, Appomattox, or Mukden in Manchuria, they not being so absolutely forever final.

Furthermore, it marks the finish of a "continuous performance" of defensive, desultory at times, concentrative at others, of a sullen foe that stood up valiantly against odds on a retreating line that covered nearly three thousand miles, from the Atlantic to the Pacific, and three centuries of defeats. A setting of a resisting Red Sun, as it were, forever, with no possible rising of the orb again even in the great rally when Gabriel sounds the reveille for the eternal awakening.

To qualify the asserted time of this unique struggle, we quote of King Philip's War in the sixteenth century in New England:

> It was, so far as the English were concerned, much such a conflict as a man might wage with a swarm of hornets. The Indians would not meet the militia in open field. Instead, they attacked parties of churchgoers, ambushed small detachments of soldiers, slew unwary men who ventured alone into the forests, swooped down on an unprotected village, and killed and burned until the settlement was in ashes. Nor were they the arrow-armed, simple folk of the Pequot War. Thanks to long association with white men, they had guns and ammunition and knew how to use them.
>
> Deerfield, Northfield, Brookfield, and other towns were the scenes of indescribable massacres. Springfield was attacked, but, being warned in time, beat off the savages. Capt. Lathrop and eighty men were set upon and butchered at Bloody Brook, near Deerfield. Throughout New England, but chiefly in Western

Massachusetts, rifle and tomahawk gleaned a horrible harvest. Women and little children, as well as armed men, fell victim to the red wave of destruction. Philip was amply avenging his people's wrongs.

Once, at Hadley, Mass., as the English townsfolk were huddled, panic stricken and leaderless, like scared sheep, before an impending Pequot attack, an old man is said to have rushed among them, formed them into military order, and by his brilliant strategic prowess enabled them to rout their assailants. Then the mysterious stranger disappeared. He is believed to have been Gen. Goffe, who (forced to flee from England for his part in the execution of Charles I) had taken refuge in a hillside cave near Hadley.

From the sixteenth to the nineteenth century, a history unequalled—a capitulation on terms with property rights, citizenship, and equality with the victors—having the advantages of every civil right and having the same self-abnegation, the traditional Saumri warrior blood will, without doubt, when occasion arises, be heard of as defender of "Old Glory."

We should now give charity to the Indian's deficiencies and lend a helping hand to his aspirations, as destiny now makes him one of us.

Our duty is done in thus giving importance to a page in American history, for when the full-blooded Indian historian writes the story of his people's last decades of swiftest decline, he will date its rapid downfall from the advent of the telegraph, the stage coach, and the Union Pacific Railroad era, whose way was paved and made possible by the first effective linking of the Great American Continent from east to west by the Pony Express.

www.ingramcontent.com/pod-product-compliance
Lightning Source LLC
Chambersburg PA
CBHW031614160426
43196CB00006B/127